DIGITAL PHOTOGRAPHY
BOOT CAMP

A STEP-BY-STEP GUIDE FOR PROFESSIONALS

KEVIN KUBOTA

AMHERST MEDIA, INC. ■ BUFFALO, NY

ACKNOWLEDGMENTS

We don't always think about all the ways in which people in our lives contribute to who we've become. Sometimes their influence is subtle or built slowly over time. Sometimes it's a great big slap in the face that awakens a side of you that you never knew existed. Sometimes you don't realize that the struggle you had with someone would have a positive effect on you in time. I've compiled a small list of key people who have influenced my life and career significantly. It is by no means comprehensive.

- Mom, for representing everything that is good in life. Your honesty and integrity are second to none.
- Dad, for infusing me with a love for photography and an insatiable thirst for knowledge.
- George Carranza, the first professional photographer I really admired. He taught me about style and good business sense. His eye for detail and quality, while eluding a comfortable, laid-back attitude, created a successful business model.
- Chuck Shahood, a fine commercial photographer who took me under his wing as an assistant. His impeccable eye for detail and quality control often left me questioning my sanity.
- Craig Strong, a mad scientist and creative soul of the highest order. Craig is the inventor of the Lensbaby and a constant inspiration to me.
- My fellow photographers and workshop attendees, for teaching me and inspiring me to keep teaching.
- Kecia Kubota, my sister and workshop manager. Her incredible eye for detail and natural people skills make her invaluable to our business—and more importantly, to all the lives she touches.
- My sons Kai and Nikko, the most precious creatures in the world to me. They inspire me to look at the world with wonderment and curiosity. May they always remind me to enjoy life's simple pleasures.
- Clare Kubota—my wife and truly better half, who keeps me in line. I love you for all you do and who you are.

Published by:
Amherst Media, Inc.
P.O. Box 586
Buffalo, N.Y. 14226
Fax: 716-874-4508
www.AmherstMedia.com

Publisher: Craig Alesse
Senior Editor/Production Manager: Michelle Perkins
Assistant Editor: Barbara A. Lynch-Johnt

ISBN: 1-58428-169-3
Library of Congress Card Catalog Number: 2005926582
Printed in Korea.
10 9 8 7 6 5 4 3 2 1

TABLE OF CONTENTS

ABOUT THE AUTHOR

Kevin Kubota acquired his interest in photography from his father, Stephen Kubota, as a teenager in the late 1970s. In 1990, Kevin committed to photography as a full-time profession and began Kubota PhotoDesign. His wife, Clare Kubota, joined the business as the studio manager in 1996.

Kevin's natural technical curiosity and acumen led him to pursue digital imaging and Photoshop with constant ardor. His early adoption of digital cameras and conversion of the studio into a full-digital workflow gave him the experience base to begin instructing other photographers in making the digital conversion.

In 2000, KubotaWorkshops.com was born and Kevin became a popular speaker at major photographic conventions. In 2002, Nikon asked him to speak for them at the WPPI convention in Las Vegas. He then formed the Digital Photographers Bootcamp™, an intensive week-long program and one of the first of its kind to teach all aspects of converting to a digital studio. This popular program is currently held two or three times a year in Bend, Oregon and other more exotic locations—like Tuscany, Italy. He also teaches at professional development schools throughout the United States and Canada.

KubotaWorkshops.com also produces training CD-ROMs, album-creation software, and Photoshop action sets, simplifying many of Kevin's most popular Photoshop techniques.

Kevin is known not only for his technical knowledge and ability to teach it in an easy-to-understand manner, but also for his artistic imagery, which has been recognized nationally in magazines, books, and advertisements.

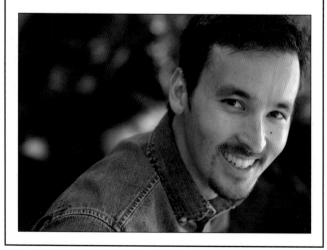

1. INTRODUCTION

"Come to the edge," he said.
They said, "We are afraid."
"Come to the edge," he said.

They came.
He pushed them . . . and they flew.

—Guillaume Appollinaire

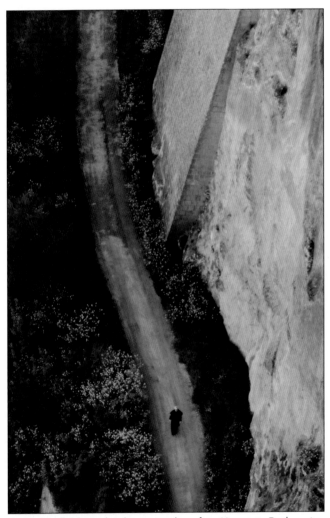

A priest walks the path. Is he coming down from Heaven to Earth or simply making his own never-ending journey?

Here's a story: A photographer I know asked me about a year ago if I thought digital was as good as film. I said, "No. It's better." "But I can make 30"x40" prints from my medium-format camera. Can you do that with digital?" he asked. "Yes, I can," I replied. After a moment of staring deep into my eyes, obviously waiting for an "although . . ." or "but . . . ," he persisted, "How? And does it look as good?" "By pushing a few buttons—and no, it looks better," I replied.

I wasn't trying to be sassy, the answer just seemed so obvious to me. We've passed that magic point in our technological timeline where digital really is "as good as film." In fact, today's 6–8MP pro SLR digital cameras produce images that are sharper and less grainy than film images, at any reproduction size. They also have a wonderful ability to capture subtleties of tone in low-light situations. 35mm negative film is still more forgiving of exposure errors, but if properly exposed, lit, and when certain camera settings are observed (see chapter 5), the digital camera can produce a visually stunning and superior image.

At the time of this writing, digital "35mm" format SLR cameras were emerging that easily surpassed medium-format film quality. How much more can we ask for? Medium-format quality in a quick handling, lightweight, SLR body with a full range of lens options. Is this a great industry or what?

■ WHAT ABOUT FILM? IS IT DEAD?

Yes, it is. For those who have made the jump to digital, there is no going back. Digital is too much fun, too creative, too good—and too many possibilities exist for taking your images to the next level. Many industry giants are already starting to abandon or reduce production of film cameras and supplies. The end is inevitable. While finding a good digital lab used to be a challenge, finding a good, full-service film lab will become increasingly difficult. Consumers are now embracing and switching to digital cameras at a rate that has surpassed film cameras. They are helping to drive the industry in this new direction. Good for them—and good for us.

As digital photographers, we now have options for sharing, selling, and displaying our images that never existed (or were extremely time consuming) with film. Popular options now include in-studio slide show presentations, DVD slide shows for clients to purchase, web proofing and ordering, browse-able image CD-ROMs, proof booklets, watercolor and fine-art prints, magazine-style albums and printed books, image collages, and more. Imagine loading an affordable digital picture frame with a slide show of ten or twenty favorite images to sell to your clients. Products like this are just around the corner as innovations like inexpensive display screens become realized.

▣ THE BENEFITS OF DIGITAL

Let's cut right to the chase. Digital has myriad benefits, not all of which can be listed here. Here are a few that can be easily brought up in polite dinner conversation:

For the Photographer

- **Multiple Originals.** Never send irreplaceable film through the mail. Create as many backups of original images as necessary.
- **Substantial Materials Cost Savings.** Shoot as much as necessary to get the shot you need. No more film, processing, and proofing expenses. Reduce your environmental waste production. We paid for our first digital camera in three months with film/processing savings.
- **Instant Review/Job Insurance.** You know the job is in the bag before you even set the camera down. Share images with clients in-camera to ensure their approval.
- **Creativity Enhancer.** Try new ideas, shoot more, experiment. Increase confidence in your creative abilities.
- **Consistency in Printing.** Reproduce a print the same way from day to day or month to month. There's no need to rely on lab inconsistencies and changing personnel.
- **Studio Control Over Image Printing and Final Look.** Prints can be given the studio's "look" with

simple Photoshop techniques. Print on demand when using in-studio printers.
- **Myriad Creative Output Options.** This facet of digital will keep you excited about your work and enjoying the impact of multimedia presentations.

For the Client

- **More Creative Images to Choose From.** Your gain here is their gain too.
- **Clean, Retouched, Custom-Printed Images.** Clients receive the best-quality images possible.
- **More Exciting Ways to View Their Images.** Viewing options include slide shows, DVDs, CD-ROMs, on websites, via e-mail, etc.
- **More Emotional Impact with Multimedia Presentations.** You can add impact to your presentations by pairing music and images.
- **Print-Ready Images in CMYK.** You can provide separation services for commercial clients.
- **Clients Receive Your Full Artistic Vision—if You Choose to Give it to Them.** They will place a higher value on your products and services.

▣ THE DIGITAL DA VINCI MODEL

I love Leonardo da Vinci. Well, actually I love what he did and what he represented. He was talented in so many different areas: art, literature, science, socializing, logic, theory, inventions, and creating systems and workflows. He nurtured all his different skills and "minds," became exceptional in many areas, and thus became an icon in the history of man. He was artistic *and* technical—an ideal model. Most of us are one or the other, but we can teach ourselves to be more balanced. We can learn anything if given the tools and opportunities.

Success in our new digital world requires a good balance of artistry and technical understanding. When these two worlds are carefully combined, amazing results can arise. No more starving-artist syndrome. Create balance and watch your studio grow. We'll assume that most of you have a good sense of artistry, since otherwise you probably wouldn't have become a photographer. But, even if you're really, really awful at the technical aspects, you can learn enough to be a mini da Vinci. Even if you have to hire someone to handle your technical work, you'll have an important understanding of what's involved and what's needed for a seamless workflow.

This book follows my Digital da Vinci concept. Nourishment for the right and left brain. Tools for creative and technical growth.

■ CHANGE YOUR MIND AND YOUR CLIENTS WILL FOLLOW

Digital is a mind-set. As with any skill, your personal confidence in your abilities is reflected in your performance and sensed by any observer. This directly translates into their increased, or reduced, confidence in your performance. This is essentially true with digital photography—at least as it is perceived by our clients.

When we display fine examples of our digital work and direct our conversations toward content in the images, rather that what they are made with, we do photographers justice by valuing our abilities to capture beautiful moments, artistic scenes, and create pleasing compositions with professional lighting awareness. We should not put more value on the equipment we use or the medium we capture with. It's still about the images, and content is still more important than pixel count. Let's not forget this as we strive to enrich our technical know-how. It's all still secondary to professionally capturing a moment in time.

Of course, as digital becomes mainstream and more professional photographers produce beautiful work, clients will stop questioning it. They will expect it. They may start to question why a photographer is not shooting digitally. Is she behind the times? Old fashioned? Afraid of change? Whether these assumptions are true or not, the clients will imagine the worst and use it against those photographers when making comparisons to others who have gone digital. Truth be told, a good photographer will make great images no matter what the medium, and I wouldn't judge the talent of a photographer by their camera choice, although clients may.

■ EVERY BOOK HAS A PURPOSE

This workbook is the by-product of a very successful workshop I developed in 2001 called the Digital Photographers Bootcamp™. The four-day, intensive program was designed to give the new or existing digital photographer a veritable "big picture" of the working digital studio. It would take them from start to finish—from setting up the studio, to setting up the camera, to taking the images, to organizing them, to enhancing, and finally to printing and presenting them. I infused my workshops with essential foundational information as well as advanced tips and tricks for those who were ready to push their imaging to the next level. We also bring in guest presenters to share creative ideas and styles and to challenge the photographers to think outside the box. The workshops are still held two to four times a year, in the mainland U.S. as well as in inspiring exotic locations like Hawaii and Tuscany, Italy. The programs consistently sell out, with many attendees returning a second or third time—a tribute to the quality and quantity of information given—or maybe it's the food and hot tub.

IS SHE BEHIND THE TIMES? OLD FASHIONED? AFRAID OF CHANGE?

This book pulls directly from the extensive workbook that is given to Bootcamp attendees. While nothing beats a live, interactive workshop, with up-to-the-minute information and surrounding oneself in a cloak of creative energy, this book is the next best thing.

I've been working with Photoshop since 1992, using it every day to prepare images for my graphic design and photography business. When the first Mac computer came out with the ability to read photo CDs (the Mac II vx), I could hardly keep from jumping out of my pants. I bought that computer and, fortunately for everyone, I had to sit still, as it took forever to simply open an image. In the following years, I dropped the design part of my business and focused on photography—my true love. In 1999, I started to use digital cameras professionally—with surprising success, considering the infancy of the technology. When the Nikon D1 was released, I was first in line to get one from my local dealer. I believe this camera started the whole evolution of digital SLR cameras as we know them. It was the first pro digital camera that was the size and weight of a pro film SLR. It handled well, shot fast, and went on location easily. I was hooked. Almost immediately I converted our studio to a full digital workflow.

One of the key concepts I share with other photographers when doing presentations is the mind-set of "just ask." Ask for what you want and don't be afraid of the consequences. This was something I wasn't always good at. However, I decided to make a change and take a chance. I submitted some of my digital wedding work to a trade magazine, and they decided to run a feature on me and also connected me with Nikon, who then asked to use my images in advertising and also for me to do a presentation at the Wedding and Portrait Photographers International's (WPPI) annual convention, which I highly recommend.

ASK FOR WHAT YOU WANT AND DON'T BE AFRAID OF THE CONSEQUENCES.

My presentation was on digital wedding photography and the work I had done with the Nikon D1. I had already shared some of the digital techniques I learned at smaller presentations, but this was the largest by far. I wanted to show people that digital was the future, that it opened the door to creative possibilities rarely seen with film, and that the workflow could be managed efficiently. Obviously photographers were convinced, and I soon began receiving requests to speak at conventions nationwide.

My life and business have never been the same since. Doors just opened. Photographic artists, as with many other types of artists, often shy away from self-promotion and, as such, they never really receive the recognition or appreciation they deserve. We all have wonderful gifts to share—either in the form of photographic talents, technical know-how, or sales and marketing skills. The more we share, the more we learn ourselves. I decided to share everything I could think of about digital and our business, and the results were surprising. Did the competition use the information to their advan-

tage? Yes. Did it hurt my business? No. My business continued to grow every year. Call it karma, call it "what goes around, comes around." Ask for what you want, and don't be afraid to share. It's a winning combination.

While this book is packed full of technical information and practical hands-on tips, I've purposely kept the techniques simple and to the point. Nobody likes to read through lengthy technical gobbledygook—except me—so I've provided the straightest path whenever possible. You should be able to jump to a section, find the technique or information you need, and get down to business.

While our photography business has consisted mainly of wedding, portrait, and commercial clients, the systems and techniques can be applied to almost any photographic discipline. Fine-art photographers as well as high-volume school studios can benefit equally. The concepts are similar no matter what you shoot and at any volume level. Similarly, whether you charge $5 or $500 for an 8"x10" print, the techniques can save you time and money, and raise your image quality as well.

My intention for this book is to provide quality and detailed technical information while also inspiring photographers at all levels to look closely at their lives and businesses to see where improvements might be made. It was supposed to be a technical manual with a "secret" inspirational message hidden within—but I guess that secret's out now. Photography is one of the best businesses/lifestyles a person could ever choose. Enjoy the ride!

DOWNLOAD ACTIONS!

Throughout this book, you'll find references to downloads that are available to readers. To access these, visit the publisher's website at www.Amherst Media.com, click on the title of this book, and enter the password K1809. A complete set of custom actions is also available for purchase from the author at www.KubotaWorkshops.com.

2. DIGITAL ESSENTIALS

Digital capture has in a sense loosened photography by demanding less, not more, technological expertise from photographers. This, surely, is a good thing: shifting photographic skills more to the visual and imaginative, and away from the technical.

—Michael Freeman

■ THE NEW DIGITAL PARADIGM

This chapter will cover the most essential digital skills and concepts, some of which may be very new to you, if you're coming from a pure film background. If you're new to digital, making the transition may be daunting at first, but hang in there—you'll be a digital guru in no time. Photographers who have a background in stock photography may find the transition quite natural and an amazing productivity booster.

We've divided our digital world into four distinct categories (see chart, next page). Each flows from one to the next. Some photographers are stronger in one area than another. For example, you may love working your images in Photoshop but have trouble with the image management part, and thus your images are scattered all over and take too much time to find, edit, or present. Each part complements the next, and the more balanced your knowledge and skills in each area, the more

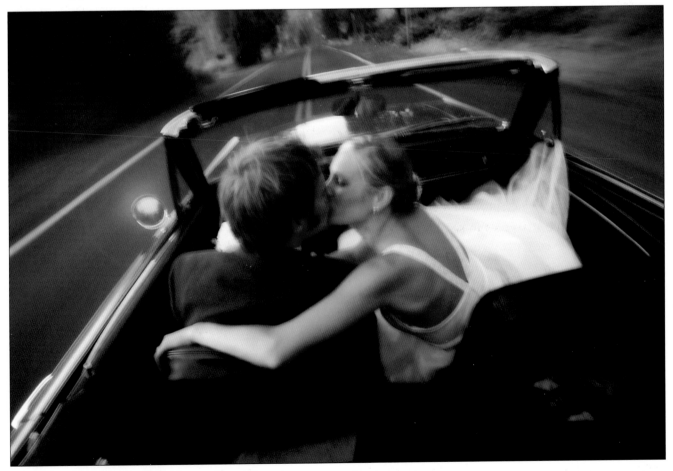

A loose, less than technically perfect image with great impact.

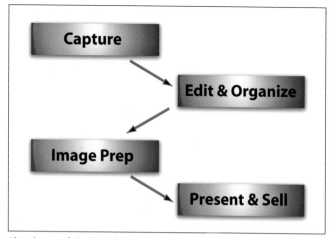

The phases of the digital system.

your studio operations will flow and the better your image quality.

The concepts that will be introduced are part of an interrelated system. Steps taken in one phase of the process are often done to facilitate movement through the next phase. Sometimes it's not completely obvious why we do something to, or with, an image until we move closer to the final presentation. Bear with me, there is a method to this madness! Take the time to educate yourself and refine your skills in each area. Balance is the key to becoming a Digital da Vinci!

While the details will be covered in the following chapters, here's a brief look at the phases of the digital system.

■ DIGITAL CAPTURE

This is probably the easiest transition to make, unless you were a negative film shooter, and I don't mean that in a bad way—pun intended. With negative film, photographers could overexpose their images by as much as three or four f-stops, and the labs could save the images. You often didn't even know how off the exposures were, unless you took the time to look at the density numbers on your negatives. We photographers just went on our merry way, thinking we could pull off a good exposure with our eyes closed—which happened quite often, actually.

Digital cameras are not as forgiving of exposure mistakes, especially overexposure. Retraining yourself to make accurate exposures is an essential first step toward success with digital imaging. On the same note, photog-

raphers who are skilled at exposing transparency film will have an easier time making the transition. Expose for the highlights and err on the side of underexposure, if at all. Moderately underexposed images (down to two f-stops sometimes) can be made printable with a few good Photoshop tricks up your sleeve (see chapter 7).

Capture also includes modifying your camera settings for the best final-image quality. Most cameras come from the factory with default settings that make your images look good when they first pop up on the screen. Manufacturers set them up for the lowest common denominator. They don't expect you to read this book and become a more refined user. It's important to keep in mind that some of the camera settings we'll recommend for final image quality may make images look less appealing straight out of the camera, but the payoff comes when making final, retouched, color corrected, enhanced, and enlarged images.

■ RAW VS. JPEG: THE MAIN EVENT

Digital images come in two basic flavors, RAW and JPEG. Each camera manufacturer has their own proprietary RAW format and the files may be named with extensions like: .nef, .crw, .raf, .tif, etc. RAW files contain the data straight from the camera's sensor, without in-camera software manipulations. This leaves the door open to modify image settings later, in the comfort of your studio, rather than at the time of the shoot. Some of the settings that can be modified later include white balance, hue and saturation, contrast, and sharpening. Many digital photographers don't take the time to do a proper custom white balance at the time of the shoot (we'll deal with you later!), and capturing in RAW enables you to correct for this after the fact.

Benefits When Shooting RAW

• RAW files are captured with 12 bits of color information, giving the best exposure latitude, tonal range, and postproduction options. These are true "digital negatives." JPEG files are captured with only 8 bits of color information (for now anyway), and thus less information is available for postproduction.

• When you shoot RAW, the only camera setting that is not changeable later is the ISO setting.

FILE TYPE	RESULTING SIZE	TIME TO WRITE FROM CAMERA TO CARD
JPG Fine	2.5 MB	.7 seconds continuous (1.43 fps)
RAW	5.5 MB	.33 seconds for first 3 shots (3 fps), 1 second thereafter (1 fps)

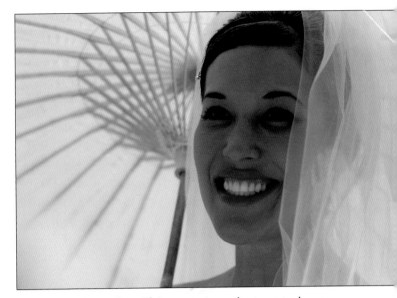

LEFT—Test performed on a Nikon D70 with Lexar 80x WA 1GB Compact-Flash card. RIGHT—A low-contrast scene shot with auto contrast ruins the image. Selecting the low-contrast mode would have softened the lines and shadows under the eyes. Fortunately, this can be somewhat improved in Photoshop.

Considerations When Shooting RAW

• The files require longer write times.

• RAW files require considerably more storage space.

• These files require slightly more post-processing time and steps.

JPEG files, in comparison, are significantly smaller and slightly faster to write from camera to card. This is because JPEG files are inherently compressed to make them an efficient image-transfer format. The compression compromises image quality, however. Compression artifacts are subtle but present in JPEG files, and therefore any further image manipulations and adjustments may magnify these artifacts. Care must be taken in capture and in post-processing to maximize image quality when shooting in the JPEG format. With this is mind, we created what we call the "raw JPEG."

The "Raw" JPEG Concept Explained. To allow ourselves as much post-processing leeway as possible, we tested various camera settings and evaluated their effect on final image quality, where typical corrections and enhancements were applied to the images in Photoshop. Our goal was to create a theoretical "raw" JPEG file—one that is as close to its original state when captured by the image sensor as possible. The following are the settings that we find essential for a "raw JPEG."

Sharpening Off (or as Low as Possible). Sharpening in camera is purely a software by-product. Real RAW files do not have any sharpening applied to them in their native form. Therefore, we turn sharpening off so that JPEG files do not receive any software sharpening either. Sharpening should always be the last step in an imaging workflow, especially after any image interpolation. It can't be the last step if it's done in the camera!

Contrast Set to Low. This protects against capturing an image with too much contrast, with blown-out highlights and blocked-up shadow detail. A low-contrast image can easily be brought into full contrast range in Photoshop, whereas an image with too much contrast is nearly impossible to completely recover from. Using auto contrast on a digital camera can also be unreliable, as it will often create a higher-contrast image from a scene that really should remain low contrast (see example above).

ISO as Low as Possible. The higher the ISO, the more shadow noise becomes apparent. Always use the lowest ISO possible for the given shooting conditions.

Make a Custom White Balance for Each Scene. To do this, use a device like the ExpoDisc or a gray/white card (see chapter 4 for details). Making a perfect white balance can be quick and easy with the right tools and the dedication to make it part of your routine. The benefits are great. Images will have true, vivid colors, with little or no color correction work necessary. Skin tones will look warm and healthy. Since JPEG files should ideally receive as little post-capture correction as possible, getting the white balance right in the camera will mean a major improvement in image quality. There is an added benefit when using two or more cameras on a job. If every camera is custom white balanced, the colors will match almost perfectly when integrated in editing.

Select the Highest-Resolution JPEG Setting and Least Compression. In most cameras, this means using JPEG fine mode and a high quality setting. Since even full-resolution JPEG files are so small when compressed, there's very little reason to shoot in a lower-resolution mode. Give yourself the most information to work with and use high resolution. Choosing these settings will minimize compression artifacts, which can be more obvious when an image is enlarged later.

Many of these settings will be covered in more detail in chapter 4. While we recommend capturing images in RAW format whenever possible in order to allow utmost image quality and flexibility, there are times when JPEG files are desired, and the above settings will help make the most of your JPEGs.

◼ MEGAPIXELS AND RESOLUTION

This is the fun stuff. No really, you'll be an expert in no time. While not the most exciting aspect of digital imaging, understanding your megapixels and resolution is key to understanding how to deliver images to clients, labs, magazines, etc. It's also important to understand so that you can properly enlarge (via interpolation, see chapter 7) an image when necessary for wall prints.

Let's see how simple we can make it. A 6MP camera has roughly 6-million pixels. When you open an image in Photoshop, the only thing that determines the file size of the image are the total pixel dimensions, not the resolution! Many people get confused or worried when they see 72 pixels/inch in the Resolution box. Not to worry. *Resolution has nothing to do with the actual size or quality of your image until it is printed.*

You can change the resolution to anything you want, without hurting the original image quality, as long as you don't change the actual pixel dimensions. The output size of the image is, however, directly related to the resolution. In other words, if you want higher resolution, the pixels will be printed closer together (for a less pixelated-looking image) and won't cover as much total area. This means the printed dimensions will go down proportionately.

When we change the resolution, we simply change how densely the pixels are displayed. A 3008x2000-pixel image will be printed at 42"x28" when set to 72 pixels/inch, whereas the same image can be changed to 300pixels/inch and the printed dimensions will go down to 10"x6.6". If the same image is set to 250 pixels/

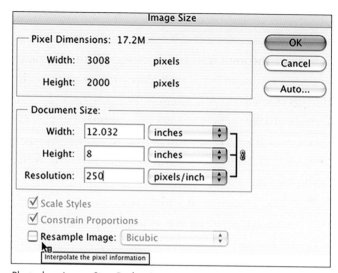

Photoshop Image Size Dialog Box. Turning Resample off allows you to see relationships between size and resolution.

Photoshop Image Size dialog box with the Resample Image option turned on.

inch, the printed dimensions will go to 12"x8". Catch the drift?

Let's use the metaphor of a piece of stretchy fabric. In this 8"x10" piece of fabric the threads are laid out so as to give us a 300 thread count—just like the fancy sheets at the linen stores, nice and silky. The threads are so tightly woven together that you can barely see them and the appearance is smooth and uniform. This is our image at 300 pixels/inch.

Now, let's take the stretchy fabric and pull it from the sides so that it's now 16"x20". As you can imagine, you'll now start to see the gaps between those threads as they are pulled apart. If we counted and measured them, we'd see that they are now spaced at 150 threads per inch instead of the original 300 threads per inch.

These gaps are like seeing pixelation in a low-resolution image.

We can theoretically stretch or squash this fabric to any size we want, and each time the density of the threads changes proportionately. We never actually add threads or take any away, right? The number of threads (pixels) of the original fabric (image) never changes, they are just observed (printed) differently. This is the fabric (or image) in its natural form.

But wait, you need a different size *and* resolution combination. No problem, this is where Photoshop uses its brain and brawn. When you need an image with different size/resolution specifications than what you get in the above scenario (e.g., you want a 16"x20" print, but with 300 pixels/inch resolution, instead of the natural 150 pixels/inch), Photoshop will resample the image—which is another term for interpolation. Simply put, this means Photoshop will add or subtract pixels to maintain the original look and detail of the image as much as possible.

Keep in mind that whenever you resample an image, you sacrifice some image detail when compared to the original in its natural form. However, the loss is usually acceptable (often unnoticeable), and it is the only way to achieve the goal of matching a size and resolution that is not in the natural proportions.

In chapter 7, we discuss the best ways to use the Photoshop Image Size dialog box to achieve your output size goals. There are specialty programs on the market to help you resize images while preserving details, but generally you can achieve comparable results using Photoshop alone and a few little tricks—which will be covered later as well.

People often wonder, "How large can I print my digital images?" The answer is simple, "How large is your printer?" In less sassy terms, that means there's really no limit to the size print you can make. Generally, the further you take the image from its natural size, the more apparent sharpness you lose. However, we've made billboard images from a 2.7MP camera before and they look great—at the proper viewing distance. Obviously, a higher-resolution original will give better detail.

If you use the proper capture settings, resample your image properly, and keep in mind your appropriate viewing distance for the size of the print, surprisingly good results can usually be achieved.

Higher-resolution originals provide the best detail in prints.

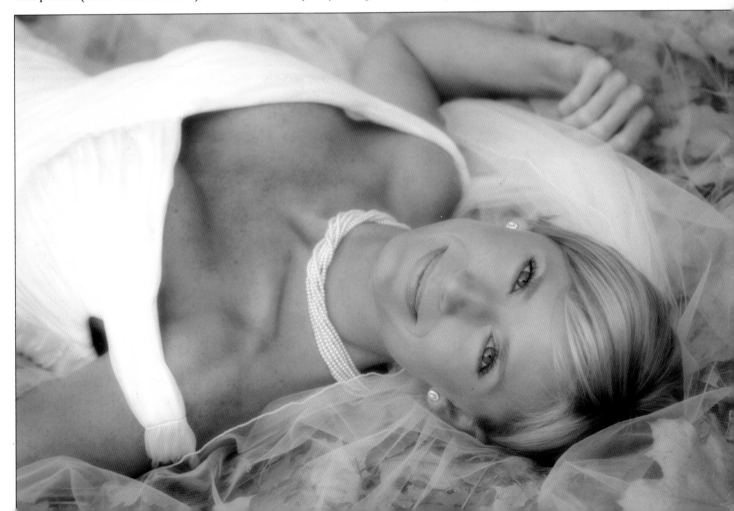

3. CREATIVITY AND INSPIRATION

Creativity is allowing yourself to make mistakes. Art is knowing which ones to keep.

—Scott Adams

■ WHERE DOES IT COME FROM?

In keeping with our concept of balance, or the Digital da Vinci model, it becomes important to remember to nourish our creative needs amidst all this digital techno-babble. Technical efficiency can be a very satisfying thing, but the real spine-tingling, goose-bumping experiences come from the creation of a really awesome image.

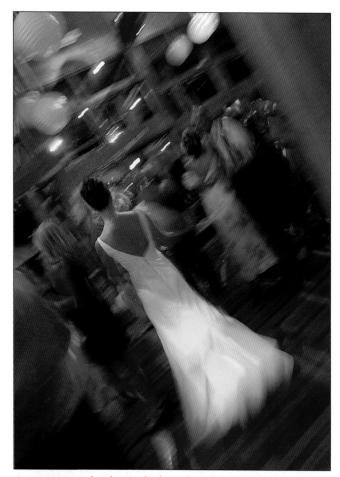

A creative "mistake" that resulted in a photo that was a keeper. Image by Clare Kubota.

When you are in the groove, you're shooting and everything is just flowing. You find yourself aware of everything happening around you. You turn just in time to capture a wonderful embrace across the room. Your exposure is dead on. You get a gut feeling and wheel around, only to immortalize another perfect moment as a father embraces his daughter with a tear streaming down his cheek. You get a wild idea to pull your bride and groom outside just as the sun is setting and climb in the back of a classic convertible. They love the idea and you create some of your favorite images. When you're in the groove, everything just flows. It seems effortless, and the ideas just seem to pour through you.

There is a classic book by Mihaly Csikszentmihalyi called *Finding Flow* (Basic Books, 1998). In it, he describes this concept of flow, as sort of a nirvana state that happens when we are completely absorbed in something we are very skilled at. It is like being on autopilot, where you no longer have to think about how to perform, you just focus on the performance. Your skills are so highly developed that they are second nature and you can react automatically.

This is what happens when we are so comfortable with the technical aspects of our craft that we can focus purely on capturing the perfect moments. Our intuition, which is immensely valuable to us as photographers, can be heard loud and clear. We can respond to hunches and ideas without the distraction of how we are going to pull it off technically.

In order to hear our true creative voice, we have to silence the technical chatter as much as possible. This only comes with time and experience, but it helps to remind yourself that learning the technical skills will help you be more creative as well.

Does this mean we have to be technical geniuses to be creative? No, not at all. I've seen wonderfully creative work from amateurs and beginning professional photographers with very limited technical knowledge. But, the more they refine their technical skills, the more creative they become. It only gets better.

◼ THE CREATIVE PROCESS

In photography, like with any other creative process, there is a simple system to help get your juices flowing. In creative writing, the final product is built in three stages.

Free Write. This is the process of letting your ideas flow to paper. No concern is given to grammar, completeness, or final usage—just open the door and let it flow. No idea or statement is too crazy.

Edit. Now we take a step back and start to edit. Rearrange sentences if necessary, make sure everything makes sense. Pick better words and refine your descriptions. Pull out unrelated or undeveloped ideas.

Rewrite. Fine-tune and put the piece into its final presentation form.

With photography, we use a similar process:

Free Shoot. Digital really has come to our rescue here. Let your imagination go wild. Try any idea that comes to your head. No concern should be given to limiting your exposures, within reason. Often when trying to capture a fleeting moment, taking three to five shots in a row will deliver that one perfect image. Don't hold back.

Edit. With the powerful tools we have for organizing and batch processing images, this task becomes less daunting. Delete the experimental images that didn't work, the fluff shots, and the warm ups. Edit down your images and save only the best of the best.

Prepare to Present. The presentation is extremely important with photography, make it count. Use Photoshop to extend your creative vision—make the images sing. Think of how your images can best be displayed or shared. Will a slide show with music enhance the mood? Clean museum-style mats? High-quality framing?

Before digital photography, the process was similar, but we were always aware that each shot cost money in film and processing. Subconsciously, we occasionally held back. Also, we couldn't immediately see the results of our experiments, and subsequently we didn't get as excited about them or push ourselves to try more.

A stack of proofs or slides makes for long work of editing down 2000 or so images. Not so with digital. We can breeze through them, mark them, hide or show what we want, enlarge or reduce, categorize, sort, etc. It's a much more streamlined and controlled process.

Making enhancements on film images was impractical or expensive at best. Each image had to be scanned, and the Photoshop skills for making the enhancements or corrections were not widely known. Everything is different now.

USE PHOTOSHOP TO EXTEND YOUR VISION—MAKE THE IMAGES SING.

Lastly, the presentation methods were limited. We basically put together contact sheets, a stack of proofs, and a typical album or folio. Not many options were available. If we wanted to go beyond the basics, considerable effort or expense was involved. Now, like Superman with his kryptonite shackles removed, we have the power to do amazing things. It's good to work digitally.

◼ TECHNIQUES FOR CREATIVITY AND INSPIRATION

Inspiration and creative ideas can come to us in many forms. Some great methods used by photographers to nourish their creative souls include:

• Going to the movies—any excuse is good, right? Isn't that a business write-off?
• Going to museums and art galleries.
• Reading industry magazines and trade publications.
• Taking "observation trips" to sit and watch people—perhaps at a coffee shop.
• Reading novels that are exquisitely written so as to evoke vivid scenes in your imagination.

- Traveling to foreign countries. Nothing stimulates the mind like immersion in an entirely new culture.
- Listening to music. Create a music video in your head. Imagine the characters, the mood, the lighting, and the angles you would shoot it with. Thinking like a cinematographer can have a positive effect on your still photography. Think of ways to capture movement and make one shot flow into the next.

In addition to those mentioned above, the following are in-depth techniques that we use to boost creativity and stay inspired.

■ SAY "BOOM" WHILE WATCHING THE WORLD

This is the process of using a mental trigger to connect your mental practice with physical performance. The idea that mental practice enhances performance is not new; in fact many studies through the years have proven it to be true, with athletes in particular. Here's an example study from *Research Quarterly* (vol. 38, 1967):

Three groups of students practiced free throws in basketball for twenty days. Their performance was tested at the beginning and end of that time period.

- Group 1—physical practice—they improved 24%!
- Group 2—no practice—no improvement at all.
- Group 3—mental practice and imagination only—they improved 23%!

What we can deduce from this is the fact that visualization is a critical tool for enhancing performance. This rings true with photography as well. The key, however, is to connect your visualization to the act of photographing. This is done with the mental trigger, "boom."

Here's how it works: When you watch the world, make a habit of taking time to imagine how you would photograph it. Watch the interactions between people, the subtle movements and gestures, the key moments when the peak of action will occur. Practice your timing and anticipation. Think about the lens you would use

and the lighting; then when a moment presents itself, say "boom!" Okay, now you don't have to shout it out and give away your stealth advantage, just say it quietly to yourself.

This verbal trigger makes a connection between what you see and pressing your camera shutter button. When you pick up your camera, say "boom" quietly to yourself again during the normal process of photographing and the connection is further strengthened.

Anticipation and timing are keys to good photography, and this exercise directly improves upon both. It can be done any time, all the time, and the benefits will grow the more you practice.

■ PROJECTS

Give yourself projects and self-assignments. It keeps you alive—creatively speaking. Remember when you studied photography in school, or started to learn it yourself. The projects were the catalyst for great ideas and portfolio pieces. They were a chance for you to do whatever you wanted, within the scope of the assignment, without the constraints of a client's expectations. Of course, we soon realized that it's not always like that in the real world—but we don't have to lose that creative excitement.

SELF-ASSIGNMENT IS KEY TO KEEPING YOUR CREATIVE BALL ROLLING.

Self-assignment is key to keeping your creative ball rolling. It's all too easy to get caught up in the day-to-day "job" of producing images for a fee. We can't forget, however, that we also love what we do and need to stay motivated. Self-assignment is a way to freely experiment with new ideas and concepts; it allows you to reconnect with the reasons you love photography. A well-executed project or self-assignment will almost always produce a new portfolio piece.

One great way to do projects is to work with your photographer friends. Set up a monthly meeting and rotate responsibility for coming up with the monthly project. Everyone does the shoot together, or separately, and shares their ideas and results. This type of group effort helps to break down those barriers to working and sharing with other photographers. Your closest competition can also be your best friend—it's actually better that way.

Here are some project ideas:

Movie Scene Re-Creation. When watching movies, we often see beautiful lighting or compositions. We don't always take the time to analyze them, however, to learn from what we see. Try renting or buying a DVD you like with great photography. Play the disc on your computer. Pause the disc at a beautifully lit scene or interesting composition and analyze it. What is it that you like about it? The mood or the unique angle of the lighting? Maybe it's a special color effect or treatment. Now, take this mental picture with you and work to re-create the key elements of it with a photograph of your own. This is a great exercise to help identify what moves you in images, then to translate what you see into a new image of your own.

Emotion Scavenger Hunt. Photo hunts are great fun. They train you to find new ways to see the world, and to be creative under (slight) pressure. Try making a list of emotions instead of objects and pick five or ten for a group or solo hunt. Look for emotions like elation, melancholy, peaceful, excited, sultry, etc. Don't limit yourself to looking for emotions in people, they can be captured in the mood of a place or scene.

Detail Collages. Instead of taking the typical overview shot of a place or scene, try to convey the feeling of the place, or its essence, with very tight detail shots. Think intimate and moody. It is often the little details that make a place (or person) so unique and interesting, not so much the big picture. Tell the story with ten or twenty images, then put them together as a collage. Chances are, you'll feel a deeper connection to your subject this way and will remember it much better.

Blur the Details. This project feels amazingly refreshing if you have always been a very controlled, technically accurate shooter. Instead of capturing images that are tack sharp, force yourself to take a series of blurry or out-of-focus shots. Some of you may do this every day anyway, so this is for the rest of you. The great thing about this exercise is it forces you to focus (not literally)

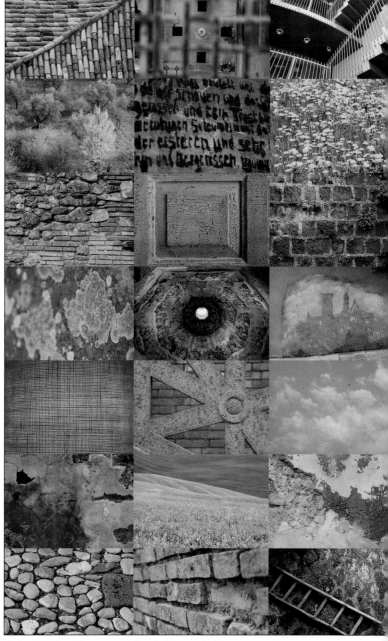

A detail collage from a workshop in Tuscany, Italy.

on composition, light, shadow, color, and form. You can think more cinematically and capture movement. Try a whole series of images this way and you may be surprised at how much you like it!

Of course, the list could go on and on. Brainstorm a little and come up with your own challenges. Make it a routine and you may never find yourself bored or at a loss for new ideas again.

◼ USE CREATIVE TOOLS

Professional Lenses. As professional photographers, we want our images to look nothing like Uncle Harry's. Chances are, Harry is using a 35–70mm zoom lens with an f4.5–5.6 aperture and flash on camera.

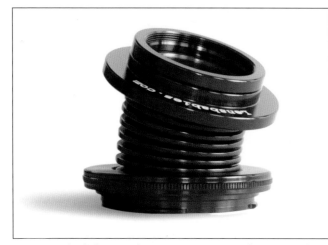

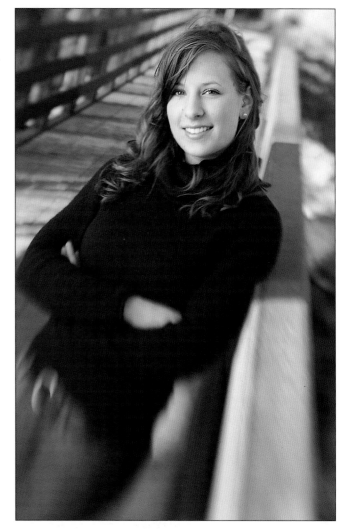

ABOVE—Portland photographer, Craig Strong—a mad scientist and creative photographer of the highest order—created the Lensbaby. This inexpensive lens is one of the most fun and unique products a digital photographer can add to their bag. (Note: The lens returns to normal, straight position when it's not being manually focused.) RIGHT—An image shot with the Lensbaby on a Nikon D70. Original color image converted to black & white using our secret formula (revealed in chapter 7).

One way to separate your images from the amateurs', other than taking better photos, is to leave no room for comparison to a "consumer" camera image. Try using wide-angle lenses in the 12–24mm range, fisheye lenses, or 85mm and above. Also use as large an aperture as you feel comfortable with—f1.4 to f2.8 if possible. Even group shots can be taken with an 85mm lens if you position yourself far enough away, and the results are quite beautiful.

Consider a Lensbaby. What's a Lensbaby? I'm glad you asked. This is a funky new lens that allows for manual control of tilt and swing effects. The simplicity of the lens and the beautiful, organic-looking effect it gives is very refreshing in our high-tech digital world. The sweet spot of focus can be placed anywhere in the frame and the other areas go out of focus. The resulting images have soft, diffused edges that look as though there is motion blur and have a dream-like feel. (See Resources for contact information.)

TTL Flash. Some cameras, like the current Nikon line, include the ability to use off-camera, wireless TTL flash. This is an awesome tool for creative lighting effects as well as for creating more professional-looking standard lighting setups. By taking the main flash off the center of the camera, you can create more depth with dimensional lighting that defies typically flat on-camera flash looks.

Use a Monopod. Find ways to get your camera into unexpected locations. One fun idea for wedding or party receptions is to mount the camera on a monopod. Then, use a wide-angle or preferably a fisheye lens and set the camera to self-timer mode with a three- to five-second delay. Focus lock the camera at a typical subject distance, release the shutter button, and lift the camera high above the crowd for a bird's-eye view. What fun! (See facing page for an example of this type of image.)

Integrate Point & Shoot Digital Movies. Bring along a compact camera that captures movies. Many current models are inexpensive and can capture full-motion, full-sized video clips (30fps @ 640x480). The point here is not to take the job of a videographer but to capture just a few little details and moments. A parting shot on the dance floor or a few great clips of people laughing are always a hit. Some cameras even have a time-lapse feature that can be used to capture the setup, use, and breakdown of a ceremony site or reception area. These are fun little tidbits to include in a slide show or DVD for the wedding client.

■ BE A GROUPIE

Shadow Shoot. If you can find the right photographer to allow you to shadow them, then this is a lot of fun. The purpose is not to be an assistant, or even to "watch" what they do, but to allow you the chance to shoot without the pressure of the job. You can shoot from the sidelines, capture completely candid images, and focus on timing, anticipation, and creative angles. Try some new exposure or lighting tricks. The key is not to get in the main photographer's way. You may also want to offer your images to the photographer to sell to their client—but don't ever try to sell your images to the client directly. This is not for profit, but purely for

the practice and the experience of shooting a different way.

Sacrifice Yourself. Be a slave for a day. It's good for you. Be an assistant and watch how another photographer works. Offer your services for free. You'll get ideas you never thought of, no matter how experienced you are. You may also discover that you are already doing some things a lot better than you initially thought—which can be a great confidence booster.

Team Shoot. Rally up a few of your photographer buddies or buddettes and plan a shooting date. Hire a model together, if needed. Pick out a great location or subject matter and plan for the shoot just like it was a real job. Acquire props, a makeup artist, and wardrobe, if necessary. You can almost always come up with portfolio-quality images, and it's great fun as well. Staying fresh and excited about photography is key to

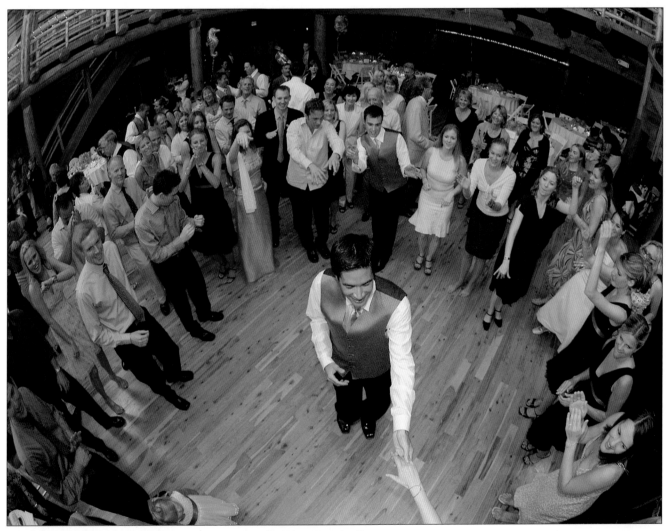

A high-flying bird's-eye view of the action using a monopod and five-second self-timer.

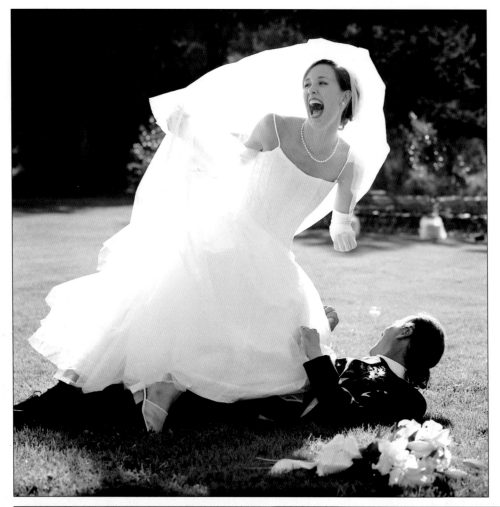

Developing intuition allows you to capture spontaneous images with little warning or planning. You simply "feel" them about to happen.

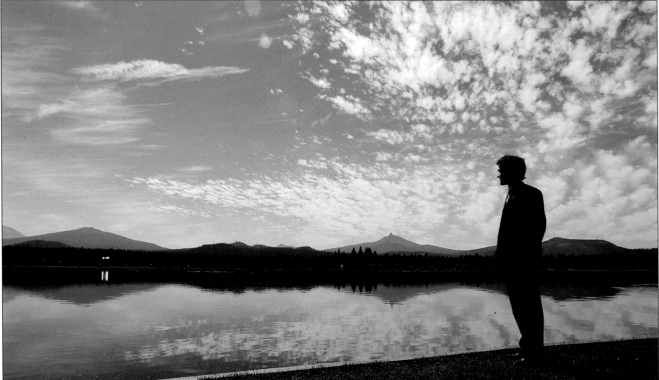

long-term success. Find ways to keep the ideas and energy flowing.

Start a Group. This might be done with the same associates that you team shoot with. Plan a regular meeting—maybe once a month. Each month, a different member can come up with a presentation for the group. They can share a new technique they've learned or style they've seen. If someone is less experienced, they can initiate a stimulating discussion on a particular photographic topic or famous photographer's work. Remember, sharing is caring, and nothing but good can come of it in the grand scheme of things.

Develop Your Intuition. As Jonas Salk said, "Intuition will tell the thinking mind where to look next."

This is one of the key skills you can master and use for every part of your business. Learning to recognize and listen to your intuition will help you to read your clients better and capture their true personalities. It will alert you when a key moment is about to happen—even if you aren't consciously aware of its significance. Your intuition will also help you with business decisions and career moves. The power of intuition is underestimated and often misunderstood.

Intuition is not a mystical, stargazers' kind of super power—it's a real and practical skill we all possess. Not everyone recognizes or trusts it, however, so it often takes some practice to make it work in day-to-day situations. The first important step toward tapping into it is to believe in it. Take it seriously. Once you're over the hump of thinking, "this is crazy hippie stuff," you can quite literally amaze yourself. It's your choice.

Some may prefer to call it "gut instinct." This is much more familiar, so if you're afraid of getting too metaphysical, feel free to substitute this phrase wherever you see "intuition." Sometimes it's difficult to put a concrete value on something so intangible, but learning to recognize and trust in your intuition can literally change your life and business. It's happened to me many times. In fact, most of the major career and life decisions I've made have been done from a "hunch"—a seemingly far-fetched idea that just popped into my head. Instead of ignoring it or rationalizing it away, I started to develop a virtual scenario in my head to see what could happen if I really followed through. The key is to keep the neg-

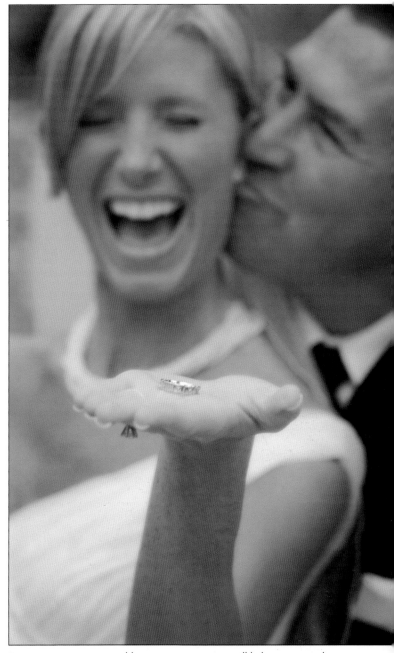

Learning to recognize and listen to your intuition will help you to read your clients better and capture their true personalities.

ative, self-doubting thoughts out of your head. Those little monsters!

Here are just a few examples of where my life or business was changed for the better by trusting my intuition—not for the purpose of being boastful, but simply to share how intuition really is effective.

I met my wife, as a teenager, through a youth program called Civil Air Patrol. I still have no idea why I decided to attend the first meeting—the program was geared toward training teens for ROTC programs—

which I had absolutely no interest in. As a teen, it was unlike me to want to go to any organized activity, but for some reason I went—and there she was. That was in 1983, and we've been best friends, husband and wife, and business partners ever since. I couldn't imagine my life without her. What drew me to that first meeting?

IF THIS IDEA ACTUALLY WORKED WHAT WOULD BE THE BENEFIT?

In 1995 we had a thriving photography business in Southern California. Business was steadily growing and we had developed a good reputation in our area. We took a road trip and stumbled upon a small town in Oregon, where we stopped to rock climb, then have dinner. We took a walk after having dinner in a quaint restaurant, and said to each other, "Let's move here."

A few months later we had bought a house in Bend and moved with no idea what to expect for the business. It was a very small town compared to the one we lived in in Southern California, and we wondered if we could even come close to the income we were accustomed to before.

After the first year in Bend, our business nearly doubled, and it has grown steadily ever since. I now realize that so many of the innovations and good business decisions we made grew from necessity—from being in a remote location. Moving to Bend was one of the best decisions of our lives, and it was based purely on intuition.

In 1998, I started to get a taste of digital cameras and immediately felt that this was our future. I didn't "wait and see" but dove right in. Although we learned many things the hard way, we learned them well. Because of our early adoption of and experience with digital, we were able to offer a product that very few other photographers were offering at the time. We also learned enough to start training other photographers in the art of digital, which has also been a wonderful complement to our photography business. Had I not trusted my gut and jumped in—despite the odds against immediate success, would I be writing this book today?

Soon after we started shooting digital, my style changed immensely, and I felt for the first time like I could really photograph the way I loved to. I followed a very small voice in my head that told me to send images in to a magazine for review. This was very out of character for me at the time. But my intuition said to do it, and I did. The years ever since have been like a whirlwind of exciting opportunities and new experiences. Doors magically opened and wonderful people walked in. I can trace it all directly to that intuitive voice telling me, "Take a chance, share your work."

Making Intuition Work for You. The hardest part of tapping your intuition, beyond learning to trust it, is learning to recognize it. Then, what do you do? Do you act on every little crazy voice in your head? Will they take away your house and family and commit you to a padded room with nothing but a cheap PC and Photoshop 3.0? Oh, horrors no! Here's a simple system for making it work:

Recognize the Thoughts. You can usually recognize an intuitive thought or idea by how seemingly random it may appear. It's not necessarily something you've worked up to, or developed, it just pops in your head. It may even appear as a totally random thought, like "walk into that store" when you are heading somewhere else. Intuitive thoughts often lead you places, they are not always the answer in themselves. Such leading thoughts are most useful when photographing.

Brief Analysis. Stop, look, and listen. Give the thoughts some thought. This should be done when a full-blown concept or idea, rather than a "leading" thought, hits you. Contemplate the "worse case *vs.* best case" scenarios. If this idea actually worked, what would be the benefit? If it failed miserably, what would you stand to lose? If the potential wins outweigh the loses, then move to the next stage.

Develop the Idea. Now it's time to write the idea down and talk it over with others you trust. Be sure, however, that your "board of directors" are not intimately involved with the results or their opinions will be biased. Unless you know they are intuitive by nature or can listen with an open mind, hold off on sharing your ideas—just for a while. When you have a firmer plan, with detailed pros and cons, present the idea. It's a good practice to keep a journal with all your ideas and the basic details that support or develop the project.

Put It into Action. If the idea has passed the last test and still looks feasible, make it happen. Take the first step now. If you wait, the energy behind the idea diffuses and it's difficult to recover. We slip back into our daily routine and habits—where we are comfortable—and the grand idea slips slowly away. Change is hard. One of the weirdest ironies in life is that change is hard, yet change can be so good. Remember this key: just because you start something doesn't mean you can't change your mind later. It is okay to abandon a project if you learn or feel that it really isn't working. If this idea came from intuition, there's a good chance that you have learned something valuable in the process or have been lead to something even more significant. Your first intuitive thought may not always be the final answer you need.

Act on Intuitive Impulses. Impulses, or leads, are a little different than ideas. They don't always give much more information than, "talk to that person" or "walk down this pathway instead." There often is no obvious reason for the thought. This is what separates them from an educated intuitive lead. For example, you may be at a party and already know that a certain person in the room would make a good business contact. Your gut tells you to go introduce yourself. This is an educated lead, and there is nothing wrong with that. Recognizing an intuitive lead is equally, if not more, important. With intuitive leads, there is rarely an obvious reason for the hunch. It remains to be discovered.

We can use this type of impulsive intuition regularly when photographing. Don't be afraid to act on an impulse when you're scratching your head for fresh images at a shoot. Worrying about what the client will think if the idea sucks will rob you of your originality.

Some of the most creative and successful people in the world are simply acting on and following intuitive impulses that others choose to ignore.

▣ INSPIRATION FROM GIVING

One of the strongest forms of inspiration can also come from giving your photography services away. Some of the most poignant and meaningful letters or comments of gratitude come from the people who receive your

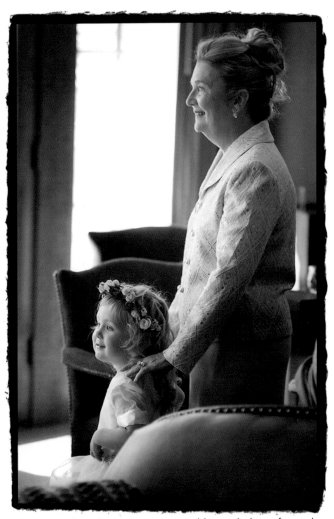

When you realize what an impact your work has on the lives of everyday people, you simply put more value on your gift in your own mind.

services through charitable work. There is immense power in a heartfelt thank you.

One thing we've noticed as well: when you realize what an impact your work has on the lives of everyday people, you simply put more value on your gift in your own mind. This is an important factor for both business success and, even more importantly, feeling that your life has a purpose. It has often been said that even more satisfying than money is the feeling that what we do matters. Wow, heavy stuff.

4. DIGITAL SHOOTING TECHNIQUES

The creative act lasts but a brief moment, a lightning instant of give-and-take,
just long enough for you to level the camera and to trap the fleeting prey in your little box.

—Henri Cartier-Bresson

■ EVERY CAMERA HAS A PERSONALITY

Get to know your camera. It's a relationship worth investing a little time in. An essential part of being able to shoot intuitively is knowing your equipment and camera settings so well that you don't have to think about them much. Each camera is significantly different in its operation and image characteristics. We often talk to photographers who don't even realize all the great features their cameras have. While we can't cover every possible setting and characteristic of every digital camera, we can cover some basic guidelines that are helpful and generally applicable no matter what camera you use.

In order for any blame for a lousy image to be placed on the photographer, not the equipment, we need to customize some settings prior to taking the camera out to play. Some of these settings were mentioned in the previous chapter, under "The Raw JPEG Concept Ex-

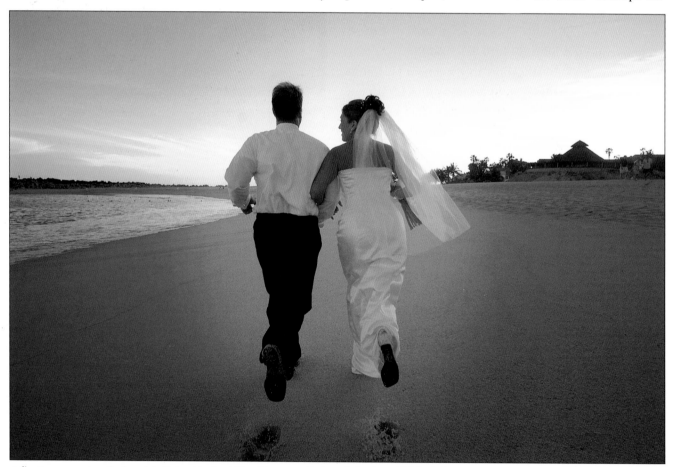

A fleeting moment on the beach in Cabo, Mexico. Nikon D1x, natural light with the digital fill flash Photoshop technique.

plained," but let's expand on those and add a few more digital camera tips.

Set Image Numbering to Continuous. This way, the numbering doesn't restart at 0 each time a card is loaded.

Time-Sync Multiple Cameras. You can set the clock on your cameras, with accuracy to the second, and this time stamp will be embedded in your image EXIF information as it's shot. With multiple cameras time-synced, they can be loaded into the cataloging program, sorted by capture date, and then all the images—from all cameras—will appear chronologically. They can then be batch renamed in this order so that the new numbers are continuous and chronological.

Set the Contrast or Tone to Low. This will protect your images from losing detail in highlight and shadow areas. See the example on page 11.

Set the Color Mode to Adobe RGB (if Available). This color setting captures richer colors and a wider color gamut. This is especially important if you plan to convert images to CMYK. Even if you plan to print to a machine like the Frontier or Noritsu (often referred to as "sRGB printers," although their true color profiles are quite different), Adobe RGB can give you better results overall. See chapter 6 for more information.

Turn Sharpening Off or to the Lowest Setting. Sharpening is purely a software enhancement and should be saved for the final step in the image workflow.

Use a Custom White Balance. Each camera is slightly different, but all allow you to dial in a perfect white balance using a white/gray card or an ExpoDisc (see above right). Read your camera manual to see how it's done, then practice so you can do it quickly on the job. It pays off in big dividends with your final image quality and color consistency. See "Custom White Balance" on page 30.

Know How to Read Your Histogram. Most pro cameras will show you a histogram for any image you've shot. This is useful for evaluating exposure.

Set Your Review Screen to Show the Flashing Highlight Warning. This is an invaluable feature on all current pro cameras. It will quickly show you, via flashing areas on the screen, what parts of the image are over-

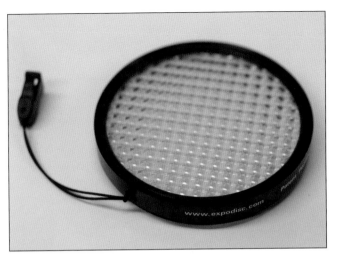

The ExpoDisc for white balance.

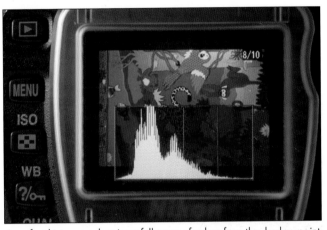

A perfect histogram showing a full range of values from the shadow point on the left to highlights on the right. Notice that the data in the histogram does not extend past the left or right edges, indicating no detail was lost.

exposed and contain no image data. You can quickly make a decision whether to lower your exposure to recapture that detail or accept the blowout. Most people leave this on whenever they shoot.

Check Your CCD for Dust. Dust on your image sensor will rear its ugly head in the form of soft black spots on the images. It will appear in the same spot on every image and is most noticeable at smaller f-stops (like f/8–f/22). Test for dust by selecting the smallest available aperture and making an exposure while pointing at a featureless white wall or paper. Add $2/3$-f-stop of exposure compensation. Open the image in Photoshop and inspect for soft black spots. If the sensor needs cleaning, take it to an authorized camera repair center or clean it yourself with a Sensor Swab, available at most camera retailers, to save time and money. Go to www.Photo sol.com for detailed instructions for each camera.

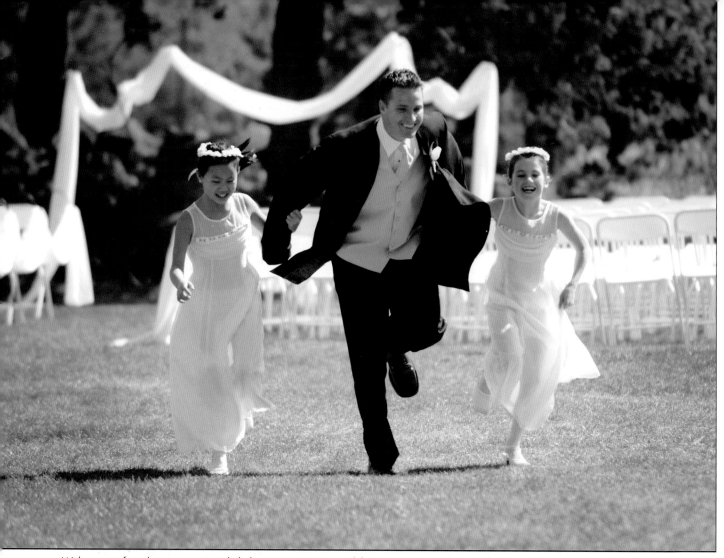

With your preferred camera settings dialed in, you can rest assured that you are getting the most from your camera.

Format the Media Card In-Camera Prior to Every Shoot. More than just deleting old files, formatting is the best way to ensure a clean directory structure for new images. It can reduce the chances of lost images or file-writing problems.

Use the Notes Field. Some cameras, like the current Nikons, allow you to enter custom text in the Notes field in your camera that will be embedded in the image's EXIF info. This information can be viewed in programs like iView and Photoshop. It helps when you want to isolate images from one camera for processing or simply to trace possible camera problems. You may find it helpful to insert the camera serial number and a photographer name, which facilitates tracking images in a multi-camera shoot. We use this text: s/n 1234599 Kevin. By default, this information will be attached to every image this camera takes, until changed or disabled.

Make it a habit to check all your camera settings every now and then. This helps to keep you familiar with where each setting is—especially the infrequently used ones. There's nothing worse than being on location and trying to find that elusive setting while your client breathes down your neck. (Okay, some things are worse, like accidentally erasing all the images while your client breathes down your neck.)

With your preferred camera settings dialed in, you can rest assured that you are getting the most from your camera. Now you can focus on technique.

■ ACTING LIKE A DIGITAL PHOTOGRAPHER

Some of these tips are unique to digital, and some are general helpful tips for any photographer.

1. Shoot several images in a row when attempting to capture key moments. Exercising control is not

always a good thing. With digital, you can free your-self. Often, that peak of the action or perfect expression will happen within a hundredth of a second. Taking just one shot severely limits your chances of isolating that perfect moment in time. Fire three in a row and you may find that the second or third frame is the one you like best.

2. Check images on the camera screen when the lighting is critical, but don't get in the habit of peeking too often—this is a great way to miss what's going on around you. Stay aware and trust your abilities. You should feel comfortable enough to know that you have a good exposure without having to look at every shot.

3. Share an image or two from your camera every now and then with your client. This is a great confidence builder for both of you. Often when creating

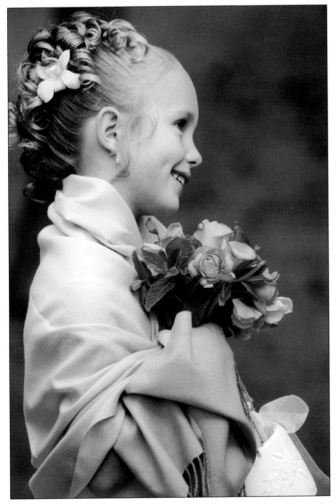

This young lady thought I was photographing her mom, the bride. I quickly swung my camera toward her when I noticed the beautiful gaze of adoration.

images, the client has no idea what you're seeing and how cool it may be. When they see the shot, it's like a switch turns on in them; "Oh, wow!" they say, "I had no idea that's what it would look like." Of course they didn't, or they'd all be photographers. This little sneak peek will help you earn their confidence and give you a little more leverage for trying new ideas with them.

4. Pose if you must, but be on guard. Often the best, most relaxed expressions happen when the client thinks you aren't watching them. It's not a conscious thing they do, it just comes naturally when they let down their guard. We often do "suggestive" posing, which is not as kinky as it sounds. Really this means we'll give a suggestion for a pose or position, and let the client naturally fall into it. We might tweak a little, but we try to avoid grabbing and repositioning body parts too much. This avoids poses that really don't reflect the client's personality and results in much more natural-looking images.

The second part of this tip is equally important. Keep shooting when the client thinks you've already captured the "pose." Look for out-takes. This is when they relax, laugh, and interact with others(see the image to the left). These are the real moments that are often the ultimate goal of the posing—they just don't know it yet. Many photographers overlook these moments, thinking they aren't what they wanted—but shouldn't they be?

5. Demonstrate your energy and willingness. There's a fine line between making a spectacle of yourself and putting the client at ease. Let's use a wedding couple as an example. They generally come to us because they are looking for fun, expressive, or emotional images. Yet sometimes when we get right down to it, they aren't much fun, expressive, or emotional at all. Yes they are! Well, most people are. Usually it takes a certain comfort level with the photographer before they will let down their guard. When you show energy and are not afraid to be a little silly, they start to mirror you. They won't do things that aren't natural to them, but they will start to open up. If you're a stick in the mud, they will be too. Don't be shy; be the mirror for the energy you want to capture.

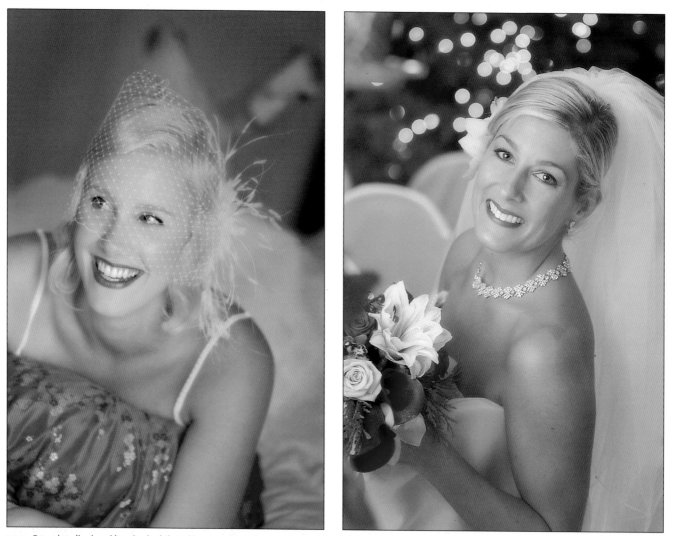

LEFT—Friends talked and laughed while I photographed. These are some of the best moments to capture. RIGHT—One off-camera flash via wireless TTL was used to the left of the scene. It was fired through a pop-up diffuser. The camera's built-in mini flash triggered the main light and gave a slight fill.

6. Experiment with various exposure methods and use exposure compensation. Using aperture priority allows for control over the look of the image, which is primarily determined by the f-stop. The camera's metering does an excellent job in most situations. When confronted with a tricky lighting situation, the exposure compensation dial comes to the rescue. We've set our cameras so that the exposure compensation can be adjusted in $^1/_3$-stop increments by simply turning the thumb wheel. No extra buttons need to be pushed. This makes for instant compensation in any situation and an almost guaranteed good exposure. Exposure is checked on the histogram on the LCD screen—a method that's quicker and more accurate than using a handheld meter. When the mountains of the histogram are pushed off the left side of the scale, "plus" exposure compensation is needed. When they are off the right side, "minus" exposure compensation is needed. With experience, the perfect amount of compensation can be dialed without having to check the histogram at all.

7. Natural-looking flash comes with finding balance. The TTL flash systems on most cameras work quite well. Using flash is no different with digital than with film. The real benefit of digital reveals itself when multiple flash units are used and off-camera TTL is employed. Now we can check the results instantly, so give some thought to trying more interesting flash setups. With wireless TTL, you can take your flash off the camera and create more depth in your single-flash lighting. Try setting it at a low power (try –1 f-stop) and using it like a fill light on

flat-lit scenes and overcast days. When positioned high and to one side, it looks like nice crisp sunlight, without the harsh shadows.

8. One great trick that commercial photographers use is to gel the flash to match the color of the ambient light. This can be used, for instance, when shooting under tungsten light indoors. You may want to use some flash to help illuminate your main subject, but also use a slow enough shutter to capture some of the natural warmth in the room. Using a normal flash will work, but the subject is very different in color temperature from the background. By putting a warm amber gel over the flash and setting the white balance to tungsten, the foreground and background will both be the same color temperature and the overall feel will be much more natural. To recapture some of the tungsten warmth, adjust the white balance to make it slightly warmer. Most cameras allow for minor variations from each white balance preset. (See example below.)

9. Wouldn't it be great if there was a secret formula for great smiles? Sharing images, posing and watching, demonstrating energy, and smiling yourself will help, but here's another tip: have someone else stand next to you and talk to or look at the subject. It could be the groom, a friend, or your assistant. I often ask the groom to stand next to me when I photograph the bride. I talk about how beautiful she looks, and how the light is perfect, and he generally agrees. This is his cue, and any groom worth his weight in plastic shoes will start laying on the compliments—and she'll smile beautifully.

When the client is not focused on the camera and is relaxed, real smiles happen. Compliments and eye contact can achieve this objective. Try this experiment: walk up to anyone, look them in the eye, and smile a genuinely warm smile. They can't help but smile back! You may even get a date or two. A compliment, a smile, and eye contact will get you anywhere. Hey, it got me my wife!

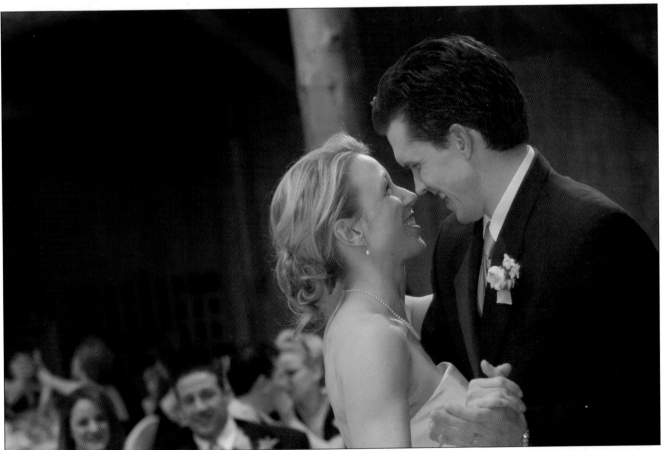

A warm gel over the on-camera flash gave a pleasing color balance with the tungsten room lights. The flash power was reduced to avoid the "flashed" look. The camera's white-balance setting was placed on tungsten.

CUSTOM WHITE BALANCE

White balance is probably a fairly new concept for the photographer making the transition to digital. It is simply the process of telling our cameras the color of our light source or letting them try to figure it out themselves by using auto white balance. Unfortunately, random results can occur with auto white balance.

In order for the auto white balance feature to work properly, the camera depends on an average scene with an average mix of colors. This may work fine on occasion, but, in general, life is not that average. Say you're taking a photo of an average scene, and the auto white balance feature works just fine. All of a sudden, a UFO lands and a very green martian jumps into your frame. Whoa! Your camera then decides the scene is too green and adds magenta. Bummer. Your beautiful green martian is now a sickly gray and the tabloids refuse to run it—it's not "realistic." Everyone knows martians are green!

This real-life tragedy could have been avoided with a simple preset or custom white balance. Presets are the icons on your camera for Cloudy, Tungsten, Sun, etc. While using one of these may not give you perfect white balance, it is usually fairly close, and at least it won't be influenced by sudden changes in your color scene—like a martian.

Better yet, make a *custom* white balance. Using a neutral gray or white card, or a tool like the Expo-Disc, you can tell the *camera* exactly what the color of the light is, and the martian will glow in all its authentic green beauty.

The ExpoDisc is our preferred tool because of its ease of use and accuracy. Within fifteen seconds, we can make a custom white balance almost anywhere. The ExpoDisc is calibrated to perfectly neutral, so using it properly almost makes it impossible to create a wrong white balance. Here are the steps:

1. Place the ExpoDisc over the lens.
2. Point the camera at the main light source and make a custom reading. Note that Canon camera users will take an exposure first, then choose that image in the white balance menu as the source. Nikon camera users will enter custom white balance mode first, then make an exposure.
3. You're all set. Continue shooting and all images captured with the same light source will be beautiful, vivid, and color accurate. The martian will thank you to the ends of the earth.

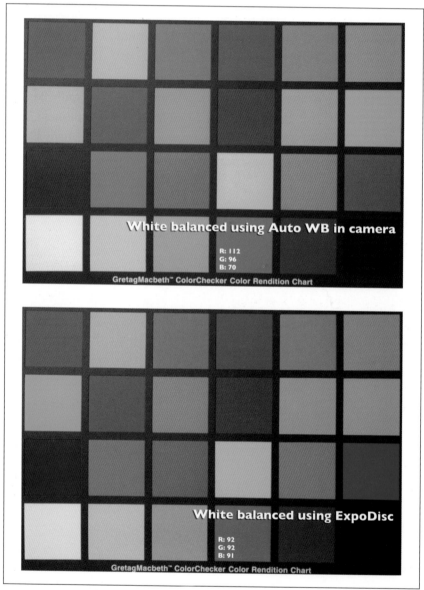

Color chart shot with ExpoDisc and auto white balance. Notice the RGB values on the gray patch. The ExpoDisc chart is nearly perfect, while the auto white balance is way off.

5. WORKFLOW

Home computers are being called upon to perform many new functions, including the consumption of homework formerly eaten by the dog.

—Doug Larson

■ OVERVIEW

"Workflow" is an industry buzzword that became popular with the advent of digital cameras. Digital photography is exciting, to say the least, but it also requires us to manage thousands of image files on our computers.

While Photoshop contains a built-in image browser, and there are other programs that allow for simple perusing of images, they are not true cataloging programs like that offered by an image-management program called iView MediaPro. (We'll discuss the difference between a catalog and a viewer a bit later.) The iView program offers an extensive feature set and professional-level tools and is considered essential by many professionals. The basic features of iView can be used by, and be beneficial to, any digital photographer. However, the real benefits come when photographers tap into its full range of capabilities.

The workflow system outlined in this chapter is ideal for high-volume event photography, like weddings, bar mitzvahs, school photos, etc., but is just as effective for small jobs. It is useful for everything from business headshots, to family portraits, to stock photography. At first the system can seem intimidating, daunting, or maybe unnatural—especially for those new to digital. It's worth the effort, however, to learn and apply the system. In the long run, it can save many hours in production time, and simplify retrieving older files.

There are four key stages in the workflow process:

- downloading/organizing
- editing
- image storage
- consistent backup to disc

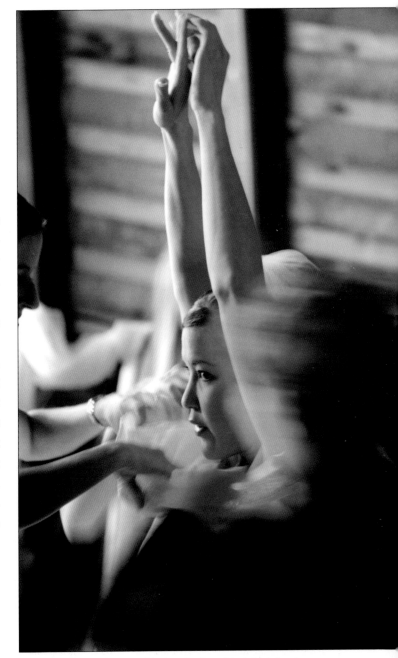

A slow shutter speed captured the busy feeling of the bride's dressing room.

Digital storage is cheap. Up-front costs on new hard drives and storage systems may seem expensive, but when amortized over the number of jobs they will hold, the cost per megabyte goes down considerably. It's best to look at buying hard drives as an ongoing cost of sales expenses, just like film, processing, and proofing expenses. When considered this way, purchasing hard drives is less stressful.

The following breakdown should help ease the pain:

- An average wedding (1500 images taken) requires 9.6GB of storage space. This includes proof copies of every image, tweaks, and slide show files, etc. With current average prices for a 250GB hard drive running $150, and DVD media at $1, this costs us $7.77 to permanently store the job on hard drive and DVD.
- Of course, we want backups of everything, so we have duplicate hard drives and duplicate DVDs. The total price to store on two hard drives and two sets of DVDs: $15.54.
- The same job, if shot on film, would require forty rolls of film, processing, and proofing. With an average cost of $20 per roll, that equates to $800.00. Ouch.

And we haven't even included the cost of purchasing dedicated boxes for storing the film.

In the above scenario, we have considered that our studio loves to create files and hates to throw anything away. For a studio that shoots less at a wedding and doesn't create all the extra files for enhanced images and slide shows, the storage requirements could go down considerably.

Let's look at an example for a typical portrait job. Again, we shoot many images for portrait sessions as well—on the average, 150 images.

- Our average portrait job consumes 2.1GB of storage space (we shoot all files in the RAW format). Assuming the same expenses as above with the wedding scenario, it would cost $2.26 to store the files on a hard drive and DVD.
- Doubling this for a backup hard drive and DVD comes to $4.52.
- The same job shot on film would cost $60, assuming only three rolls.

So, is it cost effective to factor in $15.54 for storage of each wedding and $4.52 for each portrait job? Absolutely. Even if you raised your wedding and portrait package prices by a paltry $16, you'd be covering the cost of double hard drives and DVD media. What are you waiting for?

The benefit of the above system, which entails keeping all jobs permanently on removable hard drives and DVD, plus a backup copy of both, is obvious. Access to images is nearly instant because you simply open the files from the connected hard drive, eliminating the need to retrieve the DVD from storage every time an order comes in.

When a hard drive becomes full, simply remove it from hot-swap case (see sidebar) and store it away. Buy a new hard drive and insert it in the case. If images are needed from an old storage drive, the drive is pulled from the cabinet and inserted into the case, a process that takes about thirty seconds. The DVDs are simply kept as long-term backup—they should never need to be accessed, unless both your hard drives fail. It is not uncommon for a hard drive to fail eventually, usually after extended use, so keeping a backup is very important. If a hard drive ever fails, simply replace or repair it and copy the entire contents of your backup drive to the new one. You're back in business.

■ DOWNLOADING/ORGANIZING

A Download System. Simple organizer bins make the task of downloading and backing up your memory cards foolproof. In our studio, as memory cards are brought in from the shoot they are placed in a bin labeled Ready to Download. Once the images have been copied to the computer, the memory cards are placed in a bin labeled Need to Back Up. These cards cannot be touched or reused until the backup process is completed and verified. Once done, they are moved to the Ready to Clear bin. Once cleared, they can be removed and reused at any time. While this system is quite simple, it can avoid confusion and help ensure a bullet-proof process for image backup.

Organizing Your Images on the Computer. Storing thousands of digital images requires a systematic and consistent filing system to avoid wasted time, frustration, and hair loss. A simple system for organizing your client jobs on the computer is described later in this chapter.

Long-Term Storage of Your Digital Images. The type of storage system used will depend on overall studio volume and initial budget constraints. Consider how many images will be shot in an average month, for the average job, and choose a system accordingly. Keep in mind that new digital photographers usually underestimate the number of images they will be shooting. Once you go digital, you realize the value and fun in shooting more. In addition, with each new generation of camera, resolution goes up and file storage needs inflate accordingly. *Your future file storage needs will probably be much greater than you initially estimate.* Buy now for three times more storage than you think you currently need.

■ RECOMMENDED STORAGE SETUPS

Moderate-Volume Studio. If your business falls into this category, you'll want to ensure that you have one main imaging computer with at least 1GB of RAM. A large internal hard drive is not as critical, as all jobs will be stored on external hot-swap hard drives.

Also, you'll need at least a two-bay hot-swap hard drive system connected externally via FireWire. Two bays allow for one to be used as the backup drive to mirror the main drive. RAID software is not necessary, but is optional if you are comfortable setting up and maintaining it. (If you don't know what RAID means, then you probably don't need to worry about it.) Simple automatic backup software can be used to copy the contents of one drive to the backup drive at timed intervals so the user doesn't have to think too much.

Finally, you'll also want to get the fastest CD/DVD burner available for making backup discs.

This setup should serve most small studios and single-person operations well. If you find yourself often pulling old hard drives from the cabinet to fill orders, then it may be worth investing in a second two-bay hot-swap case (or a four-bay) to keep two active hard drives mounted at all times. Usually, by the time the second drive is nearly full, old jobs on the first drive aren't needed on a regular basis and can be stored. The second drive then moves to the first drive's previous position, and a new drive is inserted.

Multiple Employees. When a second person is added to the studio mix and needs access to the images, a file-sharing setup is in order. Whether you use a Mac or a PC, it is easy to set up your system for file sharing. Once it's done, other computers can connect to them—via an Ethernet or wireless network—and use the files residing on that computer or on any connected hard drive. This allows one main computer to be the "server," and other computers can connect to it and access files on its hard drives. The server can still be used for regular work since

HOT-SWAP HARD DRIVE SYSTEMS

Hot-swap hard drive systems consist of a power supply case and removable sleeves. The bare hard drive is permanently installed into the inexpensive sleeve and the resulting unit can be mounted or un-mounted in seconds without the need for shutting down the computer. Bare hard drives are much cheaper to purchase. We purchase two matching drives at a time—one main drive and one backup for the main drive. Go to www.GraniteDigital.com to check out some great hot-swap hard-drive systems.

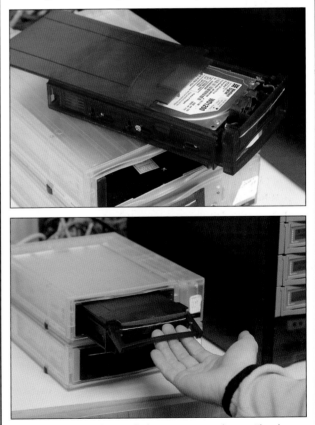

Bare drives are easily installed in inexpensive sleeves. The sleeves then mount in the power supply cases, which are always connected to the main computer.

the file access happens in the background. Frequent access to the files from other computers will start to slow down the server slightly, so regular, frequent use of two or more computers may warrant an upgrade.

At this point, it may be beneficial to use a four-bay hot-swap setup as two drives will most likely be used on a regular basis. (The four-bay setup allows for two active drives and two corresponding backup drives.)

The Next Stage. When your studio volume increases, and you have at least one other helper in your studio working on images with you, everyone will need fast access to the images, and nobody will want their computer to slow down. It's an ego thing, of course. This is where a true server system comes in. It is essentially the same principle as discussed above, except that a dedicated computer handles the file serving. File-server system software can be installed on the computer to most efficiently handle multiple users. With this, every work station runs at full speed, and access to the server files is simultaneous and quick.

There is certainly more expense involved in the true server setup: a computer must be dedicated to serving (although an older computer could be used). The server-system software will also cost anywhere from $150–$500, depending on the number of users and the computer platform. The time-saving and efficiency benefits can make it worth it, however, in a busy studio.

If you feel you need a server system, it's best to hire a computer/networking consultant to help you set it up properly. It will be money well spent as there are numerous settings and configurations to consider. Once it's set, however, it should be fairly easy to maintain and will significantly speed up your studio workflow.

The chart above represents, in a nutshell, the stages that the images pass through from initial download to final presentation. Each step will be detailed in the following sections.

■ CATALOGS VS. VIEWERS

Catalogs. A catalog is a stand-alone file that permanently stores information about your images. Catalogs also display image thumbnails instantly—once the catalog has been initially built—which is much faster than most types of viewers. It stores the EXIF information (the data

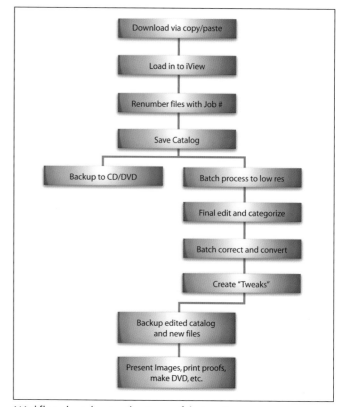

Workflow chart showing the stages of the imaging process.

about the camera, lens, and exposure settings) as well as any categories, labels, and sets the images have been assigned to in the catalog. Since the catalog only contains thumbnails (the original full-sized images remain in their original location on the hard drive or disc), catalogs are relatively small in file size. This catalog file can be saved and stored anywhere—separate from the images if necessary. You can keep catalogs on your computer, while the original images are stored offline on CDs or other media.

In addition to storing information about and helping you organize your images, iView MediaPro has basic image-editing features—allowing for a majority of your minor image adjustments to be done completely within the program.

Viewers. A viewer only shows a temporary view of images on your hard drive or mounted discs. They also provide information about the images, but when the images are removed from the computer, the viewer is pointed to another folder, or it is closed, the info is gone.

The diagrams on the following two pages illustrate the difference between a catalog and a viewer.

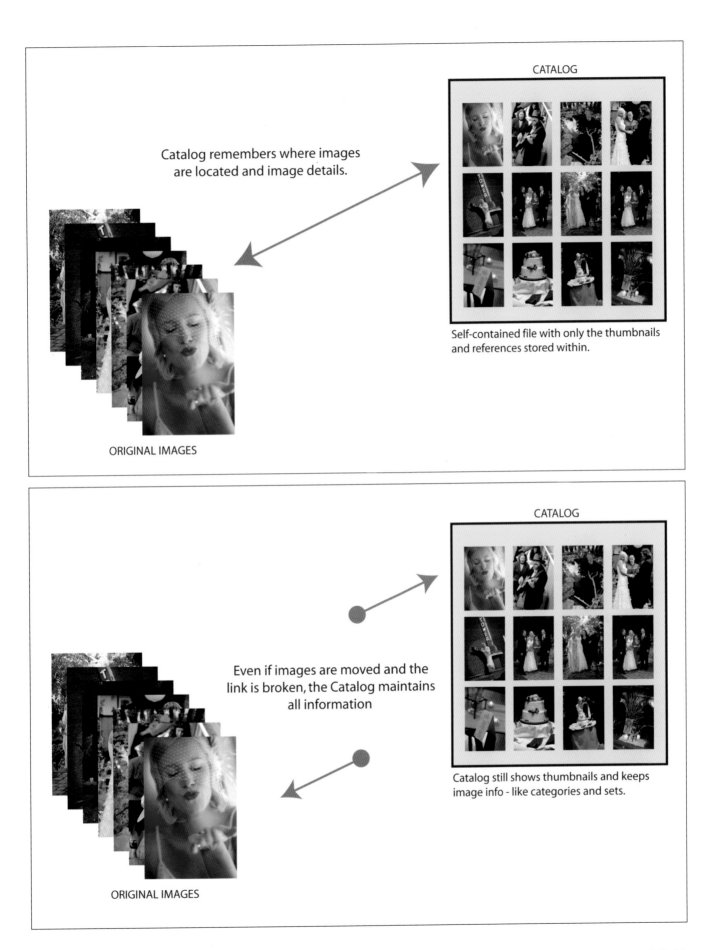

CATALOG

Catalog remembers where images are located and image details.

Self-contained file with only the thumbnails and references stored within.

ORIGINAL IMAGES

CATALOG

Even if images are moved and the link is broken, the Catalog maintains all information

Catalog still shows thumbnails and keeps image info - like categories and sets.

ORIGINAL IMAGES

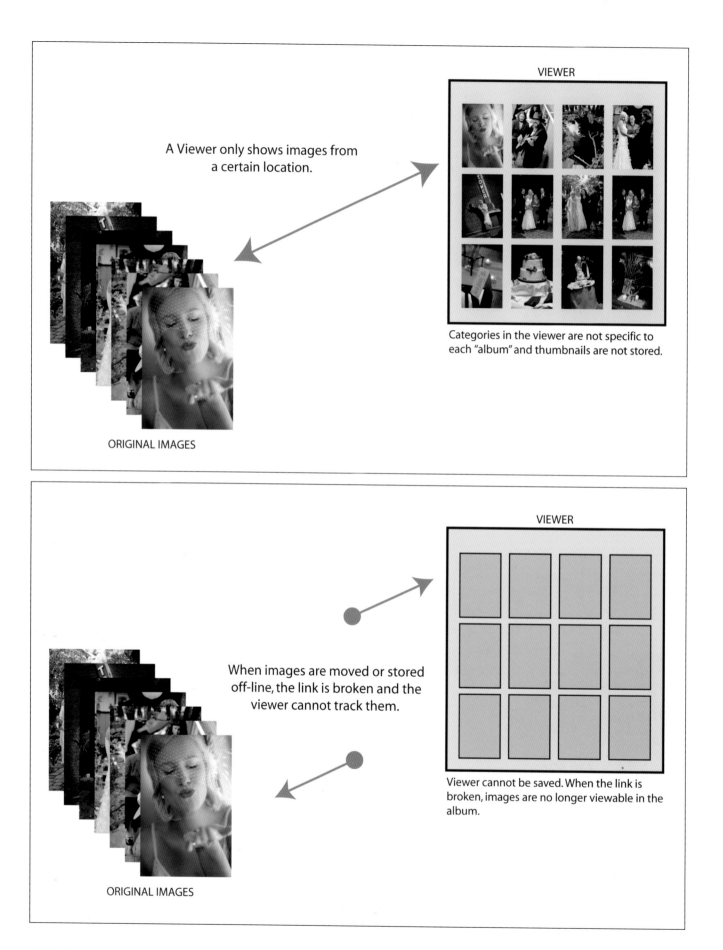

A Viewer only shows images from a certain location.

VIEWER

Categories in the viewer are not specific to each "album" and thumbnails are not stored.

ORIGINAL IMAGES

VIEWER

When images are moved or stored off-line, the link is broken and the viewer cannot track them.

Viewer cannot be saved. When the link is broken, images are no longer viewable in the album.

ORIGINAL IMAGES

Preference to let iView build new thumbnails.　　RAW files contain embedded previews.　　Labels can be assigned with a single keystroke.

IVIEW BASIC SETUP

Before we get into the workflow, it's helpful to set a few preferences in iView and to understand some of the key features. To begin, in the Preferences menu, go to Media> Images.

- Uncheck Thumbnails (above left). This will let iView build new, high-quality thumbnails from your images as they load. This will check the integrity of your full-size images and help identify corrupt images before you clear your media cards. The thumbnails will be much cleaner, larger, and sharper.
- Set rendering to Nearest Neighbor (Faster).
- Select Use ColorSync. In the same dialog box, select Camera Formats from the Type pull-down menu.
- Select Use Embedded Preview (above right). RAW files display very quickly in iView when they have an embedded preview (most newer cameras offer this). Sometimes they display faster than JPEG files. Now, click on the Labels tab.
- Each image can be assigned a label in the catalog (above right). Use the labels to mark images for deletion, favorites, etc.
- The number of the label corresponds to the numbers on your keyboard. Pressing 1 with an image selected assigns it label 1.
- You can change the name/color of your labels to suit your preferences. Try, for instance, selecting the #1/red label for Deletes. Label #5/magenta can be used to label favorite images.

Helper Applications. iView can open images directly with other programs, called helpers. You can add any applications you typically use, like Photoshop, to the list. Also, this is where you can load Photoshop drop-

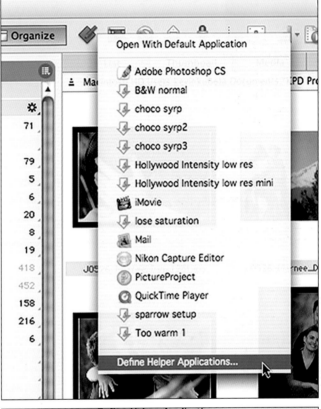

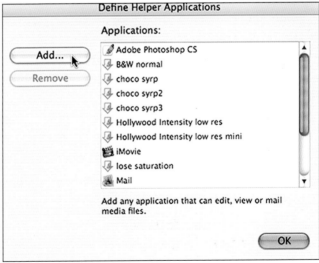

Setup helper applications and images can be opened directly with them from within iView.

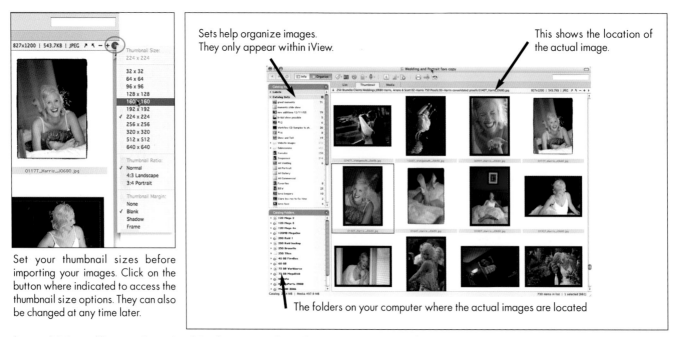

Sets help organize images. They only appear within iView.

This shows the location of the actual image.

The folders on your computer where the actual images are located

Set your thumbnail sizes before importing your images. Click on the button where indicated to access the thumbnail size options. They can also be changed at any time later.

lets, which we'll cover later in this chapter and in chapter 10.

Thumbnail Sizes. You can choose from thumbnail sizes up to 640x640 pixels. Set the size you prefer before loading your images into iView. If you want to choose a larger thumbnail once the images have been loaded and thumbnails created, then just pick another size. When going larger, you'll need to select Action>Rebuild Item to create the thumbnails at the larger size.

■ **IVIEW FEATURES**

iView allows you to do more than efficiently organize and track your images. Below are a few features and their benefits for digital photographers.

Slide Shows. iView can be used to create and run beautiful slide shows. Music files can also be added so that they start and end with the show. Shows can be self-running or played manually, allowing the photographer or salesperson to use it with clients as an image-selection and ordering tool.

Web Galleries. Complete websites can be created from images, allowing clients to browse thumbnails and enlarge images for viewing and selection online. Templates are included and can be completely customized for a look that suits your studio.

QuickTime Slide Shows. Stand-alone movie files in the popular QuickTime format can be created from iView. These single-file slide shows can be put onto

CD-ROMs for clients or imported into popular DVD-creation software.

Proof Sheets. With iView, you can print any number or size of images on a page. The print quality is excellent, and captions are customizable. This iView feature is faster than and better looking than Photoshop's contact sheet function.

Print Images. Single or multiple image layouts can be easily printed directly from iView.

Image Adjustments. iView has basic image adjustments like resize, crop, tone, contrast, color balance, red-eye removal, convert to black & white, saturation, and levels. It also has a clever system for backing up and restoring original versions of the images, in case you change your mind.

---

iVIEW KEYBOARD SHORTCUTS

These are just a few handy ones. There are many more, of course.

- Cmd+0 = Toggle between Fit to Window and 100% view when in the Media tab.
- Cmd +/– = Zooms in or out when in the Media tab.
- Arrows = Move to previous or next image.
- Number keys = Assign the corresponding label to the selected image or images.

Batch Renaming. When images are downloaded from the camera, they have meaningless names. You can easily rename a whole catalog of images in a few clicks.

Read and Modify IPTC Data. This information about the file, including notes, stays with the image and can be read by other programs like Photoshop. Handy for organizing your images even outside of iView.

Image-Browser CD-ROMs. iView catalogs can be distributed to clients with a free viewer version of iView. Clients can browse the images without making modifications to the catalog.

In addition, iView can be used to copy, move, or resize images. It can convert file types either singularly or in batches. The list goes on. It's like the Swiss Army knife of multimedia.

■ UNIQUE PARTS OF THE WORKFLOW

There are a couple of unique features in this workflow. First, lower-resolution copies of the original images are made and used for editing and proofing. They are also used for the slide shows and can be printed to proof sheets if desired. Almost every step of our process will involve working with the lower-resolution copies instead of the originals. This saves time since the proofs print faster, display better, and are more easily edited.

Using low-resolution copies of images is becoming widely accepted in various workflows. In fact, most new professional cameras have the ability to save a full-sized image as well as a low-resolution copy at capture. Manufacturers obviously recognize the benefit of working from low-resolution copies. However, it's preferable to make the low-resolution copies later, in computer, for these reasons: valuable card memory is preserved, confusion is eliminated when renumbering identical image sets later, and some cameras don't give you the desired options for low-resolution size or compression.

The second unique feature of our workflow is the creation of "tweaks." These are the favorite images from the session that have been given the full artistic enhancement treatment in Photoshop. These images represent the photographer's creative vision and should illustrate to the client what final image selections will look like when ordered. Tweaking is highly recommended. The exception may be high-volume school photography, news photography, or other jobs where enhancing images is not practical or desired.

A "tweaked" image before and after. Techniques applied: EZ white balance, digital fill flash, KevSoft, selective focus, and vignette.

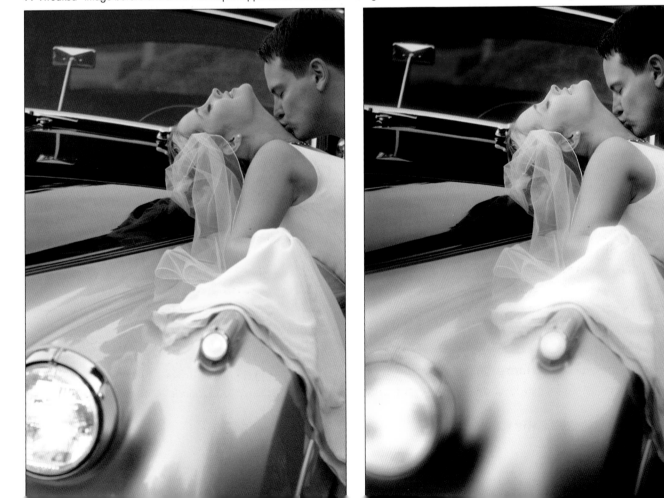

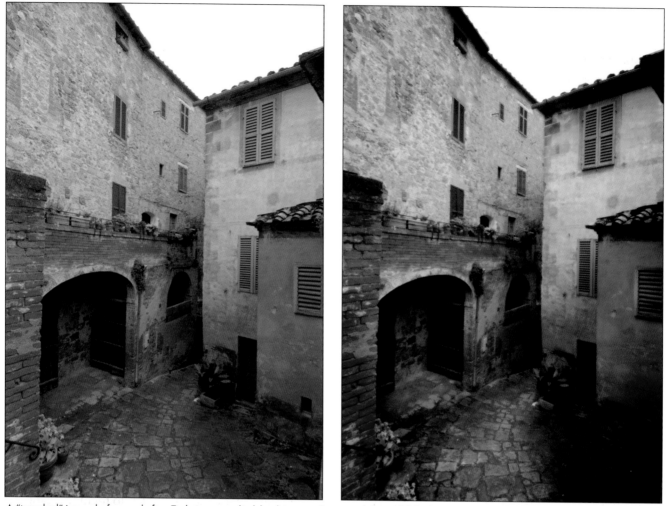

A "tweaked" image before and after. Techniques applied: landscape radiance and digital fill flash.

Above and on the peevious page you'll find some samples of images before tweaking and after. Notice the impact of the tweaked image. Often it's not apparent how significantly an image can be improved until it is seen side by side with the original. Techniques for tweaking your images will be covered in chapter 9.

Is Tweaking Worth the Effort? Absolutely. When we started tweaking images, we noticed our clients would start to buy many, most, or all of the images we tweaked. By tweaking, you show clients your full artistic vision, which shouldn't end with pressing the shutter button. They appreciate your extra work and suggestions, and the images really do sing. Many other photographers have also reported to us the more they tweak, the more they sell.

■ CHEAT SHEET

Here's a step-by-step outline of the stages involved in the iView system. Although each step will be explained in detail on the pages that follow, once you've walked through the system a couple times, you can use this list as a "cheat sheet."

1. Download images to Originals folder.
2. Load Originals into a new iView window. Sort images by capture date.
3. Batch rename using the two-step process.
4. Save catalog and back up to CD/DVD with the Originals folder.
5. If desired, do a rough edit. Mark loser images with label 1 then select all the label 1 images.
6. Use Transfer to Folder to put them in the Edit Out folder. Delete the thumbnails from the catalog.
7. In the finder, copy all images left in the Originals folder and paste them into the Proofs folder.
8. In iView, Reset Folder Path to the Proofs folder.
9. Batch resize and sharpen with iView's Image Editor. Batch without a backup version.

10. Set up a Versions folder in the Image Editor.

11. Label further edits, if needed.

12. Create sets for your image groups.

13. Batch correct images using the iView Image Editor. Be sure to check the Save in Versions Folder option (this keeps a copy of your preadjusted image).

14. You can also/instead use Photoshop droplets to batch correct the images.

15. Select images to tweak. Reset Path (not folder path) to the Originals folder. (If using RAW files, do not Reset Path, just open them in the Finder.) Open with Photoshop, tweak and save a full-size PSD and a low-resolution JPEG copy to match your proofs.

16. In iView, Reset Path again to the low-resolution tweak. Rebuild thumbnails if needed.

Setting up Folders. At our workshops, we witness far too many people wasting valuable time simply trying to remember where they put images on their computers, instead of actually working on them! Set up a well-organized folder system from the start, and use it consistently. You'll thank yourself later.

One time-saving tip that also promotes consistency is to create folder templates in your main image directory or folder that contains all the typical organizational folders you would use for a job. By creating this folder, filled with empty sub-folders, and saving it as a template, you can simply duplicate the master folder template and rename it with your client's name and job number when you start a new job.

This is an example of the folder template structure to use:

> Client folder *(this is renamed with the job number and client name)*
> Originals
> Proofs
> Edit out
> Tweaks
>   *PSD Tweaks*
>   *JPEG Tweaks*
> Versions backup
> Slide Show
> Web

Use a consistent folder structure to find files quickly.

■ SYSTEM DETAILS

Make sure to check your preferences and presets as covered in the previous sections before importing your images. If you are working with RAW files, you'll find that iView handles most formats with aplomb. Some RAW formats have a JPEG preview built into them, which iView can use. If not, iView can still show the files; they just take a little longer to view full-sized. This workflow is virtually the same when using RAW files. During the batch processing, iView will convert the RAW files into lower-resolution JPEG files, just like it does from high-resolution JPEG files.

1. **Download the Images.**

    A. Duplicate your folder template (Cmd+D on Macs or Copy>Paste on a PC). Rename the folder with your new client job number and name.

    B. Insert your media card into the computer. Select all the images and copy them to memory using Cmd/Ctrl+C.

    C. Paste images into the Originals folder in your new client job folder—there's no need to use transfer software. Software that comes with the digital camera or that is built into your system software is not necessary to move images from the card to computer. In fact, it's a good idea to avoid using any software at all; rather, simply click on the card's icon, navigate to the images, select them all, and copy them. Then, move to your client folder and paste them into the Originals folder. Using additional software simply increases the possibility for errors or corrupt files in the transfer process.

    D. Combine images from two cameras and RAW files, if any. You can keep RAW files separate from your JPEG files if desired, and you may also want to keep images from separate cameras in their own folders. It's not completely necessary, however, because iView will easily let you separate these

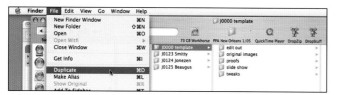

Folder templates can be duplicated and renamed for each new job, ensuring consistency.

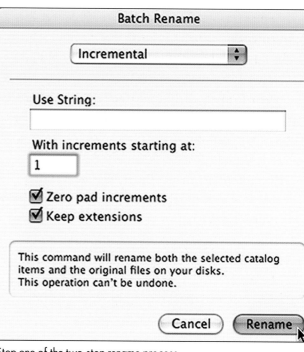

Step one of the two-step rename process.

Step two of the two-step rename process.

images later. As long as image numbers don't overlap, you can put all images in one Originals folder. If you have overlapping image numbers, then put them in separate folders for now.

2. **Load Images into a New iView Catalog.**

   A. Start iView. If a new blank window doesn't appear, go to File>New to create a new catalog.

   B. Set your thumbnail size. It's best to do this before importing, but you can change it later as well. See page 38 for tips on setting the thumbnail size in iView.

   C. Load images via drag and drop. You can drag the entire Originals folder from your hard drive into the blank iView window, or use File>Import Items>From Files/Folders. Keep in mind the basic principle of a catalog: you're not moving the images anywhere, simply asking iView to catalog them from their original location.

   D. Sort them by capture date. Use the View>Sort>Capture Date menu option to sort your images chronologically based on the second of exposure. This will put any images from more than one camera into chronological order. (You did time-sync your cameras, didn't you? If not, see "Camera Times not Synced" in the troubleshooting section.)

3. **Batch Rename all Your Original Files.** It's a good idea to use a logical system for numbering all your images. The following format is derived from systems used by advertising agencies and print shops that deal with multiple jobs, and parts of jobs, all the time. Here's the format: 123_Smith_J0288.jpg, 124_Smith_J0288.jpg, 125_Smith_J0288.jpg, etc.

   The first set of numbers (123) represents the image sequence number. Next is a client name. We use the groom's last name for wedding jobs, just to be consistent. Following is the job number, prefixed

with a letter J for "job." Lastly, the file-type extension is kept. Be sure to use underscores (_) instead of spaces in your file names. Some automated machine-printing systems prefer this old PC style of naming.

Whenever a new job is shot, simply give it the next sequential job number, no matter what type of job it is. You can then keep track of all your job numbers in a simple database, like FileMaker Pro, and enter all pertinent information for that job. This info can easily be searched, so finding an old job is extremely easy.

When every image is linked to the unique job, filing is simplified, images stay sequenced when sorted, and you can quickly jump to a particular image by simply typing the image number.

Here's how to rename the images in iView:

A. Select All images while in List or Thumbnail view (Cmd/Ctrl+A).

B. Use the two-step rename process to format the image numbers as needed. Select menu item Action>Batch Rename. In the first pass label the images incrementally, starting at 1. Click OK. Next, open the batch rename dialog again and select Add String from the pull-down menu. Put in the client name and job number.

4. **Back Up the Catalog and Folder of Original Images.**

A. Use File>Save As to save the catalog with the same job number and client name as your images (e.g., J0288_Smith.ivc—the extension .ivc identifies it as an iView catalog). Save the catalog in the top level of the client's folder.

B. Burn two copies of the client folder containing the original images and catalog to CD/DVD. It's always best to have at least two copies of your important files on optical media, like CD/DVD. If possible, store one copy in your office and the other off-site so it will be safe.

Use a database program to track all your jobs, search for old jobs by name, add job descriptions, etc. FileMaker Pro (www.FileMakerPro.com) is a comprehensive, easy-to-use database that can be customized for your needs. For basic file tracking, try CDFinder (CDWinder on the PC), which is a great little program that simply catalogs every file and disc you drop onto the program. It will keep info on the file/disc even if you remove it from your system. See www.cdfinder.de for more info. We use both in our studio as they each have unique and helpful features.

5. **Label Images for Deletion.** This is your first pass at editing. You're looking for the real losers here—not

that you take any bad photos, of course! Label all losers with 1. Just type 1 on your keyboard with an image or images selected. Type 0 to remove any label. (Note: If you set your thumbnail size to 320x320 or larger, you should be able to do basic editing without having to view the full-sized images.)

6. **Select and Move Labeled Images.**

A. Click the Organize tab; then, in the Catalog Index, open Labels.

B. Select labeled images by using the pop-up menu. Click and hold on the number following the label name. All your loser images should then be selected.

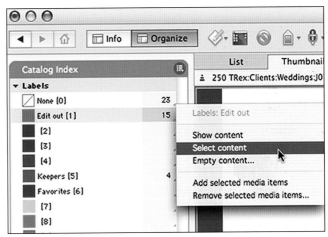

Select all the labeled images at once.

C. Go to Action>Transfer to Folder, to move the original images from their current place on your hard drive to another folder. Choose Move Files in the dialog box.

D. Click Choose Folder and send them to the Edit Out sub-folder in your client folder. You can create this folder on the fly if you don't already have it set up in the template folder.

E. Back in your catalog, click once on one of the selected images and hit the Delete key. This will remove the selected image thumbnails from your catalog only.

7. **Copy Images to the Proofs Folder.** In the Finder, open the Originals folder, select all the images, and copy and paste them into the Proofs folder. (Yes, this will take up a bit of drive space, but it's only temporary.) The goal is to leave the originals

untouched and create working copies that we can resize for proofs.

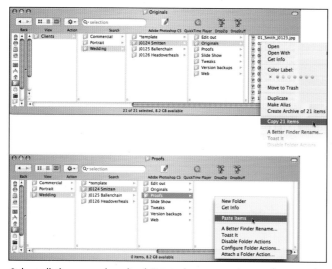

Select all, then copy the edited Original images and paste them into the Proofs folder.

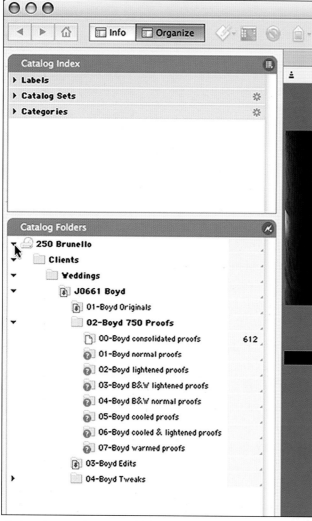

Clicking the triangle next to a folder displays all the contents within it.

8. **Tell iView to Work from the Proofs.** At this point, iView is currently working from—and showing you—the images from the Originals folder. We want to keep the thumbnails we've created intact but to tell iView to link them to the Proofs folder instead, so we can work with them from this point on.

A. Open the Catalog Folders pane. Press and hold Opt/Alt and click on the triangle next to the name of your hard drive to open and show the complete path to where your images are stored.

B. Click in the gray area (with the number in it) to access the menu of options.

C. Choose Reset Folder Path and point to the Proofs folder. Instant switcheroo! Use this when you want iView to keep your thumbnails but to reference the images from a different folder. Note that the file names in the destination folder must match exactly for this to work.

Now, iView has linked your thumbnails with the images in the Proofs folder. All modifications will be made to the files in the Proofs folder, not to the originals, which are safely tucked away.

9. **Convert the Proofs to Low Resolution.** So far, you've told iView to work from your Proofs folder, but these are all still full-resolution images. iView contains a very handy Image Editor that we'll use to make the low-resolution proofs. It's faster and easier than using Photoshop. A 750-pixel maximum (see left image, facing page) works well for printing small images (up to 3"), proof sheets, and on-screen presentations. If you plan to make larger proof prints of all images (4"x6"), use a 1500-pixel maximum.

A. Open the Image Editor from the Window menu (Window>Image Editor).

B. Select all the images using Edit>Select All (you should be in Thumbnail view), then click on the Resize button in the Image Editor palette.

C. Set the Scaling Mode to Scale to Fit, and enter 750 in both the Target Size boxes. Click OK.

Next, you'll add some sharpening to the proof images so that they will display in all their detailed glory. This is necessary if you turned the sharpening off in your camera, which is the recommended procedure.

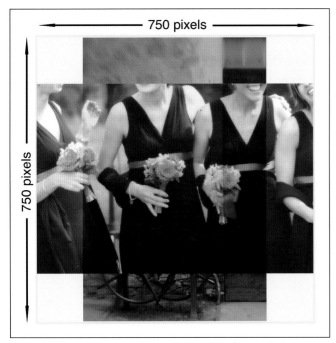

750 pixels

750 pixels

When the Fit Image or Scale to Fit options are used, images are sized to an imaginary bounding box, so they are the same size—whether vertical or horizontal. When we say "750-pixel maximum," we are referring to sizing an image to fit within an imaginary 750x750-pixel box. Vertical images will be 750 pixels tall by whatever width is necessary to maintain the original image proportions. Horizontal images will be made 750 pixels wide. Some people mistakenly think this means to make a rectangular image into a 750x750-pixel square image.

a. Click on the Sharpen Edges button on the Image Editor palette. Enter 4 in the Sharpening box, and 3 in the Edge Detection box. Lower the Edge Detection amount if it looks too "edgy" to you. Click OK.

b. Now, to apply these two adjustments—resizing and sharpening—to your selected images, click the Batch button on the Image Editor palette. When the Batch Options dialog box appears, select Format: JPEG and Settings: Highest Quality. Then uncheck the Copy to Another Folder option. This will convert your high-resolution copies (currently in the Proofs folder) to low resolution in the same folder, without creating duplicates.

c. The conversion process could take anywhere from a few seconds to many minutes depending on the number of images and the speed of your computer.

THE VERSIONS PALETTE EXPLAINED

- Once a Versions folder has been created, each version of your modified image is identified in the palette with a time stamp.
- Select an image and click the version time stamp you want on the Image Editor palette. You'll see the image change. If it's what you want, click on the Swap icon (it looks like a recycle symbol).
- In the next dialog box, choose Swap to keep the current and prior version. Choose Replace to keep this version and delete the prior adjusted one.

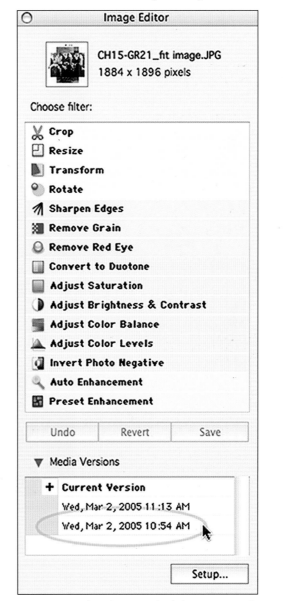

The iView Versions palette keeps track of changes you make to an image, allowing you to restore any previous version that's been saved.

10. **Set Up the Versions Backup Folder.** The Versions folder is a special folder that iView uses to keep backup copies of your images. When you make adjustments to images using the Image Editor palette, you can always return to your backup version if you don't like the adjustment or change your mind.

   A. Click Setup on the Image Editor palette.

   B. Click the folder icon, and in the next dialog box point to your Versions Backup folder. This is the folder where backup copies will be stored. You can create this folder now if you didn't use the template example. Each iView catalog uses only one unique Versions folder.

   C. Click OK. You'll notice in the Media Versions box, it will say Current Version, indicating that you have a Versions folder set up.

11. **Do a Final Edit.** It may be necessary to do a final pass through the images to narrow your selections to the "best of the best." Mark the losers with edit label 1 and move them out of the catalog. Now that your images are low-resolution and sharpened, it

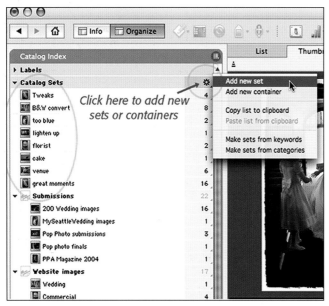

It's helpful to create sets to organize your images. Make sets for organizational groups like tweaks, black & white, too dark, too blue, too warm—or florist, venue, caterer, etc. You can add images by dragging them onto a set name or right-click on an image and use the Add to Set option. The same image can be added to any number of sets. You aren't copying or duplicating the image—only assigning it to a virtual set within iView. Note that selecting images based on their sets is done the same way you selected images based on their labels. Click on the number to the right of the set name to bring up options (Show Content, Select Content, etc.).

will be quick and practical to step through them in Media view instead of thumbnail view. Use the up or down arrow keys on your keyboard to step through images.

12. **Organize your Keepers with Sets.** In iView, sets are simply ways to organize your images—similar to categories. Sets live only within iView and do not have any bearing on how images are filed on the hard drive. An image can be put into as many sets as desired, to aid in organization. Once you have images in a set, it's very simple to show only those images in your catalog, temporarily hiding the others, or to select all the images in a set at once.

13. **Adjust and Correct Your Images in iView.** (This step can be used in conjunction with or instead of the following step.) Use the handy-dandy Image Editor to do basic corrections to images as needed. Of course, if you used a custom white balance (see chapter 4), you shouldn't need to do any color corrections. You may, however, want to lighten, adjust contrast and saturation, or convert images to black & white.

   Photoshop is generally the best tool for major image adjustments, but making minor adjustments in iView is quicker and easier.

   A. Open the Image Editor palette, if it's not already visible. Use menu Window>Show Image Editor.

   B. Select the image or images that you want to modify. Shift-click to select multiple images.

   C. Choose an option from the list of tools (see graphics 24–27 for some common adjustments and suggested settings).

   D. Click the Save or Batch button in the Image Editor palette. In the Save dialog box, be sure to check the box next to Save in versions folder. This will make a backup of your image, prior to the adjustment, in case you want to revert to it later and try a different adjustment or return to the original.

It's important to note that you can make several adjustments to an image, one after another, if desired. They don't actually get applied to the image, or images, until you click the Save or Batch button. If you switch to

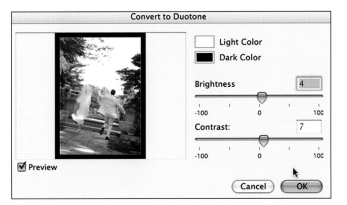

Use the Duotone tool to create black & white images. Simply set your colors to pure white and black as shown. Brightness and contrast adjustments can be made in the same window.

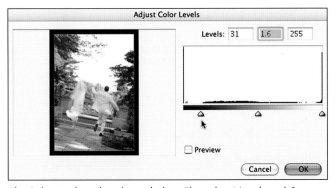

The Color Levels tool works similarly to Photoshop's Levels tool. Set your black and white points by matching the mountains. Move the middle slider to lighten the midtones.

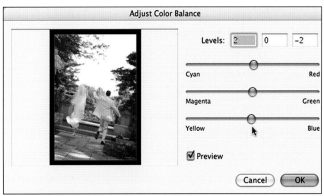

The Color Balance tool can fix slight white balance problems or simply add some warmth to your images.

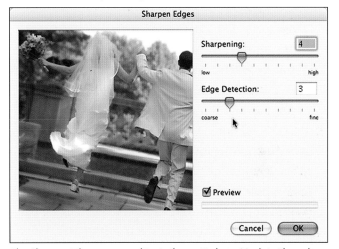

The Sharpen Edges command is similar to Unsharp Mask in Photoshop. Use it after batch-resizing images to proofs. This is especially useful if you capture images with the sharpening option turned off in camera.

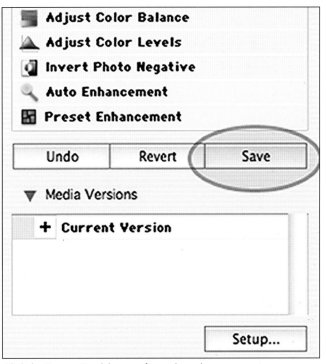

Click the Save or Batch button after making changes to an image.

another image without saving your modifications, they will be discarded. It's best to make whatever adjustments are necessary, then do one save, rather than having to adjust and save multiple times on the same image.

A good way to work efficiently is to scan through your images, adding them to appropriate sets, like too dark or too blue. Group the images so that the same amount of correction is needed for all of them in the set. Then select all the images within the set, open the Image Editor, apply the correction, and click Batch. The adjustment you make to the first visible image will be applied to all the selected images.

If you need to make unique adjustments to single images, then select them individually and apply the corrections.

The images above show some useful Image Editor tools and suggested settings to start with.

Remember to click the Save (right) or Batch button (when multiple images are adjusted together) after making any adjustments, or you'll simply revert to the originals when you start browsing the catalog again.

14. Use Photoshop Actions and/or Droplets.

Sometimes you need the power of Photoshop to make adjustments to a group of images. For example, you may have a favorite black & white conversion that you want to use on all your images. The best way to apply a Photoshop technique to a group of images is through an action. An action is a series of Photoshop procedures that are recorded and played back on any number of images automatically, without any user interaction—a great time for a coffee break!

Once you have an action, or actions, you like, you can convert them to droplets. These are little standalone programs built from an action. When you drop images onto a droplet, Photoshop opens and the action automatically runs, then stops.

Droplets can also be added to iView's Helper Application menu, so images can be opened with the droplet directly from within iView. Imagine you select a group of images in iView, right-click to pull up your Open With menu, and select the My Secret B&W Formula droplet from the list of programs. Like magic, the images begin to pop open in Photoshop, the secret black & white conversion takes place, the manipulated images close, and you return to iView. A quick Cmd/Ctrl+B, and your image thumbnails are updated to show your new beautiful black & white images. Here is the process step by step:

A. Load your droplet into the Helper Applications menu. (Assigning helper applications is described earlier in this chapter; creating the droplet is covered in chapter 10.)

B. Select the images you want to process.

C. Right-click on one of the selected images to bring up the Open With menu. Select your droplet.

D. The images will open with Photoshop, be processed, and closed. When done, return to iView.

E. Before deselecting your images, go to Action>Rebuild Item. The thumbnails will change to reflect your droplet adjustments.

Working with actions and droplets will be discussed in more detail in chapter 10.

15. Work with the Images in Your Tweak Set.
You can skip this step if you choose not to tweak your images. Tweaking was discussed earlier in this chapter, and it is highly recommended for most studios.

A. Click the tweak set that you created in your Catalog Sets panel. This will show you only your images in that set. Next, select the images in your tweak set using Edit>Select All.

B. Go to Find>Reset Paths to reset the path to the Originals folder. (This is different from the Reset

The Reset Path option allows you to tell iView to link a different file with the selected image thumbnail or thumbnails. If the new file looks different from the current thumbnail, then select Action>Rebuild Item to update the thumbnail.

Folder Path option. See graphic 29 below.) This is the only time we want to actually work from the full-resolution originals. Why? When you tweak an image, you'll put actual creative energy and time into the image, and you don't want to have to redo any of that work should the image be ordered—as would be the case if you tweaked your low-resolution copies.

C. It's best to open a handful of images at a time into Photoshop for tweaking. Try selecting four, six, or eight images then right-click on them and use the Open With menu to choose Photoshop. If you find that Photoshop slows down too much with all the images open, select fewer images.

D. Do your work in Photoshop. Save a full-sized version of the file in Photoshop format (PSD) and a flattened copy of the image, at the lower resolution, in JPEG format. Put each into the separate subfolders in the Tweaks folder in your client folder. See "Using the Tweak-Saver Action."

16. Update iView.

A. Switch back to iView.

B. With the same four to eight images selected, choose Find>Reset Paths again, but this time point them to the JPEG Tweak folder.

C. Go to Action>Rebuild Item to update the thumbnails.

D. Batch Rename to add a letter T to identify the file as a tweaked image. See "Modifying an Existing File Name."

E. Repeat from step 15C above for the remainder of the images to be tweaked.

■ **WORKING WITH RAW FILES**

Whether you shoot RAW files or a combination of RAW and JPEG files, the steps are essentially the same. iView will handle most RAW formats easily and can convert them to low-resolution JPEG files. iView uses the embedded JPEG preview to convert to low resolution, so you don't have the control over the RAW conversion

USING THE
TWEAK-SAVER ACTION

You can download actions for your use from the book website (see page 8). One of them is the "Tweak-Saver." This will save your tweaked images in two formats: as a Photoshop document (PSD) with all layers intact and as a flattened, low-resolution, JPEG copy that can be used in your iView catalog for proofing and presentations.

Each time you start a new job, you'll need to complete a quick set-up for the action so that the images are saved into that particular client's folder. Here's how it's done:

1. Start with your tweaked image open.
2. Open the Tweak Saver action by clicking on the triangle next to its name.
3. Double-click on the first Save step. In the Save dialog, find

your PSD Tweaks folder. Click Save.
4. Click once on the Flatten Image step.
5. Press and hold Cmd/Ctrl and click the Play arrow three times.
6. Double-click on the last Save step. In the Save dialog, find your JPEG Tweaks folder. Click Save.

Now you can use this action on all the images you tweak for the same job. When you're done with the Photoshop work, simply play this action and the layered PSD file will be saved along with the lower-resolution JPEG copy!

Keep in mind that the action saves the files to this particular client's folder, so it needs to be setup again when you start a new job.

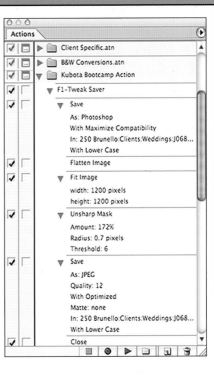

MODIFYING AN EXISTING FILE NAME IN iVIEW

This is helpful when you want to add a letter T to your tweaked image's file name. It's important to put the T directly after the image number (e.g., 123T_Harris_J2345.jpg).

1. Go to Action > Batch Rename.
2. Select Replace String from the pull-down menu.
3. Enter the T before the underscore, as shown below.

Batch Rename

Replace String

Search for:

_Harris

Replace with:

T_Harris

☑ Case sensitive

This command will rename both the selected catalog items and the original files on your disks. This operation can't be undone.

Cancel   Rename

Batch rename the tweaks with a letter T.

process that you would using Photoshop or other RAW processing software. However, your proofs can be made very quickly.

Everything would then proceed as normal, except that when images are tweaked, you won't reset paths from the low-resolution JPEGs back to the RAW files. (iView needs file names to match exactly for Reset Paths to work, and the RAW files will have a different extension in the name, like .nef or .crw.) So, instead of following steps 15B and 15C, follow this two-step approach: First, note the image numbers for the first few images in your Tweak set and switch to your client folder on the hard drive. Next, select the matching RAW files in your Originals folder and open them with Photoshop. Resume with step 15D.

If iView doesn't read the embedded previews in your RAW files (you'll know because the Image Editor won't do anything), then batch process your RAW files with your camera software or Photoshop and create low-resolution JPEG copies first. Import them into iView and work as usual.

In addition, if iView doesn't process your RAW files, modify the entire workflow as follows:

1. Follow steps 1–6. Load the RAW files into a catalog, batch rename, and do a preliminary edit.
2. Batch process the remaining RAW originals with Photoshop or your camera manufacturer's software to create low-resolution JPEG proofs. Set them to 750 maximum pixels (or your desired low-resolution size). Save them to the folder called Proofs.

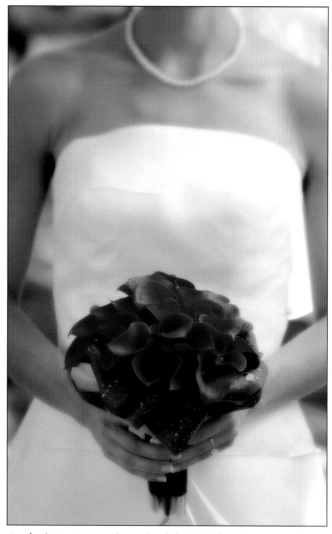

A soft, glowing image enhanced with the KevSoft technique. See chapter 9 for more on this.

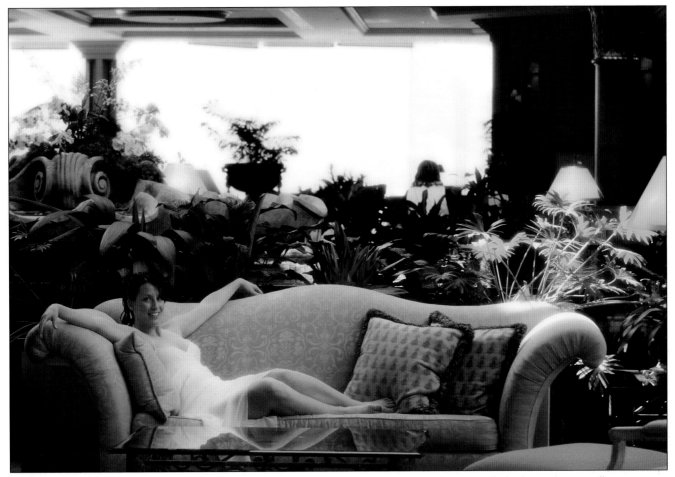

To preserve the natural light on the subject, the exposure was based on the face, allowing the window area in the background to naturally overexpose.

3. Load the Proofs folder into a new iView catalog. This will now be your working catalog.

4. Continue from step 10.

Be sure to check the iView website (www.iView-multi media.com) to make sure you are using the latest version. Support for additional RAW file formats are often added with updates.

■ READY FOR PRESENTATION

At this point, you are ready to do a basic presentation directly from iView—either through a projection system in your studio or on a large computer monitor. Projection systems are highly recommended for digital photographers, if your space and budget allows for it. Showing images in a beautiful slide show, large and on the wall, is very dramatic and impressive. It not only encourages clients to invest in larger images, it gives your entire presentation and image more impact and importance. It's a great sales tool that will pay for itself.

The images are also ready to print proof sheets, upload to a website, or be made into a QuickTime stand-alone slide show file. Chapter 11 will cover some printing and presentation options. Be sure to back up all your hard work again.

1. Save the newly edited catalog.

2. Copy the full-size Photoshop tweaks, JPEG Tweaks, and the edited catalog to a final CD/DVD. Store this with your Originals CD/DVD.

Phew! Did all of that seem confusing? Honestly, it is— at first. Once you've become familiar with the system, however, it can really speed up your workflow. Many photographers are often intimidated by all the specific steps when they start out, but patience and practice will pay off. This system has been implemented by photographers all around the world—with tremendous success. When you've gone through the whole process a few times, it starts to become second nature, and you may wonder how you ever lived without it! Nothing worthwhile ever comes easy, right?

6. COLOR MANAGEMENT

Artists can color the sky red because they know it's blue.
Those of us who aren't artists must color things the way they really are or people might think we're stupid.

—Jules Feiffer

■ COLOR IN THE DIGITAL WORLD

Sometimes dealing with color, at least as our computers see it, can tend to make us feel stupid. But we're not dumb. Computers just deal with color in a different way. They need it to be clearly spelled out, by the numbers, like computers always do. So let's take a minute to look at color from a computer's point of view.

A digital camera cannot capture the entire world of color, which is far greater than our eyes can see. The world of color also cannot be displayed on our monitors nor printed on any paper. In fact, our computers can't even work with the colors we humans can actually see. Computers really are dumber than we are. They have a more limited color palette, so to make them happy we set limits to the range of colors that we will work with. This is known as a color space.

The graphic at the top of the facing page shows a comparison between the wide world of color and a color space within it.

No device can capture, display, or print all the colors that the human eye can see (Aha! We really are smarter than computers!), so programmers had to set limits on

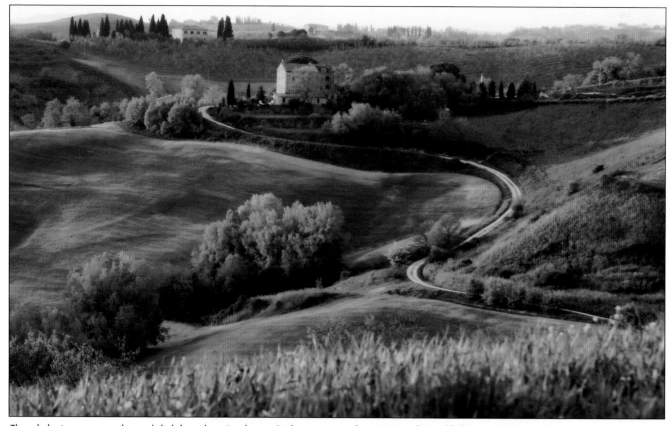

Though the image was enhanced slightly with my Landscape Radiance action, the existing color and light were phenomenal.

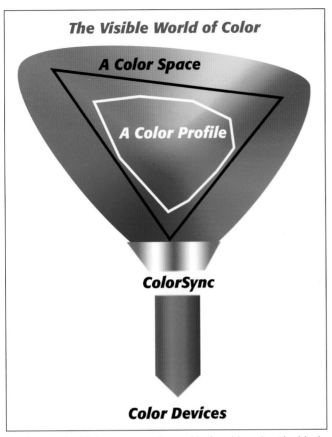

The large color blob represents the world of visible color. The black-lined area represents a standard color space, and the white polygon represents a device's color profile.

the gamut of color that cameras, computers, and printers work with. The term for this gamut of color is "color space."

PIECES OF THE COLOR PUZZLE

In order for color management to be simple, all the pieces must be in place from capture to print. The user must also be consistent in following the steps. With these components in place, predictable color is quite simple—although grasping the underlying logic may not be. That's okay, though, as it's the end result that photographers really need to focus on.

Here are the components of the color management puzzle:

• Understand your camera's color space.
• Calibrate and profile your display monitor.
• Decide on a Photoshop working color space.
• Obtain and use printer profiles (or, know what standard color space to convert images to for the lab).

That's it. Simple, right? It really *can* be simple, especially as color-management implementation gets more refined and universal. Apple Computer Inc. has made great efforts to simplify the mysteries of color management by integrating it into their system and many of the Apple applications. It works behind the scenes to make sure what you see is what you get. Even Apple's e-mail program and web browser (Safari) are color managed so that images you view in either program will appear correctly to the viewer (assuming the monitor is profiled and the images contain a color profile).

COLOR SPACES

There are really only two color spaces that photographers need to be familiar with: Adobe RGB and sRGB. You've probably heard discussions about both—sometimes quite heated discussions—as every digital professional seems to have an opinion about which is best. Let's take a quick look at each.

Adobe RGB. Adobe RGB is a standard color space that is designed to encompass the full range of colors that professionals will need to work with. It covers the color needs of the CMYK printing press nicely, as well as high-quality photographic printed output. Most professional digital cameras allow the option to capture in Adobe RGB color mode. It is a good choice when the widest gamut of color and saturation is desired or when images will be reproduced in CMYK print.

sRGB. sRGB is a color space designed to closely mimic the color capabilities of a typical computer monitor. It is a smaller color space than Adobe RGB and does not quite cover the colors in the CMYK print range. Think of it as the "least common denominator" color space. All consumer digital cameras, and most pro cameras, default to using this color space for capture. The richer, more saturated colors of the Adobe RGB space are not covered in the sRGB color space. In fact, printers like the Fuji Frontier, which are very common in digital labs, are actually capable of more color than the sRGB color space will provide. This is also true of better inkjet printers, like the Epson 2200 and above. Therefore, using an sRGB color space is certainly adequate, but may not maximize the capabilities of your camera or printers.

Many photographers like to use the sRGB color space, however, because of its universal implementation and "safe" color palette. This is primarily true with portrait photographers, whose subject matter mainly consists of people (skin tones). If portrait images will be passed through Photoshop with little or no corrections involved and printed solely to an sRGB-type printer, then a pure sRGB workflow may be perfectly adequate. It is certainly a little simpler to employ for the beginning digital photographer. The two workflows are outlined below.

sRGB Color Workflow

1. Set your camera to sRGB capture mode.
2. Set Photoshop to use sRGB as the working color space.
3. Send images to labs/printers with an sRGB profile attached.

Adobe RGB Color Workflow

1. Set your camera to Adobe RGB capture mode.
2. Set Photoshop to use Adobe RGB as the working color space.
3. Send images to labs/printers with Adobe RGB or convert them to sRGB as needed.

Other studios, ours included, advocate a workflow that is based on Adobe RGB. One of the primary reasons we do so is to avoid limiting images to an sRGB space when a multitude of output needs may be filled by the same image. Any given image may be used for magazine printing, high-quality photographic output, medium-quality photo output, inkjet printing, web use, etc. By using the "highest common denominator," each output receives the best color translation possible from the original image. Here's an example:

In our studio we shoot everything in Adobe RGB. Our wedding and portrait images will often be used in magazine ads, brochures, or books—which require CMYK conversion. Adobe RGB provides the best color base here. The same images will also be ordered as loose prints, which we send to a lab that requires images in the sRGB color space. We can easily "downgrade" the images to the sRGB space and send them to this lab, and they look fine. Next, these same images will be placed in the client's heirloom album. For this we use a different lab, which prints from a higher-quality machine. These images are sent in Adobe RGB color, and the resulting prints are noticeably better than those from our sRGB lab. These prints are used for the albums. We may then make inkjet prints on our Epson printer. The profile for the Epson is more closely covered by the Adobe RGB color space as well, so we get the most from our images and printer here too.

DO YOU WANT TO LIMIT YOURSELF TO THE LEAST COMMON DENOMINATOR?

It is a simple matter to convert images from a larger color space (like Adobe RGB) to a smaller one (like sRGB). No loss of quality occurs (as compared to shooting it in sRGB to begin with). However, converting an sRGB image to Adobe RGB will give no benefits. Moreover, the extended potential color range of the original, if shot in Adobe RGB, would not be realized.

Set Your Camera. So, the first step is to decide which color space you wish to use and set your camera accordingly. Check in your camera manual for instructions on how to change the custom settings and choose your color capture space. Some cameras even offer different "flavors" of a color space, e.g., sRGB I, sRGB II, etc. Consult your manual for the specific uses of each. If the camera has an option for Adobe RGB, it's worth a try. Run some comparison tests on typical subject matter and compare the results. Keep in mind too that the lab you use today may not be your lab of choice tomorrow. Do you want to limit yourself to the least common denominator?

Imagine this: you have all the money you need and you've given more than your share to charity. You live in a city where everyone drives a Honda to scuttle about town. The Hondas are great, efficient, and reliable. You could get a Honda too. Or, you could get a Mercedes—which would scuttle about town just as well as the Hondas during the week. The weekend comes, however, and it's time to open it up and go for a long, beautiful drive through the empty country roads where there are no speed limits. The Mercedes will really shine here, and you'll be glad you bought it. You have the best of both worlds. Back in our real world of digital capture, it doesn't cost any more to capture in Adobe RGB, but you still have the best of both worlds.

Calibrate and Profile Your Monitor. This is probably one of the most important things you can do to simplify your life, end frustration, and facilitate world peace. Why doesn't everyone profile their monitor? Many people think a monitor is a monitor—which it is. However, every display device, just like every camera and every printer, has a unique way of showing color, and it needs to be profiled in order to show an accurate representation of an image on-screen. Our good buddy, color management, does all the work behind the scenes, using the image's color profile and your monitor profile to show you accurate color.

Using an un-profiled monitor to judge color in a digital image is like holding a transparency up to Christmas tree lights to evaluate the color quality—you just don't know what you're going to get.

Calibration and profiling is best done with a hardware device, affectionately known as "spiders." Color-Vision started the trend with their device, called the Spyder, but several other companies make comparable products as well. Most will work fine with both CRT (tube type) and LCD monitors—laptops included. Keep in mind that not all laptop screens can be accurately calibrated. Many have a very narrow viewing angle, meaning the colors and brightness appear to shift when you move your head off center of the screen. Some just don't have the inherent quality to display accurate color—even with calibration and profiling. We have found that most Mac PowerBooks have high-quality screens that respond well to profiling.

Here are a few companies that make popular and affordable hardware devices. Most run between $200 and $300, including the necessary software:

- GretagMacbeth—www.i1Color.com
- ColorVision—www.colorvision.com
- Monaco by X-rite—www.xritephoto.com

Using the device and software is very easy and takes only about ten minutes. You should plan on recalibrating your monitor monthly, as the color tends to drift and change somewhat over time. All of the above manufacturers also allow you to use the device and software on all the computers in your studio, so you can create harmony in your little world.

Speaking of LCD monitors, they are highly recommended for professionals for the following reasons:

1. High-quality units are stable and color accurate. Colors and brightness drift less over time compared to CRT-type monitors.
2. LCD technology is much easier on your eyes for extended use. These monitors do not have a high-frequency flicker like the CRT-type do, and they are sharper, reducing eye strain and possible headaches. How much are your eyes worth?

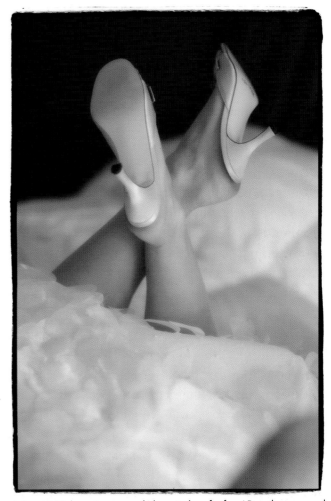

A "portrait" doesn't necessarily have to be of a face! Details can reveal much about an individual's personality.

3. The have no electromagnetic radiation, reducing possible health concerns.
4. They last twice as long and use $^1/_3$ the energy of a typical CRT monitor—saving money and reducing environmental waste.

Keep in mind that a good-quality LCD monitor is necessary for accurate color work, while inexpensive models can be used for second monitors that will not be used for color correction. An efficient setup is to have one main monitor for viewing images and a second monitor—attached to the same computer as an extended desktop—to put all the palettes or other program windows on. Most current Macs have this ability built in, and PC computers need only to have a second video card installed.

YOU'LL NEED TO DECIDE WHAT COLOR SETTINGS TO USE IN PHOTOSHOP.

Instead of spending money on a giant monitor, purchase a high-quality, medium-sized monitor and an inexpensive small- to medium-sized monitor for the palettes. This combination yields more screen space than the largest of monitors, yet costs less. It's a very efficient way to work, and you'll easily find yourself spoiled by the breathing room. The dual-monitor setup is also a great way to work if you only have a laptop computer as your main workstation. You can attach a second, larger display to the computer for the images and use the built-in screen for palettes. Again, Mac Powerbooks have this capability built in, and some PC laptops do as well. Be sure to check the specifications of your computer before buying the second monitor.

Here are some resources for high-quality LCD monitors that can be used for photo editing work (all of them can be used with Mac or PC computers):

• www.Formac.com—Very high-quality and affordable LCD monitors. We use these in our studio. They represent some of the best deals in the industry. Cool designs too.

• www.Mac.com—Apple monitors are arguably some of the most beautifully designed on the planet. They aren't cheap, but you get what you pay for. We also use these in our studio.
• www.LaCie.com—Known for their high-quality graphics products.

These manufacturers often sell a companion hardware calibration device that is tuned to work best with their displays. If you don't already own a Spyder, this would be a good time to get one.

Decide on a Photoshop Working Color Space. Similar to choosing your camera working space, you'll need to decide what color settings to use in Photoshop. By doing this, you set up predefined limits to the colors you'll be working with. Chapter 7 details setting up the Photoshop working color space.

Printing from Photoshop. A calibrated monitor does not, in itself, guarantee every print will match your original image on screen. Calibration does, however, allow Photoshop to display colors accurately so you can see a true representation of your photo in Photoshop. By using the Soft Proofing feature, described in the following section, Photoshop can provide a simulation of what your particular printer will create from that image. In other words, sometimes your printer simply cannot match the colors of your original image exactly, but with a calibrated monitor and the Soft Proofing feature, you can at least see what you *will* get before printing.

Each printer has different capabilities and characteristics. Not all will be able to print the exact same color range. Therefore, certain printers may be preferred for different projects and color ranges. "Soft proofing" means that you can see on screen, with a profiled monitor and printer, what a particular printer can do. So, while we cannot make every printer do our bidding, we can at least know what they will do.

The first ingredient you need is a color profile for your printer. You can use the factory-installed profiles or have a custom one made. The actual profile is a small file with an extension of either .icc or .icm. They must be installed in the correct place in your system before they are available to Photoshop. Here's where to install them on your computer:

- MAC OS X—System drive>Library>ColorSync> Profiles
- Windows XP—C:\WINDOWS\system32\spool\ drivers\color

With the profiles properly installed, you are ready to soft proof in Photoshop. Follow these steps:

1. With an image open, go to View>Proof Setup>Custom.

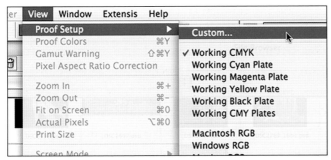

Choosing a custom proof setup.

2. In the dialog box, open the Profile list and find the profile for the printer–paper combination that you want to use. Set the other options as shown.

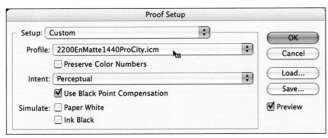

Choose your printer under Profile and select the appropriate item under Intent in order to see on screen what your print should look like.

The Intent describes how colors are translated from one color space to another (from your working space to the printer profile, for example). The two Intent options that are most suitable to photographic images are Perceptual and Relative Colormetric. Perceptual is more suited to photographs and will generally give only a very slight visual shift in colors—if any. We usually use Perceptual, but it is okay to try both to see which is more pleasing to you. You'll see the differences, if any, on screen immediately if you have the Preview option checked.

When you print your file, or send it to a lab, make sure to use the same intent in the print dialog

box or the Convert to Profile dialog box. Both of these are discussed later.

3. With the Preview button checked, you should now see a simulation on screen of your printed output. How does it look? It's a good idea to save proof setups for your common printer–paper combinations so you can access them quickly from the bottom of the Proof Setup list. Click OK.

4. Your window is now in active Preview mode. (You can always check this by going to View and verifying that Proof Colors is checked.)

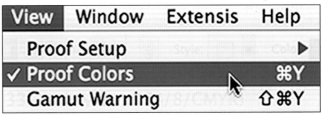

Turning proofing on or off.

5. If you don't like the way your image looks, you can alter it using any of your adjustment layers.

Keep in mind that the Proof Colors option will only be active for the current window. If you open another image and want to proof it, you'll need to turn it on again.

Now it's time to print this image. Use Photoshop's Print with Preview option from the File menu. In the dialog box, select your printer profile again in the Print Space: Profile section. Make sure that Perceptual (or the

The Print with Preview option is the best to use from Photoshop, rather than the standard Print command.

intent you soft-proofed the image with) and Black Point Compensation are also selected. Click Print.

In the Print dialog box you have options for the quality, paper choice, etc. When using a color profile, it's necessary to use the same settings that were used to make the profile originally. If this is a custom profile for your printer, then the service that made the profile will supply specific settings to use. If using factory profiles, for printers like the Epson 2200 or 4000, then choose the matching paper and be sure to turn off any additional print-driver adjustments, as shown below:

Turn off all printer color controls so you can get consistent results, allowing only Photoshop to manage your color.

If your monitor is profiled and you have used good-quality printer profiles, then your on-screen proof should match your printout quite nicely. If it is significantly different, then go through this quick checklist to see if you've missed anything:

1. Monitor profiled.
2. Accurate printer profile installed in system.
3. Printer–paper profile selected in Photoshop's Print with Preview dialog box.
4. Matching paper for profile selected in Print Driver dialog box.
5. All auto corrections turned off in Print Driver dialog box.
6. Print is being compared to proof view, not normal image on screen.
7. Print wasn't made on the backside of the paper. (Don't laugh, I've done this.)
8. Computer and printer both turned on. (ha, ha)

If all the steps seem to have been followed, but still the print doesn't closely match the screen proof view, then it's likely the printer profile in use is not very good. It may be time to invest in a custom-made profile. Unless you need to make many profiles for different printer–paper combinations, you'd be better off paying for good profiles one at a time. It's possible to buy the hardware packages to make your own custom-color profiles, but they are expensive and time consuming to use. Save your sanity and let the profiling services do it for you. The process is simple with most companies: you download a target file from their website, print it according to their instructions, then send the printout to them via mail for scanning and profiling. Within a day or two they will e-mail you the custom profile with instructions for use.

Here are a couple resources for custom printer profiles:

- www.Drycreekphoto.com—$50 per profile. Money-back guarantee.
- www.Chromix.com—$100 per profile. Money-back guarantee.

Most printers come with factory profiles in the box. However, their quality can vary. They are usually acceptable, and better than no profile, but a custom profile will squeeze every bit of color-matching accuracy out of your printer as possible. Printing doesn't have to be complicated or time consuming. Be consistent and follow the steps, and you should never again have to scream, "All I want to do is print a picture!"

7. PHOTOSHOP ESSENTIALS

The negative is comparable to the composer's score and the print to its performance.
Each performance differs in subtle ways.

—Ansel Adams

The darkroom, as many of us knew it, has forever changed. The smell of developer has been replaced by the smell of leather office chairs and aromatherapy candles. Hallucinating under extended periods of red-light cave dwelling has been replaced with an electronic hum and an iTunes visualizer screen. Instead of backaches from standing, we get backaches from sitting. Yes, everything is really the same, but completely different. Having worked on images both in the dark and via LCD illumination for many years, I have to say I like the new digital darkroom a lot better. I still disappear into my cave, but at least now I don't have to freak out when my kids open the door unexpectedly.

Photoshop is as much an artist's tool as is the camera. Just as film photographers would seek out the best darkroom artists to reproduce their work, digital photographers can apply artistic enhancements to their own work. I like the epigraph from Ansel Adams because it

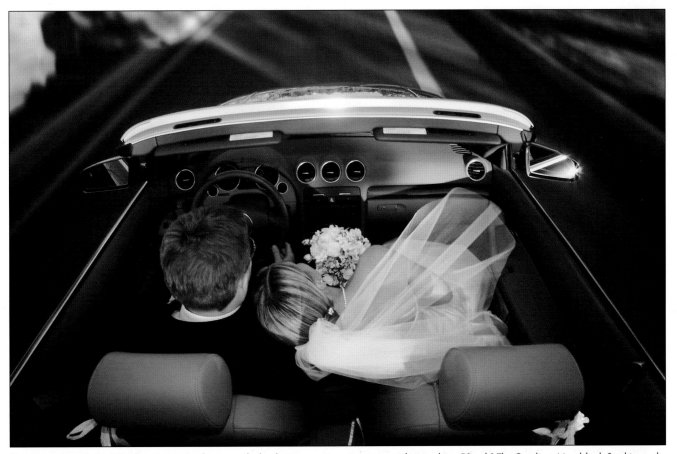

Do not try this at home! I love movement in photos, and what better way to get movement than to drive 50mph? The Gradient Map black & white technique worked beautifully with the gleaming chrome. Image made with a Nikon D1x, 14mm lens, and slight fill flash on camera.

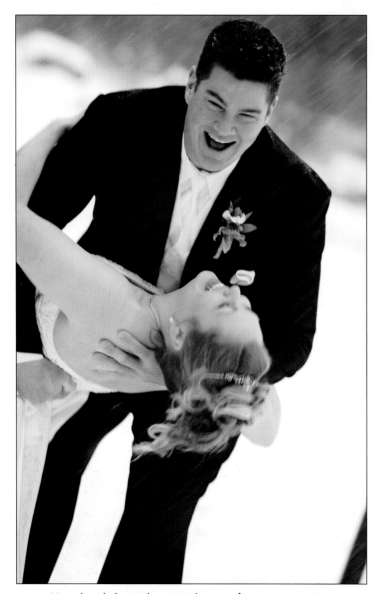

Never let a little weather get in the way of a great moment! Image converted to black & white with the Gradient Map technique.

easy. It takes the creative power away from the "elite" who invested the time, space, and money into a darkroom setup—who studied, and often learned via trial and error, the "dark art" of printing their own images.

Let's face it: Photoshop is really fun. And it's not that hard to learn. In fact, in a single day it's possible to learn some essential imaging techniques that would take weeks or months to master in the old darkroom. Moreover, the pressure is now upon photographers to produce better work to begin with. Fancy Photoshop tricks don't impress much anymore. Good images must be made in capture and enhanced in Photoshop. Everyone is expected to be able to produce good clean work, at the very least.

In this chapter, we'll take an extensive look at some essential Photoshop techniques. If you want simply to fine-tune an image for best output, you'll find the required techniques here. When it's necessary to correct problems in images, retouch, reshape, or remove—then the Photoshop Corrective chapter is the place to go. When it's time to add the artistic touch to an image, to really customize it, then the Photoshop Enhancing chapter will give you some great ideas and techniques.

■ THE BASICS

While this chapter is not a "Photoshop 101" type of instructional—it assumes some knowledge of Photoshop 7 or newer—it is broken down into simple-to-follow steps. Don't be deceived by the simplicity of these techniques. They are critical building blocks to outputting the perfect image. Many books have been written on the use of Photoshop, but not many get straight to the point: "this is what you need to do every day, in a busy photography studio, to make your images look great."

Before diving into the well of knowledge with Photoshop, please print the following mantra and pin it up above your computer:

bridges traditional thinking and artistic thinking. Most people think of Ansel Adams as one of the finest and most influential "traditional" photographers of our time. Yet traditionalists often frown upon any sort of "manipulation" to photographic images.

What many photographers may not realize is that photographers like Ansel Adams—and most other famous photographic artists—spent *hours* in the darkroom manipulating their photographs! Every time a photographer puts a filter in front of her lens or changes film stock, she is essentially manipulating a scene or photograph. Anything done prior to capture or in the darkroom to achieve the artistic vision was fair game, yet Photoshop manipulation was considered "cheating" or labeled "manipulated." Why? Maybe because it is

- The temptation to wander is great. I will focus on day-to-day necessities: efficiency and production—yet allow the right brain equal satisfaction.
- I am digital, therefore I have more options available than any film photographer. I will exercise them.

- I will not be a slacker and let the open door to creative opportunities slam on my foot.

Now let's get started.

Setting Up for Success. Photoshop has preferences that should be tweaked a little. Here are some settings that should be changed from their defaults, and an explanation of each. It is not a complete run-down of every option—just the settings that will make the most difference for the workflow and techniques used on a daily basis. If a preference is not discussed, then it can be assumed that it is left at the default.

1. Go to Photoshop>Color Settings (Edit>Color Settings on PC) and apply the following important changes. Check on Advanced Mode (see facing page) if you don't see all these options. Leave the other settings at the defaults:

- Working Spaces: RGB>Adobe RGB (or keep at sRGB if you've decided on an sRGB color workflow).
- Color Management Policies: RGB>Preserve Embedded Profiles.
- Profile Mismatches: check on Ask When Opening and Ask When Pasting.

Make sure to check Advanced so you'll see the options as listed here.

- Missing Profiles: check on Ask When Opening.
- Conversion Options: Engine>Adobe (ACE) and Intent>Perceptual

2. Open Photoshop>Preferences>File Handling.

The File Handling preferences.

A. Click on the Ask Before Saving Layered TIFF Files check box. This file format is not universal, and some programs may not properly read them. If saving layered files is needed, keep them in PSD format. "Asking" prevents unintentional saves.

B. Maximize PSD File Compatibility: Never. This can reduce file size when saving layered PSD images. With it on, layered files are saved with a flattened copy of the image embedded. This increases the file size by the amount of the original image.

C. Click OK.

3. Go to Photoshop>Preferences>Display & Cursors.

Display & Cursors preferences.

A. Painting Cursors: Brush Size (this is the default).

B. Other Cursors: Precise. This will give an exact-point crosshair instead of a picture of the tool, which is rather useless for precise work.

C. Click OK.

4. In the tool bar, there are a couple of settings that should be changed as well:

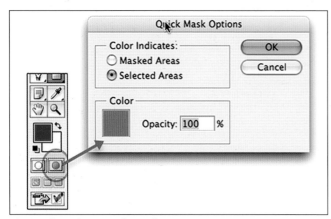

The Quick Mask icon on the toolbar.

A. Double-click on the red circle to open the Quick Mask options. Change the opacity to 100% and the Color Indicates option to Selected Area. This is helpful when you use a Quick Mask (a.k.a. Red Blob) mode to see an actual feathered selection area. This will be covered in more detail later. Be sure to click on the Normal Mode icon box after closing the dialog box.

B. Click on the Eyedropper and change the Sample Size to 5x5 Average instead of Point Sample. This gives a more realistic representation of an area of color as seen by the eye.

The Eyedropper settings.

■ WORKING EFFICIENTLY IN PHOTOSHOP

Once you start getting a grasp on all the amazing things you can do with Photoshop, you may actually enjoy working on the computer. However, it's still a good idea to make your time spent as efficient as possible. After all, time is money. Here are a few ways to work faster:

Learn and Use Keyboard Shortcuts. By taking the time to remember a few key combinations, you can greatly reduce time and energy spent mousing around and digging through layers of menus. Here are the most essential keyboard shortcuts from Photoshop's built-in set. Try to memorize these, at the very least, and your productivity will go up by 68.23%!

- Space bar—produces the Hand tool, which allows you to move the zoomed-in image around in the window for close inspection of various image areas
- Cmd/Ctrl+space bar—Zoom In tool (click with mouse to zoom)
- Cmd/Ctrl+Opt/Alt+space bar—Zoom Out tool
- Cmd/Ctrl+0—fit entire image on your screen
- Cmd/Ctrl+Opt/Alt+0—see actual pixels or 100% view
- D—reset default colors (black foreground, white background)
- X—switch foreground and background colors
- Opt/Alt+Del—fill with foreground color
- Cmd/Ctrl+Del—fill with background color
- [or]—each press reduces or enlarges the current brush size (up to four steps total)
- Shift+[or]—each press softens or hardens the brush edge (up to four steps total)
- Cmd/Ctrl+Z—undo your last step
- Cmd/Ctrl+Opt/Alt+Z—move back through your History states one step at a time. Multiple undo.

Customize Keyboard Shortcuts in Photoshop CS. If some of your commonly used menu items don't have keyboard shortcuts, you can assign them whatever you

Custom keyboard shortcuts can be created to suit the way you work best.

want. Go to Edit>Keyboard Shortcuts and you'll see a list of every available menu item. Assign your favorite menu item your unique key combination. You can then print out a summary of all your keyboard shortcuts with the Summarize button. Almost anything can be given a shortcut! Choose your own key combinations to use with these:

• Make new Levels adjustment layer
• Make new Curves adjustment layer
• Unsharp Mask
• Gaussian Blur
• Play Action
• New Layer Mask

Add Function Keys to Your Favorite Actions. Double-click just to the right of the action name to bring up the options box. Add a Function key combo here. Then, on the keyboard, tape a hint tab with the name of the action to help you remember.

Use a Programmable Mouse or Wacom Tablet. You can customize them to play your shortcuts or actions by clicking certain buttons on the tool.

Use a Larger Monitor. Although not a free option, using a larger monitor, or ideally adding a second monitor, can really boost your efficiency as well. Much time is saved when it's not necessary to scroll around in a large image.

■ THE PHOTOSHOP WORKFLOW

As in life, Photoshop has what's known as the Path of Least Resistance. This is the sequence of steps that should generally be followed when working on an image. Following this sequence will help preserve image quality and minimize corrections—and stress.

1. Tonal correction.
2. Color correction and/or balancing.
3. Retouch.
4. Enhance.
5. Save a master file.
6. Size/crop for intended output.
7. Sharpen. (From the official Adobe Photoshop documentation comes this advice: ". . . if you plan to edit

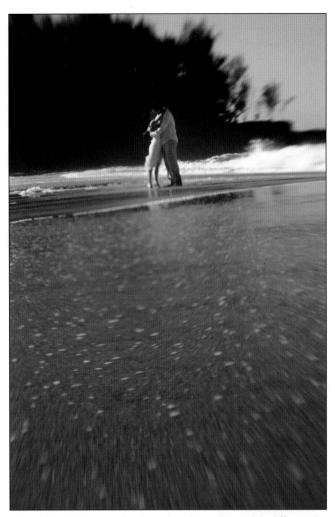

A Lensbaby 2.0 was used to keep the subject sharp while diffusing the rest of the image.

the image extensively in Photoshop, turn off the Camera Raw sharpening [or camera sharpening], and later use the sharpening filters in Photoshop as the last step after all other editing and resizing is complete.")
8. Resave a copy for output.

Often the first two steps can be combined into one. For example, a Levels adjustment layer may be used to inspect and adjust the histogram to create the perfect tonal range. In the same dialog box, the white balance can be done using our "Single-Sample Neutralizer" technique shown later in the chapter. If both will be done together, it is easier to do the white balance first, then adjust the tonal range in the same dialog box. It is possible to use either a Levels or Curves adjustment layer for this purpose. Both will be discussed later.

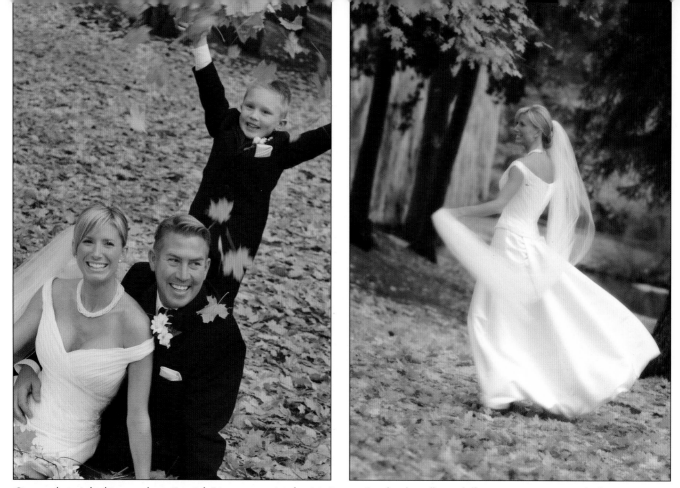

Once a photo is looking good as a "straight" image, meaning that it is "correct" and technically ready for print, it's time to start looking at ways to improve it.

Once a photo is looking good as a "straight" image, meaning that it is "correct" and technically ready for print, it's time to start looking at ways to improve it. This is where the retouching and enhancing come in. It's best to have a clean image before adding the spice.

Retouching could simply mean blemish removal, stray hair trimming, removing distracting objects (like the mother-in-law), or more complex things like cloning and head swapping. These techniques will be covered in chapter 8.

Enhancing is where creativity takes over. The image can be made black & white or handcolored, digital fill-flash can be applied, the image can be softened, etc.

After all the main image work is done, a master file should be saved in the PSD format with all adjustment layers intact. This will give you a starting point for any sized image that needs to be made in the future. Notice that cropping, sizing, and sharpening the image have not been done yet.

When a file is needed for printing—either at an outside lab or on an in-house inkjet—the master PSD file can be opened and sized appropriately. Sharpening should then be applied. The resulting file can be printed directly or saved in the lab's preferred format.

This is a brief and simplified view of the process, and each part will be covered in more detail. Let's start with some Photoshop essential concepts and image basics.

■ 8 BITS VS. 16 BITS

In Photoshop, the user has the option to work in 8-bit or 16-bit mode. As of Photoshop version CS, users can also maintain layers and still work in 16-bit mode, a feat that was not possible in versions 7 and earlier. This feature is a key component to a simple imaging technique we developed that can be integrated into your daily routine. The technique is called "8-16-8." Before delving into this, it's important to have a basic understanding of what bit depth means.

In 8-bit mode, Photoshop has 16.7 million colors at its disposal. This may seem like more than enough, but really it is just barely enough. Occasionally, when major color corrections or enhancements are done—including techniques like vignetting—an image can show signs of posterization. This monster rears its ugly head in the form of "stair steps" where smooth transitions of color should normally be. For example, imagine a rich blue or amber sky that is lighter at the horizon and graduates to a darker shade at the edges of the photo (see next page).

The posterization happens here because in 8-bit mode there really aren't enough shades of the particular color to allow for a seamless transition. This is especially obvious after an already graduated sky is enhanced with a vignette.

Now, take this same image in 16-bit mode (RAW camera images are captured in 12 bits, which translates into Photoshop's 16-bit mode): there is now more than enough color to fill in the gaps and eliminate posterization. Even if the final image must be converted down to

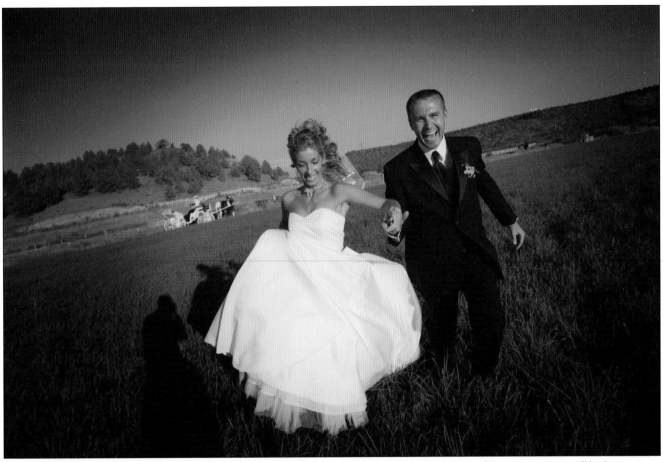

The full 8-bit JPEG image. (Note: Posterization is more apparent in high-quality photographic prints than in offset press production [like the images in this book], which tends to camouflage it somewhat.)

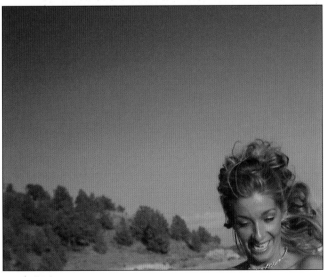

Normal 8-bit image.

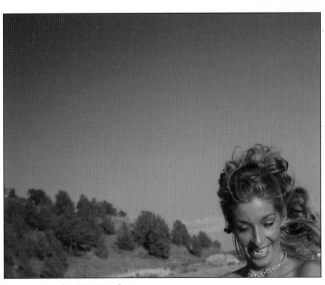

Image using the 8-16-8 technique.

8 bits in order to send to your lab or printer, the best 8-bit color palette can be created from the 16-bit data.

What if you shot the original image as an 8-bit JPEG file? Is all hope lost? No. Actually, we can reap some of the benefits of a 16-bit workflow even if starting with an 8-bit original. In the case of an original 8-bit file, we can apply our corrections while in 16-bit mode, and Photoshop will have the extra colors available to fill in any potential gaps in the color gamut with the best possible 8-bit palette. Here are the simple steps to take advantage of the "8-16-8" concept:

1. Work on your image as normal in 8-bit mode by using adjustment layers for tone and color corrections as well as any enhancements.
2. Save the master image as normal.
3. When it's time to print or send a copy of the file to your lab, convert the image to 16-bit (Image>Mode>16 bit).
4. Flatten the image.
5. Convert the image back to 8-bit mode (Image>Mode>8 bit).
6. The resulting 8-bit file should now show improved gradations and a full histogram, sans gaps.

The image crops on the previous page show the difference between the traditional 8-bit workflow and the improved "8-16-8" workflow. The left image was done purely in 8 bits, while the right image used "8-16-8." Both started as an 8-bit JPEG file. Look particularly at the graduated area of the sky where posterization is obvious in the 8-bit version.

The following are the final histograms for each image. Notice that the gaps in the histogram, indicating missing information, are gone in the "8-16-8" version.

Using adjustment layers is key to this technique. With them, the image can be worked as normal in 8-bit mode and doesn't actually need to be converted to 16 bits until print time. Why? Because an adjustment layer simply shows a simulation of what will happen to the image when it is flattened or saved in a flat format. When you move the image into 16-bit mode and flatten it, this is when the adjustments are applied to the image data—for good.

When working in Photoshop 7, layers cannot be used in 16-bit mode; however, there is a viable (though not as flexible) way to work around this to improve image quality. Here are the steps:

1. Open the 8-bit image and go to Image>Mode>16 bits/Channel.
2. Go to Image>Adjustments and select Levels or Curves to do your major tone and color corrections. You may also want to use Hue/Saturation or Color Balance as needed.
3. Convert back to 8-bit mode and continue as usual, adding layers if needed.

The limitation here, as compared to doing the same process with layers in Photoshop CS, is that once you make the corrections via the Image>Adjustments menu, they are applied and done. This is not usually a big deal, but keeping them as active layers does allow the flexibility to go back and readjust the settings at any time. They can be changed as many times as necessary before actually flattening the file.

The "8-16-8" technique can easily be made an action, which can then be assigned to a function key. From then

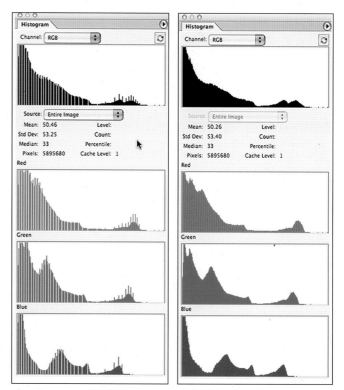

The 8-bit histogram vs. the "8-16-8" method histogram.

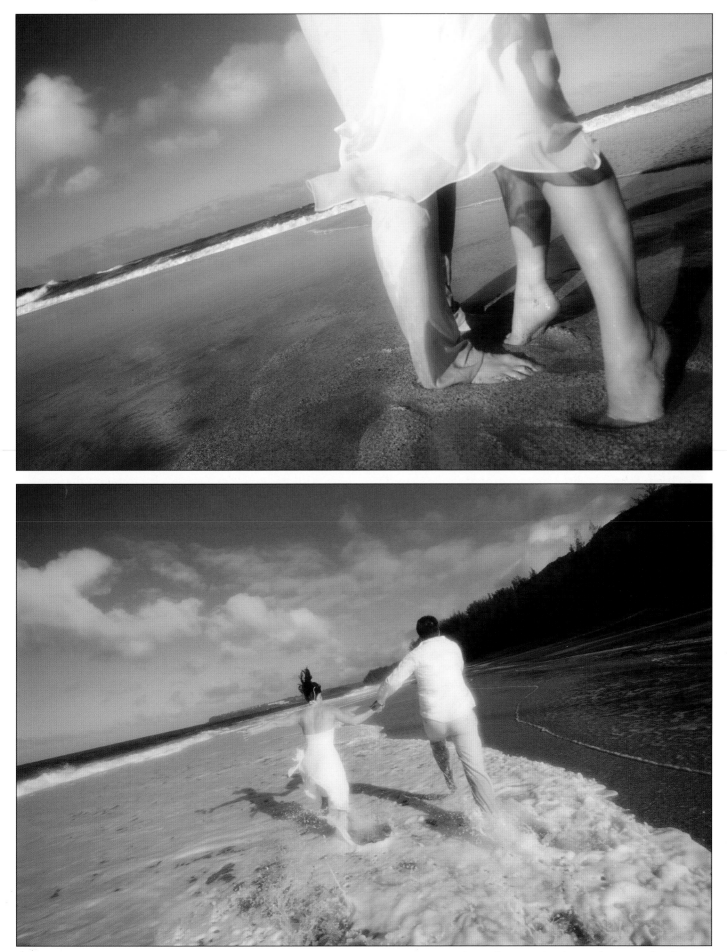

In 8-bit mode, Photoshop has 16.7 million colors at its disposal. This may seem like more than enough, but really it is just barely enough—especially when capturing images with graduating blue skies.

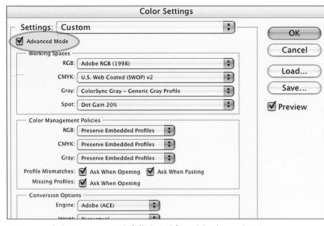

A "normal" histogram with full detail from black to white.

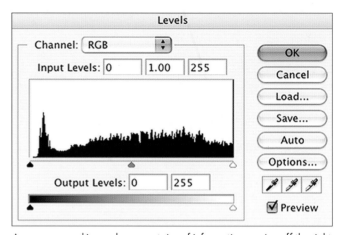

An overexposed image has mountains of information running off the right edge of the histogram.

on, it's a simple matter of pushing the appropriate key and waiting five seconds or so for it to complete the steps. It can easily be the last step before sending off any image for print.

■ EVALUATING OVERALL IMAGE QUALITY

You open an image in Photoshop—then what? The first step is to go to Image>Adjustments>Levels and peek at the histogram. The image may be a little low in contrast (especially if you shoot in low-contrast mode as recommended). You may also notice right away that the color is off a bit—perhaps too warm or too blue, indicative of an improper white-balance setting in camera. Both problems can be addressed using Levels or Curves, if you prefer.

The Histogram. Photoshop CS (and newer editions) has a helpful feature known as the Histogram floating palette. To access it, go to Window>Histogram. As with the other floating and dock-able palettes, it can be visible all the time and will update whenever an adjustment is made to an image. This can come in handy when working with adjustment features like Curves, which do not show a live histogram. The previous technique using the "8-16-8" conversion showed the floating histogram palette.

The histogram is basically a type of graph indicating where the tones in your image lie in relation to the pure black and pure white points. The left side of the histogram represents pure black, the right side pure white. The higher the black hump in the middle (a.k.a. the mountain), the more pixels in the image that are in that tonal range. For example, a low-key image with a lot of shadow information will have a large hump on the left side of the scale. In contrast, a high-key image with very few dark tones will have a hump toward the right end of the scale.

A "good" image will have all its mountainous regions within the confines of the left and right edges, with data that starts and ends right at the corners of the scale.

The key thing to look for, which may indicate problems with the image exposure, is a mountain that runs off the left or the right edge. Mountains running off the left edge indicate underexposure, and those that run off the right edge indicate overexposure. Keep in mind, however, that some images have highlights that simply must be overexposed to maintain important detail in other areas of the image. An example of this would be a photo of a person backlit by a bright-white sky. Without fill lighting, the exposure must favor the subject, and the sky will naturally blow out. In this case, the histogram will have mountains running off the right edge of the scale, but this is really unavoidable.

Generally it's best to see most, if not all, of the mountains within the histogram. When shooting with a low-contrast setting in camera, it is not uncommon to see a histogram where the mountains are within the range but don't quite reach to the corners. This is a typical low-contrast histogram, and it's really just fine. It is a simple matter to extend that tonal range and increase the contrast to a pleasing level. The opposite is not true, however. If the mountains extend past the edges, indicating detail that has been lost, there is no way to really

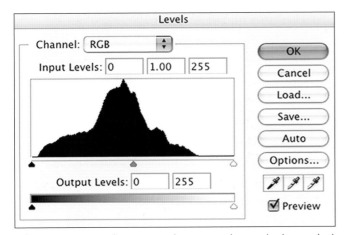

A low-contrast image histogram with mountains that need to be matched.

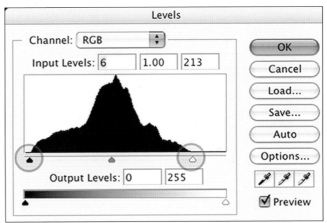

The low-contrast histogram with mountains matched. The black- and white-point sliders were pulled in to the edges of the mountain.

recover that detail information—other than reshooting the image.

1. **Set the Tonal Range.** Now that you have an idea of what a good histogram should look like, it's time to tune the low-contrast image to give it the snap it needs. This is known as "matching the mountains" and simply involves pulling your black- and white-point sliders in to the scale and matching them to where the mountain starts and ends. Of course, it makes sense to use your judgment and visual preference as well. You may like the image's low contrast—and you're the boss. Here's how to "match the mountains."

   A. Open a Levels adjustment layer.

   B. Drag the white-point slider to the right edge of the mountain. When you place the slider, any image information to the right of it will be pushed to pure white with no detail. If there is an area that looks like a flat line extending toward the right from the base of the mountain, this represents specular highlights. These are normal, and it's okay for some data to fall in the pure-white range.

   C. Drag the black-point slider to the left edge of the mountain. Generally, it's best not to have information on the left side of the black triangle, as this indicates a pure black with no detail. Featureless black areas in an image are generally more objectionable than specular highlights, which are often expected and acceptable.

Here's a trick to help see how far to pull those triangles in. With the Levels dialog box open, hold down the Opt/Alt key and drag the white triangle in toward the left. The image area will go black, and as you near the mountainous region it will reveal a bright color. This is the color channel information that will get "clipped," or pushed off the scale, if the slider is released there. Back off a bit so that just a hint of color shows. These areas will be your brightest spots in the image. If large areas of color appear, then releasing the slider there will wash out the highlight detail. The same works on the black end of the scale, except that the screen will turn white, and dark areas will appear to indicate the clipped areas.

If the image feels a little dark in the midtones but the contrast range looks correct, then sliding the midtone (gray) slider to the left will open up the midtones and give an overall brightening effect to the image, without

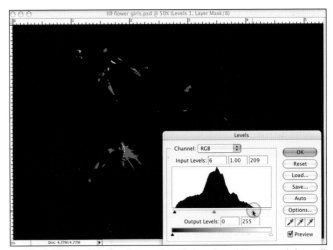

Holding the Opt/Alt key down while sliding the white-point slider will show image areas that are affected by clipping.

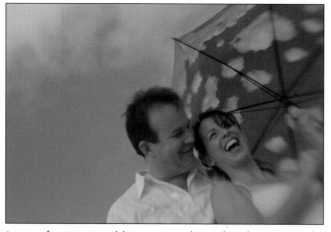

Images often come in with low contrast—due partly to the settings on the camera. This is okay, as the tonal range can be quickly Optimized.

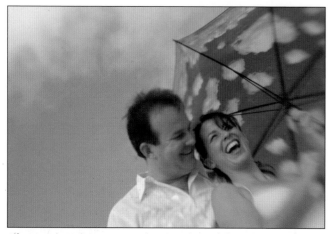

After matching the mountains, the image has a full tonal range with values from 0–255. (Image made using a Lensbaby.)

washing out the dark and light areas. With this accomplished, click OK and rest assured you have a nice tonal range.

2. **Set the White Balance.** If everyone remembered to make a custom white-balance setting in their camera prior to shooting, this step would not be necessary. However, the truth is that everyone forgets—or should we say the camera forgets? In fact, many images that initially look quite good may look even better when a white balance is done. The following technique simply and accurately neutralizes any color cast brought about by an inaccurate white-balance setting. It is called the "Single-Sample Neutralizer."

Keep in mind that this works great for images that are slightly off and works fairly well for many images that are grossly off (like an outdoor shot done with a tungsten white-balance setting). However, it is not a replacement for proper white balance in camera! Images corrected with this or any other technique will never look as bright, clean, and color accurate as those captured with a proper white balance. Photos needing significant adjustment with this technique may also benefit from some Color Balance adjustments, explained in the next section.

If an image will need both a color balance and tonal adjustment, it's easiest to do this technique first. Then in the same dialog box apply tonal corrections with matching mountains.

The first step is to identify an area or object in your image that should be neutral. Areas like a bride's white dress, a gray card, a concrete sidewalk, a white shirt, etc., can be used.

A. Make sure your eyedropper is set to 5x5 Average. Also, go to Preferences>Display & Cursors and make sure you've selected Precise under Other Cursors.
B. Open a Levels adjustment layer.
C. Press Shift and click on the image to set a neutral sample point. Be sure that the sample point has image detail (no blown-out white spots). The RGB values on your Info palette should all be between 50 and 200 for this point.
D. Double-click the white eyedropper in the Levels dialog box to open the Color Picker.

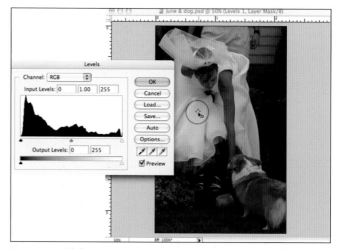

By pressing Shift and clicking on the bride's dress, we created a sample point to correct the white balance.

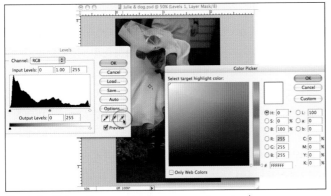

The Color Picker allows you to choose a new target color.

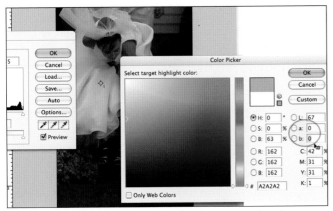

The "off" color was sampled into the Color Picker for neutralizing.

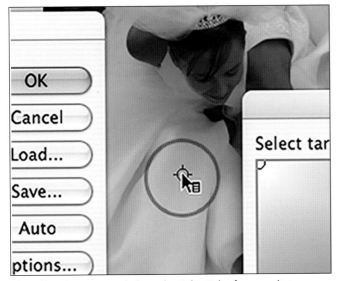

Changing "a" and "b" values doesn't affect luminosity, only color.

E. Position your cursor just over the sample point on the image so that it disappears, indicating perfect alignment with the sample. Click once.

F. In the Color Picker, the top swatch will indicate the color of the area you've clicked on. The color cast may be more obvious now. Set your "a" and "b" channel values to 0 (in the Lab boxes).

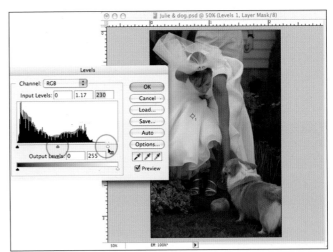

Final adjustments to the midtone brightness after matching the mountains.

G. Click OK to close the Color Picker dialog box.

H. Click again on the same sample point in the image. The color cast should disappear.

I. Match the mountains on the histogram, if needed, then click OK.

What's happening here? Essentially we are telling Photoshop, "This is an area that should be neutral. Keep the brightness of this point the same, but shift the colors to make it neutral." When this happens, all the other colors in the image should fall into their natural places.

It can be helpful when shooting to simply include a gray card, or gray frame captured with an ExpoDisc, whenever the lighting conditions change. These can be used as reference images for all other images captured under the same lighting conditions. Of course, it's still best to create a custom white balance using a gray card or ExpoDisc at the time of exposure.

3. **Fine-Tune the White Balance with Color Balance.**
Sometimes a perfect white balance is not desired; perhaps the mood of a certain color bias would enhance the image. It's generally best to start with a clean, neutralized image and adjust from there. The Color Balance adjustment layer is a great tool here. It is also helpful after using the "Single-Sample Neutralizer" technique on an image with a severe color cast, as occasionally it will still need help.

Color Balance is also helpful when there really is nothing in the image that can be used for a neutral reference point. In this case it will need to be balanced by eye, and this tool makes it most intuitive for photographers.

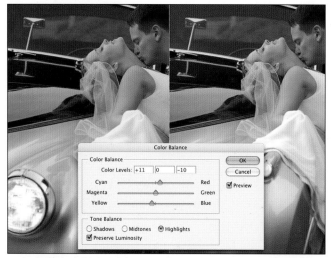

Color Balance adjustment layer applied to the midtones and highlights.

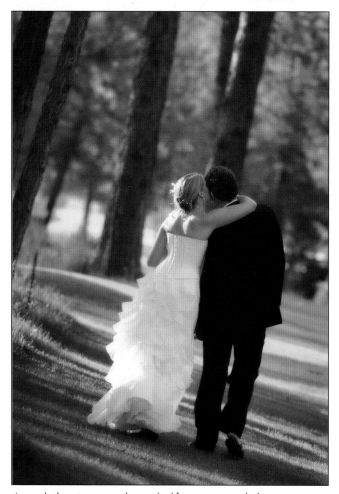

A good, clean image can be readied for print in very little time.

A. Go to Image>Adjustments>Color Balance.
B. Start in the Midtones (the default). Images that are too blue (this is common when shooting under overcast skies) generally need warming with a touch of red and yellow. Move the top slider toward Red and the bottom one toward Yellow.
C. Click on the Highlights button to adjust them separately from the Midtones. Add the same type of red and yellow adjustment.
D. The Shadows generally need less or no adjustment. Experiment to see what's needed.
E. Click OK.

Images that are too warm will generally require moving the sliders toward Cyan and Blue. Images with a green cast, like those shot under fluorescent lighting, can usually benefit from moving the middle slider toward Magenta. As before, working in the Midtones and Highlights will usually give the most obvious correction. The Shadows will probably need a smaller adjustment.

The three techniques that are described in steps 1–3 will probably handle 95 percent of your basic image needs. A good, clean image can be readied for print in very little time. Occasionally, though, corrective techniques will need to be applied (cover in the next chapter), or an image will be converted to black & white.

4. **Convert to Black & White from a Color Image.** Capturing every image in color, and applying a black & white conversion in Photoshop, gives the most flexibility in terms of the tonal quality of the black & white image. It also allows for simulated handcoloring techniques to be easily applied. There are myriad methods for converting color images to black & white, and it seems every experienced Photoshop user has their own "best" way. Really, though, the best way is the way that gives you the look you like. You're the boss, remember?

After trying most methods commonly used— grayscale mode, desaturation, channel mixer, channel mixer with pre-filters, Lab-mode conversion, etc.—we've developed a method that consistently

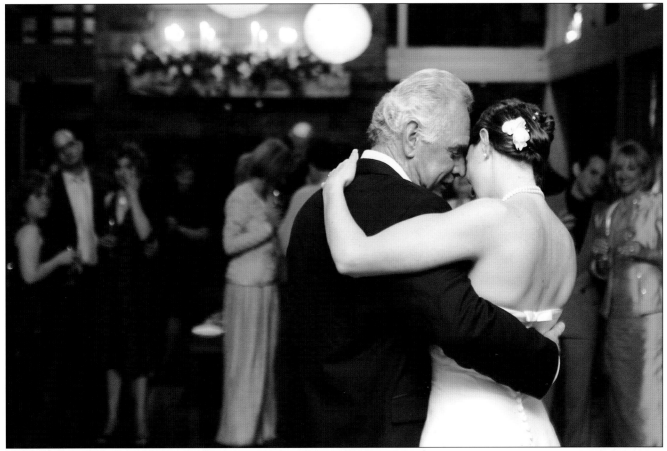
A color image converted to black & white using the warm Gradient Map technique.

gives us the look we like best. This technique uses a Gradient Map adjustment layer as its key. One of the nice things about the Gradient Map technique is that it bases the conversion of an image to black & white on tones rather than colors in the image. It also allows for an intuitive way to adjust the tonality of the new black & white image interactively. Lastly, it allows for warming or colorizing to be quickly applied. A slightly warm black & white, reminiscent of selenium-toned darkroom prints, has a much richer feel than a completely neutral black & white image. These warm black & white images also print beautifully on inkjet printers, offsetting the common green cast that can occur when attempting a neutral black & white. Here are the steps:

A. Reset your Color Swatches to black over white (press D on your keyboard).
B. Add a Gradient Map adjustment layer to a color image.

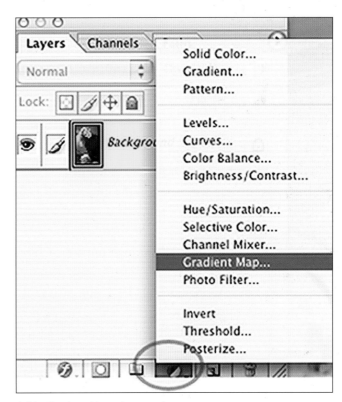
Add a Gradient Map adjustment layer.

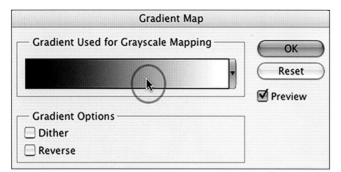

Click anywhere in the gradient to change it.

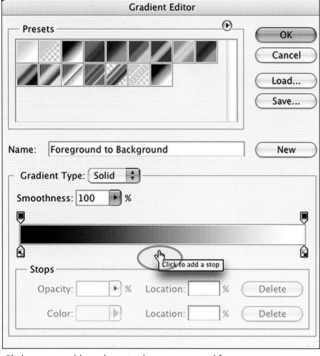

Click once to add a color stop that you can modify.

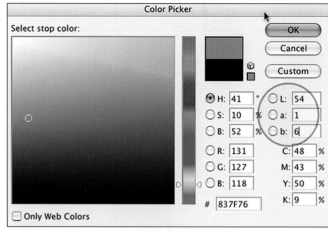

Entering a 1 and 6 in the "a" and "b" fields created a warm gray.

Shifting the tonal ramp by dragging the middle slider to the left.

C. Click in the gradient area to bring up the Gradient Editor palette.

D. Put your cursor just under the center of the gradient. Photoshop will give you the finger when you have it in the right place.

E. Click to set a color stop.

F. Double-click on this color stop to open the Color Picker.

G. In the Lab section, enter 54, 1, 6, respectively. This gives a warm-tone black & white. For slightly less warmth, use 54, 1, 4. For a completely neutral black & white, use 54, 0, 0.

H. Click OK.

I. Now you can adjust the overall tonality by grabbing your new color stop and dragging it to the left. Notice how the midtones and highlights open up without losing detail. The image has a nice "pop" to it, and the shadows stay deep and rich. Try setting the Location amount to 42% for starters.

J. Fine-tune the overall contrast by adjusting the Smoothness slider. Values less than 100% effectively lower the contrast.

The Gradient Map is cool. I mean it's warm . . . . Anyway, the reason it works so well is that it allows the tonality to be shifted so that the midtones and highlights get a longer ramp—effectively "brightening" the image and giving it more snap. The warm gray color is mixed with neutral gray as it moves from black to the middle of your tonal stop and then fades back to neutral gray and white as it reaches the highlights. The overall effect is clean—pure blacks in the shadows, warmth in the midtones, and clean white highlights. Most photographers find the adjustments very intuitive once they've done the technique a few times.

5. **Add Color to a Black & White Image.** Colorizing an image is just as easy once you have the Gradient

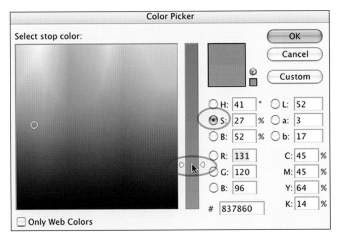

Sepia, or any other color tone, can easily be created by adjusting the H (hue) and S (saturation) sliders.

Map in place. Sepia, blue tone, or even split-tone effects are easily achieved. Here's how:

A. Reopen the Gradient Map adjustment layer if it's been closed (Image>Adjustments>Gradient Map).
B. Click in the gradient bar.
C. Double-click on the midtone color-stop slider.
D. In the Color Picker, click on the S (saturation) button.
E. Move the saturation slider upward to create a sepia tone. To create any other color toning, simply click on the H button to adjust the hue, then move the slider up or down to find the hue you like. If you only use the slider, instead of clicking in the color square, then the brightness value will stay consistent.

An added benefit of using the Gradient Map is that shadow noise is often minimized in the conversion, whereas it can be made more obvious using other methods. See the following example for two methods of converting an image to black & white. Notice the shadow smoothness and detail in the Gradient Map.

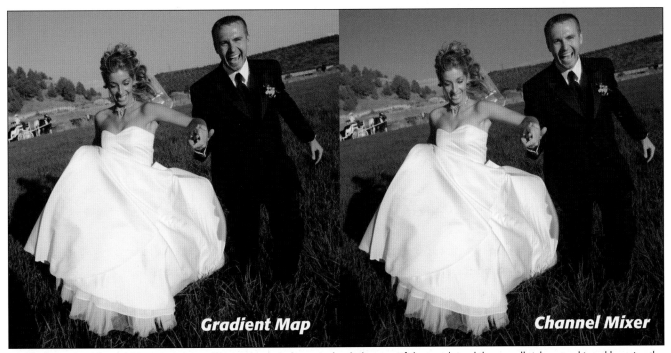

Gradient Map   *Channel Mixer*

Gradient Map vs. Channel Mixer conversion. Notice the smoothness in the dark areas of the tuxedo and the overall richness achieved by using the Gradient Map method.

■ SAVE A MASTER FILE IN PSD FORMAT

Now that the handiwork has been completed, it would be wise to save a master file with your adjustment layers intact. The master file should be kept in PSD format to preserve all the layer information. It is not uncommon to want or need to revisit the image later and make changes to the tone or color—especially if re-purposing it for different uses. Keeping the layers allows for infinite adjustability.

At this point, the image has not been cropped, sized, or sharpened. The same logic applies here as well: keep a master file and make a copy in the size, crop, and resolution you need for each type of output. This is also beneficial when working with certain labs that prefer you send an original, unsized, unsharpened file to them. They will use this master file for any size print. The lab may prefer to use their proprietary software to do the sizing and sharpening. This is great for photographers, as we need only keep one file and can send it for any image size.

When saving the master image, be sure to check the Layers and Embed Color Profile options.

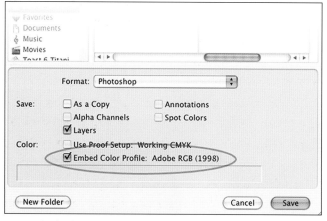

Saving the final master file, with layers intact and profile attached.

■ PREPARE TO PRINT

With the master file safely preserved, proceed to making the print-ready file. Keep in mind that if you use a lab like mentioned above, they will prefer you to send them the unsized, unsharpened image file. In this case simply save a JPEG copy of the image, and off it goes. The following steps would then not need to be taken.

Cropping and Sizing. These steps can usually be combined into one motion with the help of the Crop

tool and tool presets. The exception would be when an image will need to be enlarged more than 200%; in this case, a helpful technique is Step Interpolation. For most images (those needing less than 200% enlargement), the process of cropping to the right print dimensions and applying the correct resolution setting can be done with one simple tool—the Crop tool.

It is helpful to zoom out so that there is gray window area around the image before cropping. This way, the Crop tool can be placed outside the image area and pulled across it—and it will automatically snap to the edges of the image. You can change your window view by typing F on your keyboard. This will cycle through the Floating Window, a single image on gray, and single image on black—helpful for cleaning up your view and analyzing the image without distractions. Speaking of distractions, hit the Tab key and watch your palettes hide from view, leaving a lone image to inspect. Hitting Tab again will bring them back.

Select the Crop tool and in the options bar at the top of the window, enter your desired width, height, and resolution. You can type 5 in. for 5"(or type "px" to use actual pixel dimensions if needed [e.g., 750px]). Next, click outside the top-left corner of the image (or any corner) and pull down and across the image. The cropping border will snap to the edges of the image, and the proportions you set will be locked. When you have the crop you want, release the mouse and then hit Enter. Your resulting image will be exactly the dimensions you asked for.

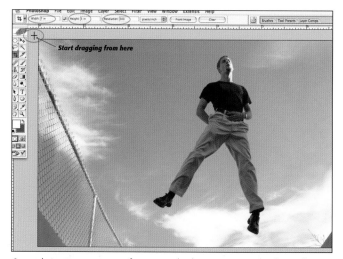

Start dragging your crop from outside the image area and it will snap exactly to the image borders.

Tool presets go hand in hand with the Crop tool. A preset allows saving of favorite crop combinations—for example, 5"x7" at 300dpi, or 10"x8" at 240dpi. With the presets made, all that's necessary is to select one from the list, drag across the image, and press Enter. Presets are located at the far left of the menu options. To create a new preset, type in the desired number combinations and choose the Create New Tool Preset button. Give it a name, and it's done. Horizontal and vertical crops of the same dimensions will each need their own preset.

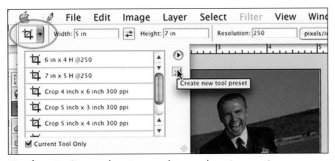

Your favorite Crop tool settings can be saved, saving you time.

Sizing an Image to Over 200% Larger or 50% Smaller. When an image must be increased to over 200% or decreased to under 50% in size, Photoshop needs to do some serious resampling, known as interpolation. "Resampling" and "interpolation" are techy terms for making up new pixel information. When this happens in small increments, it is easier for Photoshop to figure out what the in-between pixels should look like. It's like taking baby steps instead of a giant leap. For Photoshop to "leap" to a 300% larger image requires quite a bit of guesswork, however, because the program needs to fill in rather large gaps in the pixel information. A better solution is to let Photoshop take it "one step at a time," essentially moving up toward 300% in 10% increments. The first part of the technique is to decide what size the image needs to be, in total file size. This is easily done with the Image Size dialog box:

1. Go to Image>Image Size.
2. In the dialog box, make sure Resample Image and Constrain Proportions are checked.
3. Type in the new desired dimensions and resolution in the size boxes.
4. Make a note of your new file size, indicated at the top of the window after Pixel Dimensions. You

should also see "(Was XXMB)," indicating that the image will be resampled. This new file size is your target size.

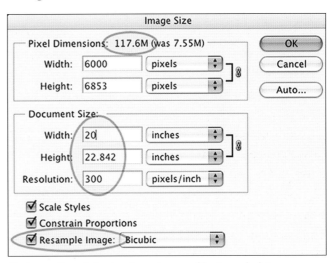

The Image Size dialog box is used as your file-size calculator.

5. Now, change the top menu from Pixels to Percent and enter 110%.
6. Click OK to close the box, and your image size will increase 10%.

Now, you just need to repeat the 110% enlarging process until the target size is met. The goal is to get just below your target size, without going over. Then, the last image size adjustment should be to enter the exact final dimensions needed (e.g., 20"x30" @ 250 pixels/inch).

To check your progress as the image grows toward the target size, make sure to set your image window to Floating Window mode (using the F key, remember?) and set the status area to Document Sizes (you'll find this to the right of the Percent field in the left-hand corner of the screen). Watch the number on the left of the slash as you increase your image size.

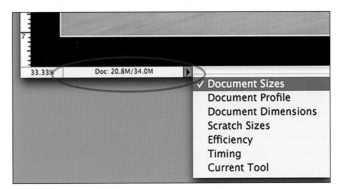

Watching the document size while you res up the image.

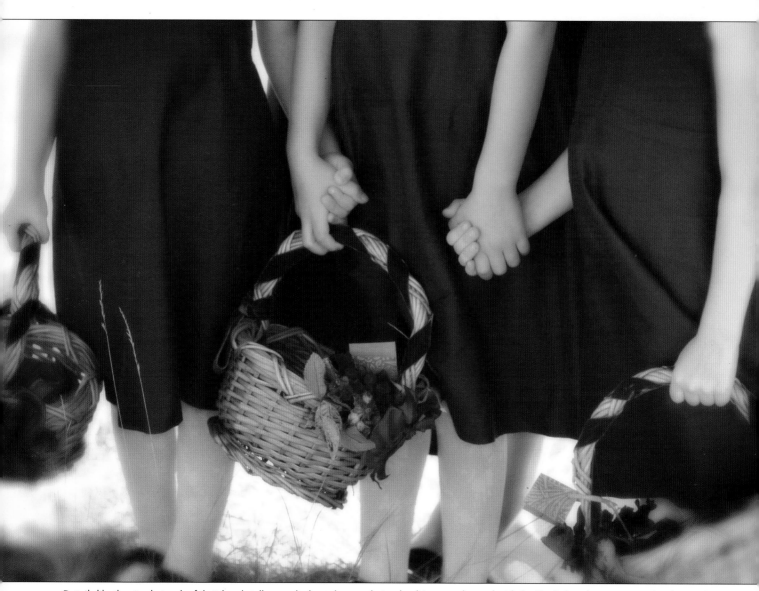

Details like the simple touch of their hands tell so much about the people involved. Image enhanced with the KevSoft technique covered in chapter 9.

If this whole process seems tedious, it is. But only the first time. After that, you can make an action to automate the process for you. Simply start recording, change the image size by 110%, then stop recording. From then on, simply hit Play and your image will increase to the desired 110%. You might be thinking ahead now, "Hey, can I make an action to do that increase five times in a row? How about fourteen times?" Of course you can! (If you don't feel comfortable with actions, wait until you finish chapter 10.)

Since an increase in image size to over 200% will require at least eight steps at 110%, it makes sense to save actions that will increase one, five, eight, and ten steps. These can be used in combination to reach your target size. If using a five-step action makes the image too large, open the History palette and step back one history step at a time until you are just below your target size. Then, open the Image Size dialog box one last time and enter your exact finished dimensions.

Images resampled using this 110% method will retain finer details better than images that are resampled in one giant step. However, the difference is only really noticeable when enlarging beyond 200%.

Sharpening: The Final Step. Sharpening, which incidentally is accomplished via Photoshop's Unsharp Mask filter, should be the last step after all image manipulations have been done. Sharpening is merely a software trick, done either in the camera or in Photoshop. It accomplishes its magic by increasing contrast along the edges to make them stand out more, effectively giving the sense of sharper edges. It does not magically find detail where there was none, but sometimes it really can appear to do miracles.

When image resampling is done on an image that is already sharpened, like a magician doing his tricks in slow motion, the illusion becomes obvious and magnified. The artifacts from the sharpening process become resampled as well, and the resulting image can look "edgy" or oversharpened (see graphic). With this in mind, it's best to reserve the sharpening until after the image has been resampled.

Unsharp Mask works by creating contrast along the edges it finds in an image. If you want to see this in action yourself, open an image and go to Filter> Sharpen>Unsharp Mask. Push the Amount all the way up and then move the Radius slowly up until you can see the edges gaining contrast.

The amount of sharpening is also dependent on the final image size and resolution. Here are some guidelines and starting points for sharpening images that are about 6MP. These settings are applied in the Filter> Sharpen>Unsharp Mask dialog box. Begin with the following settings—Amount: 225, Radius: .7 or .8 pixels, and Threshold: 8.

The Amount setting used may vary with the image resolution and content—higher amounts may be needed for images that don't have distinct edges. The Radius setting will generally vary with the image resolution. Low-resolution images, like web images, will need settings in the .3–.5-pixel range. High-resolution images, like 300dpi, may require .8–1 pixel.

The Threshold setting is the only one that should generally stay in the 6–8 range, no matter what the size and resolution. Threshold is the amount of contrast necessary before Photoshop considers pixels a line that should be sharpened. You'll find that any threshold less than 6 or 8 will start to show sharpening artifacts, or graininess, in areas of smooth tone—like skin. This is generally not pleasing. If a low threshold is used, digital noise is enhanced and made more obvious. Try this experiment:

Too low a Threshold setting reveals noise in areas that should be smooth. A higher setting keeps edge sharpness, but smooth areas stay smooth.

1. Open a digital image in which the subject's face is visible.
2. Open the Unsharp Mask dialog box and zoom to 200%, keeping the face in your preview window. Set your main image area to 100% for an overall view.
3. Set the Amount to 500.
4. Set the Radius to 2 pixels so you can clearly see the effect.
5. Set your Threshold to 0 and notice how "noisy" the skin becomes.
6. Move the Threshold slider slowly up until the skin smooths out but the line detail is still enhanced. Usually this will be at about 8 or more.
7. Zoom back to 100% view for accurate assessment.
8. Now go back to the Amount and Radius and lower them to appropriate numbers.

For web images, try these settings for starters: 225, .3, and 8. To find the best setting for any image, it generally works well to move the Amount up as high as is pleasing, then start moving the Radius. If the Radius is too large, dark lines appear to border detail, obscuring it.

When done, save this image copy in a format appropriate for your lab. Be sure to check Embed Color Profile. If it will be in a TIFF format, *do not* include layers. JPEG files should be saved with the highest-quality setting.

Now that the basic image is complete, we're ready to move on to bigger and more exciting things.

8. PHOTOSHOP CORRECTIVE TECHNIQUES

The aim of art is to represent not the outward appearance of things, but their inward significance.

—Aristotle

Not every image is just perfect right out of the camera. It may not be perfect even after doing the image basics in the previous section. Sometimes it just needs a little more help. Some of these techniques are designed to address exposure and camera-specific problems, while some are simply for making a scene or person look a little better. One thing is for sure; in portrait photography, everyone wants to look good. Your judgment will be the guide as to how far you want to go.

In portrait studios, there are many schools of thought as to the best approach for handling retouching. Should it be done before the client sees the image? Should we wait for them to ask, then charge a retouching fee? Should we point out problem areas and then offer to fix them—for a fee? Our studio's philosophy is to take care of corrective retouching before showing the image to a client. We don't want them to have to feel uncomfortable asking, and we feel that first impressions are very important. We also price our prints so that we can do

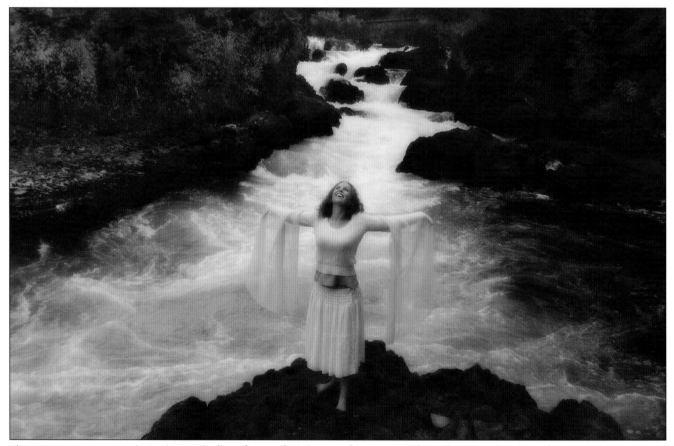

This young woman seems to be soaking up the flow of energy from the powerful river around her. Nikon D1x and 17–35mm lens.

basic retouching without having to tack on an extra charge. However, complex retouching done at the client's request will usually incur an additional fee.

■ UNDEREXPOSURE FIX

It was mentioned earlier that digital images should be exposed similarly to transparency film. It is always safer to err on the side of underexposure, if at all. Therefore, underexposure correction is not an uncommon task. Fortunately, even extreme underexposure problems can be corrected with decent results. Images will never look as good as when captured properly, but then again, it's not always possible to capture the full dynamic range desired in one photograph. It is better to capture the highlight detail and adjust the underexposed areas than to have no highlight detail due to overexposure.

This technique is one approach that works well for a variety of images. It also works well when used in batch processes to fix multiple images at once. We call the technique "Under-X Fix." Start with an image that looks too dark in the midtones and shadows, typical of under-exposure.

1. View the Layers palette.
2. Type Cmd/Ctrl+Opt/Alt+~.
3. Inverse the selection by typing Cmd/Ctrl+I.
4. Add a new Levels adjustment layer (Layer>New Adjustment Layer>Levels).
5. Click OK to close the dialog box without making any adjustments.
6. Change the layer's blend mode to Screen.

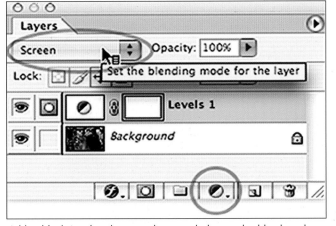

Add a blank Levels adjustment layer and change the blend mode to Screen.

Notice that the image will lighten about the equivalent of $^2/_3$ of an f-stop. The nice thing about using this method is you get nice lightening, similar to an exposure change, without hurting contrast or making the image look washed out. It opens the shadows, midtones, and shifts the highlights gingerly toward white—but keeps the blackest blacks, well, black. It also preserves color intensity, where other methods—like a Curves or Levels adjustment—will wash out the color and often some highlight detail.

The following images illustrate the difference between using Curves or "Under-X Fix."

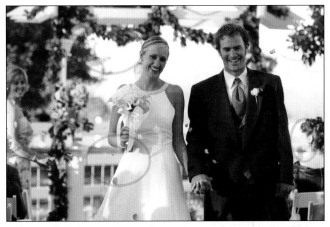

Curves was used to lighten this underexposed image. Notice the washed-out highlight detail. Key areas are circled.

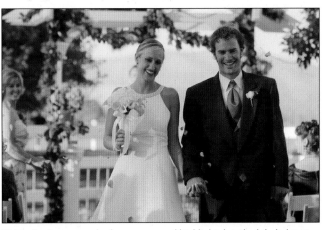

Using the Screen method, we preserved highlight detail while lightening shadows and midtones to an acceptable level. Notice the subtle blue of the sky was preserved. Two layers of "Under-X Fix" were applied, the second one at 59% opacity.

More Power to the "Under-X Fix." As you may have noticed, this trick is quite slick. The first part of the technique created a selection (Cmd/Ctrl+Opt/Alt+~) based on the highlights. Then we inverted the selection (Cmd/Ctrl+I) to target the shadow areas. This helped to

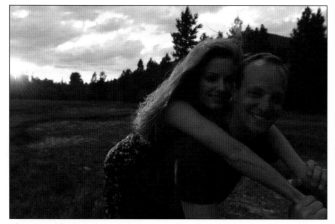

The original image was underexposed...or was it?

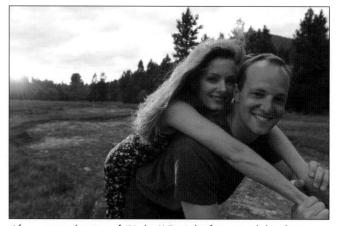

After one application of "Under-X Fix," the foreground detail starts to reveal, but the dramatic sky started to wash out.

isolate our lightening to the darker parts of the image, preserving highlight detail in the process. Loading the highlights or shadows as a selection, before creating an adjustment layer, automatically uses that selection as a mask for the new adjustment layer. It's perfect whenever you want an adjustment to affect primarily highlights or shadows separately.

However, there may be instances where you want to keep parts of an image dark—totally unaffected by an adjustment—and open the shadows in the rest of the image. To do this, we'll add some additional layer masking to the technique.

Layer masks allow for selective blocking and revealing of parts of the active layer. By painting on the layer mask on the "Under-X Fix" layer, parts of it can be blocked (using black paint on the layer mask), essentially showing the original image beneath it through this "hole." See the layer mask sidebar for details.

This is very cool when, for example, an image was shot against a bright sky—a typical backlit-type scene. The sky may look beautiful, but the foreground subject is very dark. Using the "Under-X Fix," the foreground can be opened up and detail revealed; however, the sky will also lighten somewhat and lose its drama (see the images above).

Let's bring back the sky with a simple layer mask adjustment.

A. Create your "Under-X Fix" layer as above.

B. Choose a fairly large soft-edge brush.

C. Paint with black on the layer mask to block the lightening effect in certain areas (like a sky). The

layer mask is automatically created when you add an adjustment layer, so all you need to do is start painting on the image area.

D. Use a smaller brush as you get closer to the edges of the area you don't want to block. By using soft brushes and selecting smaller brush sizes as you near the edges, no tedious selecting is necessary. The edge will blend smoothly and require very little time to complete.

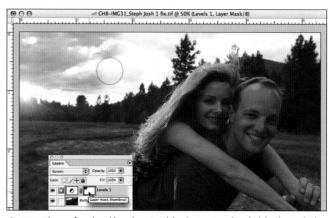

Paint with a soft-edged brush, using black, to completely block any lightening in the sky area.

Let's take this trick one step further. Suppose you want to lighten the image even more than one application of "Under-X Fix" does. Simply select the "Under-X Fix" layer and duplicate it. Adjust the opacity of the layer if it's now too strong, or duplicate it again to lighten it even further. You could also add a Curves layer to fine-tune the contrast at this point.

If multiple layers are used, then masking them all together (as in the above instructions) can be tedious.

Here's how the gurus do it:

    a. Link all the "Under-X Fix" layers together by selecting one of them, then clicking the link box on all the other "Under-X Fix" layers.

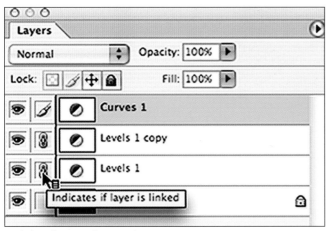

Link the adjustment layers only.

Create a set based on the linked layers.

    b. Go to Layer>New>Layer Set From Linked.

    c. Add a layer mask to the set and paint away as usual.

Now the mask will affect all the layers in the set as a group, saving you from having to mask each one separately and identically.

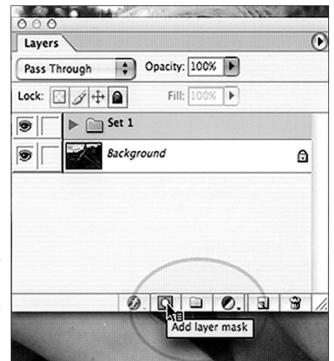

By adding a layer mask to a set, you can mask all the layers at once.

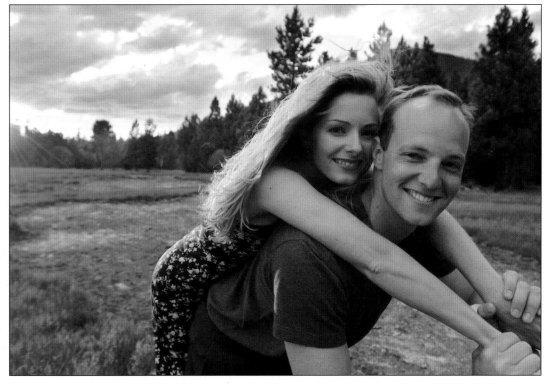

The image after application of the "Under-X Fix." Curves was used to fix the contrast, and masking was utilized to bring back the sky. Had I overexposed the image to begin with based on the subjects' faces, I never could have recovered the dramatic sky.

THE LAYER MASK REVEALED

The layer mask is one of the secrets behind Photoshop guru status. Once understood and integrated, it seems that anything is possible, including world peace—but that's another story.

Here's the skinny on layer masks: think of a layer mask as a transparent piece of plastic attached to your layer. It always stays with the layer, and when the mask is white (the default), it is essentially invisible.

If we take black paint and apply it to the transparent sheet, it will block the area on the layer, allowing the layer or layers below to show through. It's like an eraser, but not permanent.

To restore the mask, or reveal what was blocked by the black, simply paint with white. By using the default colors (hit the D key) and

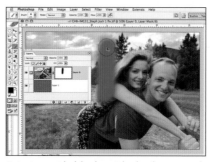

Painting with black, with the layer mask active, blocks whatever is on that corresponding layer. Notice how the green from the background is showing through.

the key for swapping foreground/background colors (X), it's easy to switch between black and white while "painting" on a layer mask. If you accidentally erase part of the image with black, type X to swap to white, and paint it back.

To make an area partially blocked, paint with a shade of gray.

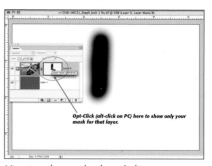

Opt-Click (alt-click on PC) here to show only your mask for that layer.

Viewing the mask alone helps you to see where you've painted.

The darker the shade, the more it blocks. A layer mask can be affected with any shade from white to black.

Tip: To see just your virtual layer mask, press Opt/Alt and click on the Layer Mask icon. To return to normal view, press Opt/Alt and click again. This is helpful for cleaning up a mask and inspecting your handiwork.

■ CLARIFY CUTS THE HAZE

Here's a neat little trick to help clear up some of the "haziness" that can be inherent in certain digital images. This technique, called "Clarify," adds a subtle type of localized contrast that brings in just the right amount of snap.

1. Open the image and choose Filter>Sharpen>Unsharp Mask.
2. For the settings, use Amount: 20, Radius: 60, Threshold: 4.
3. Notice the haze disappear and a nice edge contrast appear. (To increase or decrease the effect, adjust the Radius amount.)

This technique can be used in combination with a normal Unsharp Mask application—which is used to create overall sharpness in the image. It's generally a good idea to use the "Clarify" technique first, after overall tonal

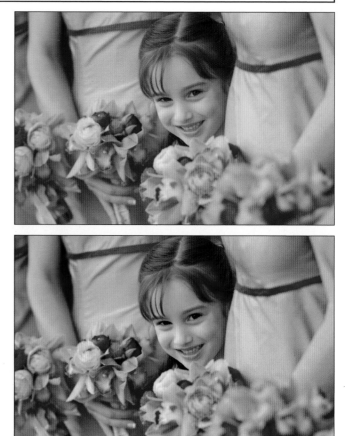

The top image is the original. The results of the "Clarify" technique are shown in the lower image. Notice the subtle contrast and crispness.

corrections have been done, but before applying the normal Unsharp Mask (which should be done last, remember?).

HOT YELLOW FIX

No, this is not a drug. It's just good, clean fun. This works great on images that have what may be called "color staining," which often shows up in the highlight areas where the image is verging on overexposure—or has ventured unrecoverably into "blown out." It can also be used to colorize areas to match similar objects in the scene. For example, brown grass can be matched to living green grass, or sunburned skin can be given a more natural coloration. This technique works by sampling the color of a good area and applying it to the area that needs fixing—without changing the detail or tonality of the destination area.

1. Open the image to adjust and look for a color you can use that represents your "good" color.

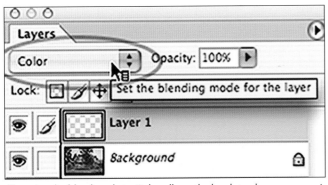

Changing the blend mode to Color allows the brush to change an area's color without impacting detail.

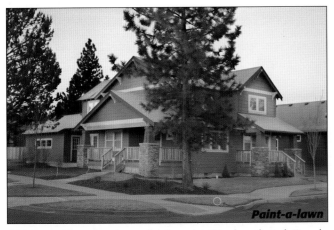

Painting on a layer in color mode allows detail to show through. Sample the good color with the eyedropper, then paint where needed. The left side of the lawn has been re-greened. Digital Miracle Grow!

2. Create a new, blank layer above the main image and change the blend mode to Color.
3. Select a medium-soft brush and then press Opt/Alt and click on the image where the good color is. This will load the color into your foreground swatch.
4. Paint on your new layer over the area that needs the good color. Feel free to reload a new color sample by pressing Opt/Alt and clicking, to vary the painted effect.
5. Use the layer opacity, if necessary, to adjust the intensity of the newly colored area.

RETOUCHING BASICS

Photoshop has some great retouching tools, and I'd like to personally thank the genius that created the Healing Brush for us. What a great tool! Alas, it's still not perfect, but we can adapt. This section will cover some basic retouching skills and tips for using the tools more efficiently. While not an extensive course in retouching, which is a book in itself, the techniques should cover most of your day-to-day needs.

The Healing Brush. For general blemish removal, the Healing Brush really shines.

1. Zoom your image area to 100% view.
2. Select the Healing Brush and choose a hard brush that is just barely larger than the blemish you want to remove.
3. Press Opt/Alt and click on an area of skin that has good, clean texture and would make a good patch for the blemish area. It does not have to be exact in tone or color, but being close helps.
4. Click on the blemish and it is blended away.

This works great if the area to be healed needs complete obliteration. But what if you want to soften an area, like lines or wrinkles? It's generally a good idea to minimize wrinkles and lines rather than completely re-move them (some of your clients may think otherwise, however!). The Healing Brush does not offer an opacity adjustment, allowing for partial replacement of an area. To do this, we need to add a simple step.

If Photoshop CS or newer is used, there is a handy new option that allows for applying the healing onto a new blank layer, rather than a full duplicate of the original. The advantage here is reduced file size and complete adjustability of the retouching.

A. Select the Healing Brush.

B. In the options bar, check Use All Layers.

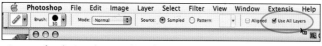

Options for the Healing Brush tool.

C. If there are other layers in the image, besides the background layer, turn them off now, or the retouching results may be unpredictable. You can turn them back on later when done retouching.

D. Create a new blank layer above your background layer.

E. On the blank layer, use the technique above to remove lines or wrinkles. However, for lines it may be helpful to pull short strokes along them to erase them, or dab a little at a time. If you pull across them, notice that your sample point (where you pressed Opt/Alt and clicked) also follows you as if tied to the area you are replacing. Be careful not to let this sample point run into a different textured area. Short strokes or dabs work best to keep it in the same sample area.

F. You have now made your subject look like a Barbie doll. Unless you're doing before-and-after ads for a plastic surgeon, you probably want to simply minimize, not remove, these lines. Adjust the opacity of the top layer and watch as the lines fade in and out. Pick a realistic balance, and you're done.

Retouching Tips. *The Healing Brush.* Use a hard-edged brush when using the Healing Brush and a soft brush when using the Clone Stamp. The Healing Brush automatically blends the edges nicely, so a hard edge gives more accurate feedback as to where the actual border of the brush is.

The Clone Stamp. This used to be the tool of choice for retouching, and it still has myriad uses. The Healing Brush does not replace detailed areas well—for example, cloning a patch of grass over a distracting object. Enter the Clone Stamp.

Using the Clone Stamp. To use this tool, press Opt/Alt and click to sample an area to use as your source, then start dabbing or dragging across the area to be replaced. Notice, too, that the source point will follow when you drag to replace an area, as if connected to the brush by an invisible string. If you want the source point to remain in the same spot, then turn off the Aligned option in the options bar. The source point will then still move with the brush when dragging, but it will always return to the same starting point.

The Clone Stamp with the Aligned option selected.

■ SWAPPING BODY PARTS

If only it were this easy in the real world. Digital imaging has opened many doors for portrait photographers. It is now a simple matter to take the eyes from one image, the legs from another, and the head from a third and replace these parts on a fourth image to create the perfect composite. Is it cheating? Of course it is! So

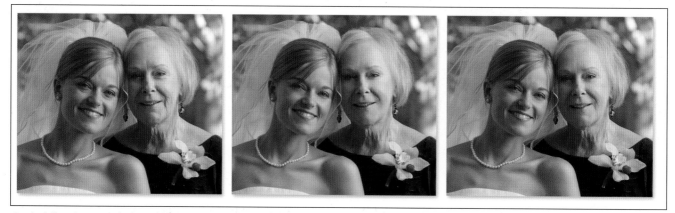

On the left is the original. The middle image was made with the Healing Brush's default settings; can you say "plastique"? On the right is the more natural image with the healing layer faded about 50%.

what! Clients love it, and we can give them exactly what they want. The trouble is, buyers of portrait photography are all too aware of what's possible now and they often start asking for the stars and the moon.

With this is mind, our studio will often make a judgment call to decide whether an image could be significantly improved by an eye- or head swap. If so, we'll do it before the client sees the image. This way, we don't have to make statements in the sales room—like, "we could easily swap the head from number 6 onto number 4 if you like it better, or . . ." When you quickly start making suggestions like that, the customer begins thinking about changing things at the slightest whim. It's best to wait until they really seem to need a push, then you can offer to make the swap—especially if it will save the sale (or create one from nothing).

Fortunately, swapping body parts is quick and easy in most cases. The hardest part is making sure you don't get carried away and accidentally put Aunt Jane's head on Uncle Bob.

To make this trick work, it's best to have two (or more) images that were shot in the same lighting conditions and from the same angle and distance. We generally shoot a few more images when we take group photos, just to make sure we have a good expression from everyone. Then we can grab a head here or there if needed. Here are the steps involved for a closed-eye swap, but any other body part could be Frankensteined too:

1. Open both images, good eyes and bad eyes.
2. Use the Lasso tool and draw a rough selection around the good eyes.
3. Press Opt/Alt and drag the selected area to the image needing new eyes.
4. Release the mouse when over the destination image, and the new eyes should be visible—although probably in the wrong place.
5. Type 5 on the keyboard to make your new eyes layer 50% opaque.
6. Select the Move tool and drag the good eyes precisely over the old ones. Use a common point for reference, like a nose or eyebrows.
7. When the new eyes are aligned, type 0 to return the new eyes to 100% opacity.

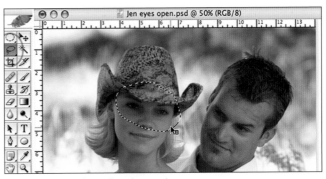
Use the Lasso tool to select the good eyes.

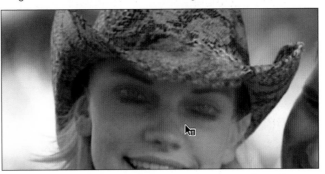
Drag the selected area into the second image.

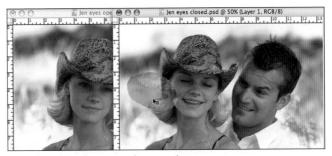
Making the new eyes layer temporarily 50% opaque allows for easy alignment of the old and new. Kind of freaky too.

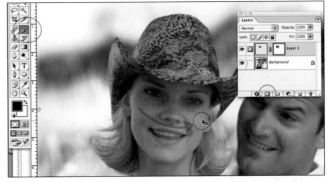
Use a soft brush to paint away the edges of the new layer. The soft brush allows the new area to blend nicely with the underlying image with no effort at all. (The mustache shows the masking stroke, not my juvenile delinquency.)

8. Add a new layer mask to the good eyes layer.
9. Choose a soft black brush, a little larger than one eye socket, and paint away the edges of the new eyes that aren't needed!

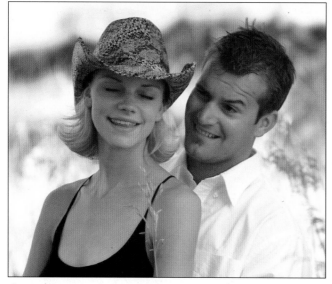
Original image.

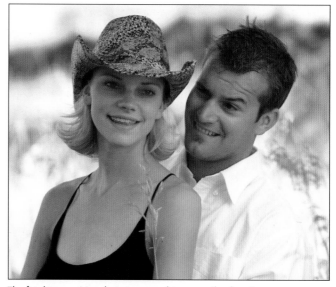
The final image. Now he's got something to smile about!

Sometimes the source and destination parts are not exactly the same size. In this case, when the new part is brought over (step 6 above), use the Free Transform command (Cmd/Ctrl+T or Edit>Free Transform). With the transform active, corner handles will appear.

A. Grab a corner, hold down the Shift key (to maintain proportions), and size it as necessary.
B. The part can also be moved to the right position with the Free Transform active by grabbing inside the boxed area (but not right on the center mark) and placing it where needed.
C. The part can be rotated by placing the mouse just outside the transform box. When the curved arrow appears, click, hold, and drag in the direction of rotation needed.
D. When it's the right size and in position, hit Enter to set the transform.

■ DIGITAL LIPOSUCTION

What power we hold in our hands! This technique can certainly be used for good . . . or evil, so be careful. It is also one of the most fun—and profitable—tools available in Photoshop.

The process of reshaping a person or object should be considered thoughtfully. It is not something that should be done automatically; in other words, the client should request it or have expressed concern about a particular feature that they are sensitive about. Some clients are a

little shy about asking to be slimmed or trimmed, yet they would be more than happy to see their picture presented that way. Sometimes you have to carefully read your client and make an educated guess. You certainly don't want to offend them by removing something they are quite proud of!

Here are some examples of how this technique, which uses the Liquify tool, can be used:

• slimming and trimming
• weak chin shaping
• straightening crooked noses
• love handle removal
• large ear or nose reduction
• comic relief and alien creation

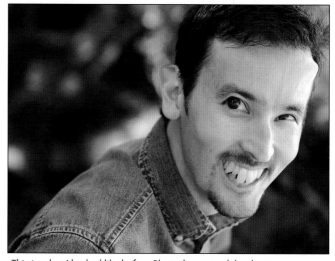
This is what I looked like before Photoshop saved the day.

The Liquify Tool, found under Filter>Liquify, offers an extensive set of options in the control window. However, we only use a few of them for basic needs.

The Forward Warp Tool. The actual instrument that does the deed. Its size and properties are determined by the settings in the options bar.

The Freeze Mask Tool. This is used to protect areas from any accidental warping and reshaping.

The Thaw Mask Tool. Erases the Freeze Mask where applied.

Here's a sample image and the workflow used to correct it. The beautiful bride was a little self-conscious about her neck and chin and how they photographed in profile. She felt the area could use a little more definition. The image captured a beautiful moment, and we didn't want her to be distracted by any concerns for the way her profile appeared here. So, let's get busy:

1. Make sure you are on the main image layer, not an adjustment layer.
2. Go to Filter>Liquify.
3. Set the Brush Pressure to 100.
4. Set the Brush Size to the width of her arm.
5. Choose the Freeze Mask tool and paint over her arm to protect it from correction (protected areas will show as transparent red).
6. Be sure to keep the red protected area just over her arm without going too far into the area we need to work on. (See example.)
7. Switch to the Forward Warp tool and change the Brush Pressure to 20.
8. Set the Brush Density to 50.
9. Set the Brush Size interactively so that it is large enough to cover the area that needs correction. Too small a brush will create uneven, bumpy edges.
10. Position the brush so that ⅓ of it is over the area to be corrected. Then click, hold, and push to reshape. A few small movements may be needed to achieve the desired effect. Too many separate movements will start to blur edges and smear the texture or grain in the image. Keep them to a minimum.

If the texture does appear lost after the manipulation is done, it can be restored in certain areas by using the Reconstruct tool (found just below the Forward Warp tool). Select a smaller brush with a Density of 100 and a Brush Pressure of 100. Paint over areas of lost texture,

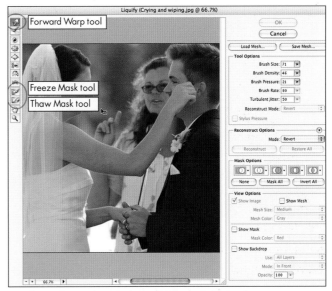
Liquify window with tools that will commonly be used.

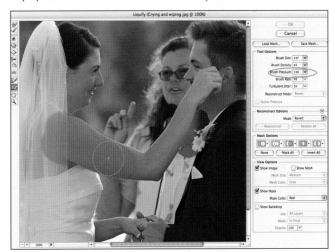
Use the Freeze tool to protect areas you don't want modified.

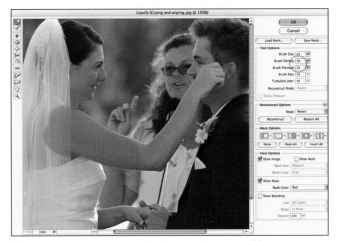
Gingerly reshape the area with as few strokes as possible.

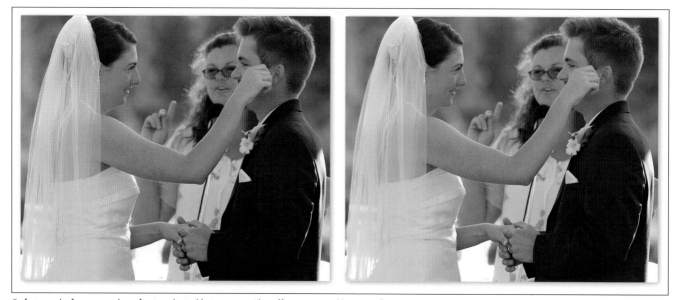

Before-and-after examples of using digital liposuction. The effect is natural but significant.

and the original texture will return. Be careful not to paint over reshaped lines, or they will return to their previous state too!

Areas that cannot be retextured with the Reconstruct tool may be fixed with the Healing Brush or Clone Stamp once the image is returned to the normal Photoshop window.

Tip: To see the before-and-after effects in the Liquify window, check the Show Backdrop box at the bottom right of the Liquify window. Make sure these options are selected—Use: All Layers, Mode: In Front, Opacity: 100%.

In all honesty, we have recovered the cost of Photoshop many times over with extra profits made using the corrective tools in this section alone. With practice, everyday corrections should not take more than a minute or three per image. Consider factoring the cost of doing these corrections into every image (many of them probably won't need any corrections). If you can give your client a better product, without them having to ask for it, then the overall perception of your image quality in general will be improved.

9. PHOTOSHOP ENHANCEMENTS

Pictures must not be too picturesque.

—Ralph Waldo Emerson

This is where the fun really begins in Photoshop—not that digital liposuction wasn't more fun than a barrel of monkeys! Enhancing images is also affectionately known as "tweaking." In the minds of many photographic artists, an image is not ready for public display until it has been tweaked in some form—either simply and subtly, or given a full artistic work over. For many, myself included, half the creative fun of photography is creating the perfect print after it's captured. We can use the unlimited tools we have in Photoshop to extend our creative vision and create what we really envisioned in our minds when we took the photograph.

With Photoshop, we can somewhat blur the lines between photographic realism and painterly impressionism. In fact, I like to use the term "photo impressionism" to refer to the images I create in camera together with Photoshop. The feeling of the image is more important than the exacting details. If an enhanced color palette or light-painting technique will convey the feeling more convincingly, then I will do it. If a soft, gentle glow gives the image more mood, I'm all over it. Now, this may not be appropriate for a pure photojournalist, but it can certainly apply to most other forms of photography where we are expected to take some artistic license—whether at the time of capture or

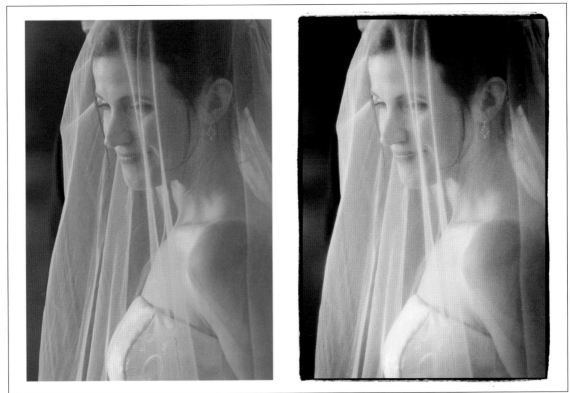

A normal image speaks. A tweaked image sings.

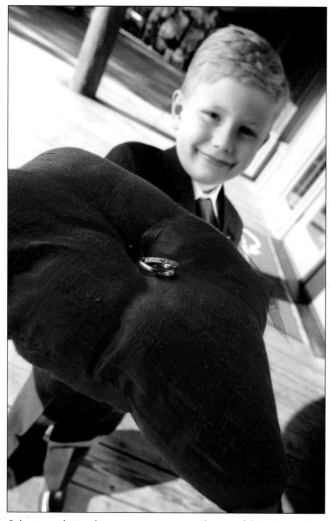

Selective coloring draws attention to special areas of the image.

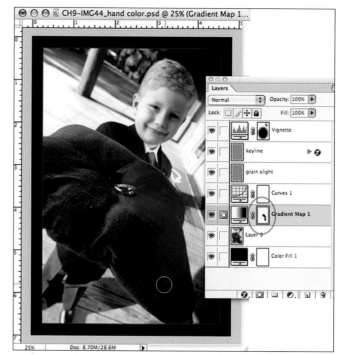

"Painting" with black on the black & white layer's mask reveals the color below.

in our digital art studio.

When shown both versions of an image, tweaked and normal, the client will inevitably prefer the tweaked version. The difference in quality and appeal is glaring and undeniable. Tweak more, sell more. Don't be a slacker, tweak it!

■ HANDCOLORED BLACK & WHITE IMAGES

Let's start with a best-selling technique that is fun and easy to do: black & white with handcoloring. The term "handcoloring" is used loosely here, as it is not the same as traditional handcoloring where paints are used to simulate real colors on a black & white photo. The look of this traditional technique is wholly possible in Photoshop as well, it just takes quite a bit more time and some practice to make it look right. For day-to-day production work in a busy studio, the luxury of that

kind of time is not always available, so here's the easy way. This may be more appropriately called, "selective coloring" as that's essentially what we'll do.

This works best when you have an image that can stand on its own as a black & white photo but also has an important element of color that would love to be revealed. It works great in advertising to focus on the product in a scene, in portraits of children with colorful outfits, and, of course, on flower girls with bouquets.

1. Start with a color image.
2. Add an adjustment layer to make it black & white. (The Gradient Map technique works well.)
3. When adjustment layers are created, they automatically have a layer mask attached to them in white—indicating the adjustment is entirely revealed. We are going to block part of this adjustment layer to let the color from the main image below show through.
4. Choose a medium-soft brush and black paint. Paint on the image where the color should show. Voila!
5. If you paint outside the lines and reveal color you don't want to, simply switch your color to white (X key) and paint it away again. As you get close to the finer details, reduce your brush size.

■ SOFTENING WITH KEVSOFT

Okay, so the name may be a little corny, but the effect is nothing short of beautiful. This technique softens skin and adds a little glow—as much or little as you want—for a flattering look and a little moodiness. Unlike other types of softening, this minimizes blurring in the darker areas, where the edge detail lies, giving a soft glow with full edge clarity.

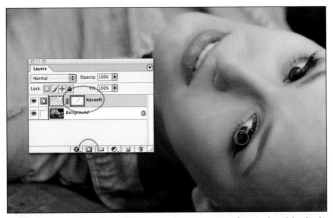

Add a layer mask to the soft layer so that portions of it can be "blocked" with black paint. Paint over the eyes to reveal full sharpness.

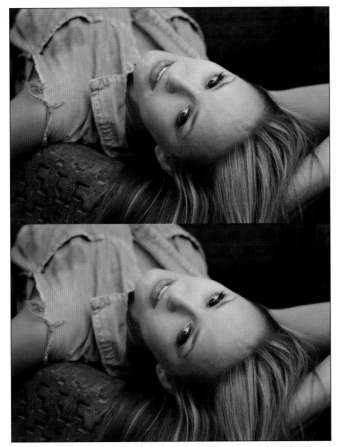

The effect is a beautiful softness that doesn't obscure fine details or reduce overall contrast.

1. Start on your main image layer.
2. Press Cmd/Ctrl+Opt/Alt+~ to load the highlights of the image as a selection mask.
3. Copy the selection to a new layer by selecting Layer>New>Layer via Copy (shortcut: Cmd/Ctrl+J). This will take the highlights from the image and copy them onto a new layer.
4. Go to Filter>Blur>Gaussian Blur. Start with a radius of 3–6 pixels. Adjust to suit your tastes, then click OK.
5. You should now have a nice, touchy-feely image with glowing skin and highlights. But, we want to make sure there is full clarity in the eyes and around the lips and teeth. Therefore, we'll need to add a layer mask to this soft layer.
6. Choose a soft brush and black paint. Size the brush to one eyeball.
7. Paint over the eyes and eyelashes to restore full clarity.
8. Paint over the lips and teeth as well. Try using a 50% brush opacity for this part.

■ DIGITAL FILL FLASH

One of our most-used techniques, this is a type of dodging and burning on steroids. It does wonders for bringing attention to the important elements in your image and works much more naturally than the Dodge and Burn tools. We sometimes refer to it as a type of "light painting" too, as you really do paint with light, opening shadows where needed and adding dimension to the image. It also allows us to use natural light as much as possible, knowing that slightly dark areas can be opened up using this technique. It is then possible to reduce the dependency of fill-flash on camera, which can tend to flatten an image and make it look a bit artificial. If you love natural light photography, you'll love this trick!

1. Open an image that needs a little fill.
2. Create a new Curves adjustment layer. Name it Lighten. (You can name a layer by simply double-clicking on its default name in the Layers palette.)
3. Lift the curve so that you see the maximum lightening that you'll need anywhere in your image. Don't

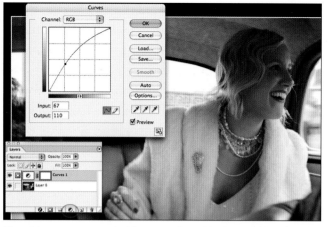

The midtones are opened with a curve shape like the one shown here. It's okay to go a little lighter than you think you might need.

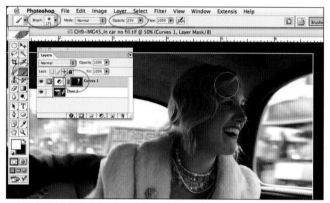

Painting with light using a soft brush at 20% opacity.

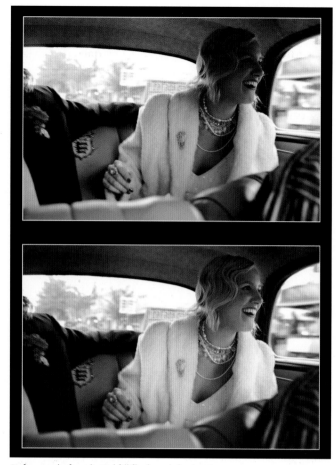

Before and after digital fill flash and shadowing.

Click on the Layer Mask icon, not the image icon, before painting.

be afraid to go a little too bright, as this is the maximum lightening that will be available, not what the final image will look like. Click OK.

4. Immediately type Cmd/Ctrl+I to invert the layer mask (or go to Image>Adjustments>Invert) so that it is completely black, or blocked.

5. Select the softest, white brush. Set the opacity of the brush to 20%. Size it according to the area you'll be working on—larger for broad expanses, smaller for detailed areas. The secret is to use as large as possi-

ble, as the feathered edge is softer on a larger brush, and reduce the brush size as you get closer to detail areas. When the brush is used right, tedious selections are not necessary.

6. Paint over the areas that need lightening. Since the brush is set to 20% opacity, only partial lightening will occur. The more the area is painted over, the lighter it gets. Keep in mind that until the mouse button is released and pressed again, the lightening will not increase—only the area covered. To make an area lighter still, release the mouse button, press it again, and start painting.

Using this technique really is like painting with light. The more you paint over an area, the lighter it gets. Think about shaping your subject, gently bringing brightness and attention to areas that need it most.

7. If an area becomes too dark, you can undo your last brush stroke with Cmd/Ctrl+Z, or switch your color swatch to black (X) and paint over it again. Applying

black paint will darken the image in 20% increments, toward the appearance of the original image.

Most images may only need a few dabs or strokes of light here or there to make a marked improvement in the depth and attention focus. If you really want to be a light-painting artist, you can add a darkening layer as well. It's simple:

A. Make another Curves adjustment layer. Name it Darken.

B. This time, pull the curve in the opposite direction so it's more of a dip. Be sure to go darker than you think you'll need anywhere in the image. Click OK.

C. Invert the layer mask as before (Cmd/Ctrl+I).

D. Use the same soft, white brush at 20%. Painting now will darken areas instead of lightening.

E. Switch layers depending on whether lightening or darkening is needed. Just click on the layer you want to work with. Be sure to click on the Layer Mask icon, instead of the first icon.

Using these two layers, an image can be shaped and lit exactly as you need it. Think about the basic rules in photographic lighting: lighter areas tend to come forward, or be more obvious; darker areas recede. Darken areas that need to be minimized or hidden. Think about how shadows can shape the human form, making it slimmer looking where needed. Flat lighting tends to make round shapes look wider.

Paint in shadows around a neckline or jawline to slim the face. Increase shadows on the dark side of arms or bodies to make them look slimmer. Add highlights to the bright side to give it more depth as well. Darken distracting objects to minimize their visual importance.

The best feedback is a before-and-after view; to do this, click the eyeball icons on the Layers palette off or on. Both the Lighten and Darken adjustment layers can be put into a layer set, then turned off or on together. Sets also help to clean up and organize your layer view.

■ CLEANING UP THE EYES AND TEETH

Now that we have the above steps down, let's use them for another classic retouching technique: enhancing eyes and teeth by brightening and removing color stains. The whites of the eyes can occasionally be bloodshot, which is an obvious thing to want to remove. Teeth could often use a little digital dentistry in the form of whitening. Traditional portrait retouchers will also make the whites of the eyes lighter and whiter, to increase their draw and attention. While we won't be going as far as to paint the eyes, like artists do, we'll use a similar concept to quickly enhance the eyes, while keeping them natural looking.

A simple dab of the brush in the whites of the eyes and across the teeth makes a subtle but noticeable difference.

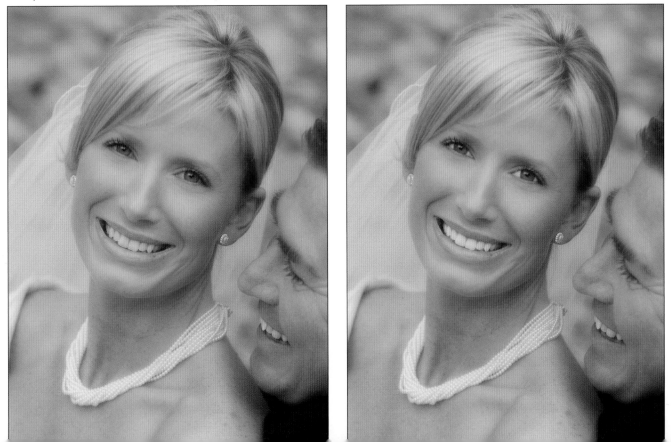

1. Open a portrait image and zoom in to at least 100% so the eyes and teeth are large enough to see clearly.
2. Create a new Curves adjustment layer and create a curve like you did in the digital fill flash technique. Click OK. Name the layer Lightening.
3. Invert the layer mask (Cmd/Ctrl+I).
4. Choose a small, soft, white brush, set to 20% opacity.

Dab gingerly in the whites of the eyes. Paint across the teeth as well. Build up the brightness as needed, being careful not to go too light so the enhancement does not look fake. Switch to black and paint if you go over the wrong area or want to restore.

Often, when the before-and-after view is toggled, the eyes and teeth may seem overdone. The easiest way to adjust the overall lightening is to change the layer opacity instead of the brush opacity.

Now the lightening is complete; eyes and teeth are shiny and bright—but wait, are those coffee stains and blood vessels from too much partying last night? Let's clean up a little.

Since we've already made a layer mask for the lightening, and essentially need to affect the same area again for stain removal, we'll reuse what we've already done.

A. Duplicate the Lightening adjustment layer. Label it Bleach.
B. Choose Layer>Change Layer Content>Hue/ Saturation.
C. In the Hue/Saturation dialog box, move the Saturation slider to 0. Click OK.
D. Yipee! You've now used your existing layer masking on a new saturation-reducing layer to get the

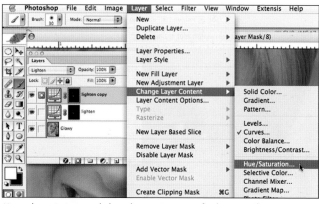
Keep the existing mask, but change its type of adjustment layer.

stains out. If the effect is too gray, reduce the layer opacity. If the effect needs more color removal, paint over the eyes and/or teeth with the soft white brush to build up the "bleach."

■ SELECTIVE FOCUS

Another great way to bring attention to the main subject area, selective focus is similar to using a large-aperture lens wide open. However, we're not limited to imitating film and camera effects, remember? We're working digitally and we have unlimited options.

Selective focus allows us to see clearly only what we want to. We'll apply it here with the intention of simulating lens depth of field, where the area in front of the subject is blurred and the area behind the subject is blurred. Our blur will also gradually fade in and out like depth of field.

1. Duplicate the background layer.
2. Apply the Lens Blur filter by selecting Filter>Blur>Lens Blur. Set the Radius to the maximum amount of blurring that you would like to see in the image. Click OK. (If you have Photoshop 7, instead of Lens Blur [which was not available until CS] use Gaussian Blur.)
3. Add a layer mask to this new blurred image by clicking the layer mask icon at the bottom of the layers palette. Select the Gradient tool. In the options bar, choose a black-to-white gradient and select the icon for the linear gradient.
4. With the layer mask still active, click on the image where the blur should start and drag a line to where the blur should be heaviest. A gradient will appear on your mask, blocking the blur where you started to drag and fully revealing the blur where you let go. This is the foreground blur.
5. If you aren't satisfied with the blur fading, then click, drag, and let go again to redo the gradient. Each time you apply a new gradient, the previous attempt is replaced.
6. Duplicate the blurred layer.
7. On the duplicate layer, click on the Layer Mask icon to make sure it's active, then drag your Gradient tool again in the opposite direction. The old gradient

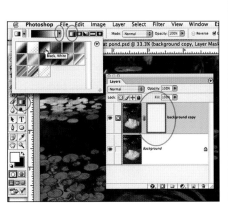

Select a black-to-white linear gradient from the options bar.

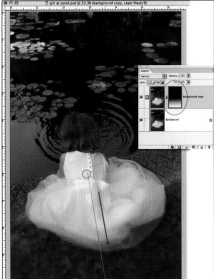

Applying a gradient to the layer mask on the blurred layer will gradually reveal the sharp layer below.

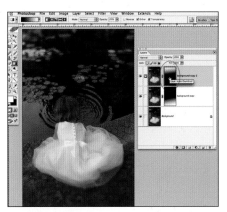

The final image with the gradient applied in both directions.

will be erased. On this second layer, we are creating the background blur.

8. At this point the effect is fairly complete. On images that don't have a distinct foreground/background, it may take some experimentation to get the blur graduated just right. It's also nice to simply paint in blur at the edges of the image—without consciously simulating a depth-of-field effect. Use a soft, larger white brush at 20% opacity and paint any other areas that should be blurred. Since the opacity is at 20%, more painting will increase the blur—up to the total amount of the Lens Blur filter.

◼ HIGH-SPEED BLACK & WHITE FILM

Here's another film-like favorite technique that has carried over into the digital domain. Grainy black & white films have always been popular for the raw, artistic feel in the images. High-speed black & white films have a couple of identifying characteristics: higher contrast and noticeable grain. Let's get some speed!

1. If the image is still in color, create a black & white version using the Gradient Map technique.
2. Above the Gradient Map layer, add a new Curves adjustment layer, and call it Snap.
3. In the Curves dialog box, create an S curve to increase contrast. Click on the line $^1/_3$ from the bot-

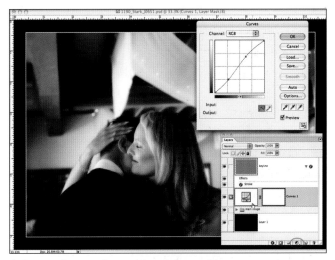

A Curves adjustment layer with an S shape adds contrast to the image.

tom and pull down slightly, then click $^1/_3$ from the top and push up slightly. Click OK.

Now for the grain. This method creates an adjustable and more organic-looking grain than other standard methods. It also preserves shadow detail better than simply applying noise directly to an image. Even if you don't quite understand what's happening when we create the following layers (it's a little wacky), don't worry—just follow along and see how you like the result.

A. Start with your top layer active (simultaneously pressing Opt/Alt+Shift+] is a quick way to jump

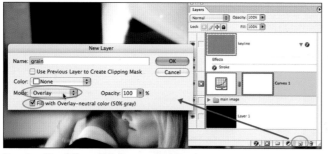

Pressing Opt/Alt and clicking on the New Layer icon gives you options before it is created.

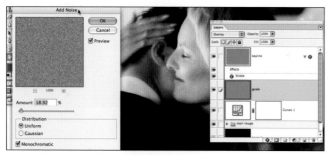

Noise filter with the initial "grain" settings.

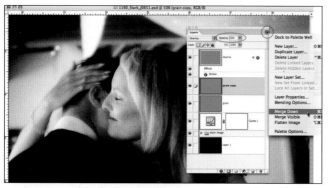

Choose Merge Down from the layer options menu to combine the two grain layers.

to the top of your layers). Press Opt/Alt and click on the New Layer icon. A dialog box will appear.

B. In the dialog box, change the Mode to Overlay, then check the box next to Fill with Overlay—neutral color (50% gray). Click OK.

C. You'll now have a new gray layer that visibly does nothing. Not yet. Go to Filter>Noise>Add Noise. Set the Distribution to Uniform and check the Monochromatic box. Adjust the Amount to suit the image. 10–15% is a good starting point. Make sure to view the image at 100% for best evaluation. Click OK.

D. You now have a nice grain pattern, but let's make it a little more organic. Duplicate the Noise layer.

E. Choose Edit>Transform>Rotate 180°.

F. Set the layer opacity to 50%.

G. Select Layer>Merge Down.

H. Yummy! Now that looks good. Adjust the opacity of this new grain layer to reduce the effect if needed.

I. Keep in mind that the amounts used in these examples are generally good starting points for high-resolution images around 6MP. If you are working on lower- or higher-resolution images, you may need to vary the amounts to get the results you like best.

The final image with high-speed film effect.

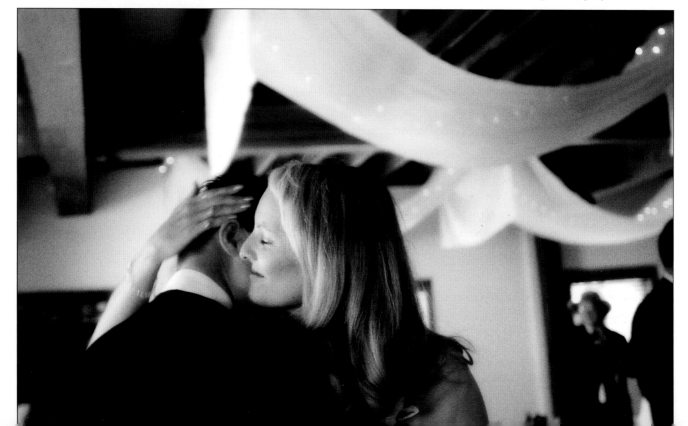

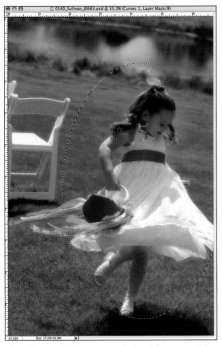

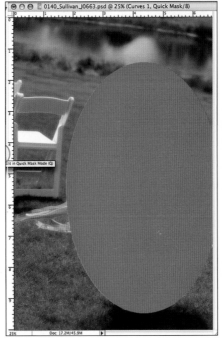

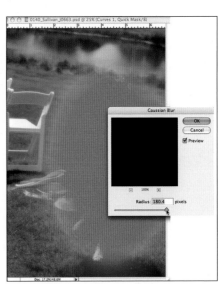

The elliptical Marquee tool should surround the subject but not come too close.

The Quick Mask icon, also known as the "red blob."

The red blob should be blurred enough to create a very smooth transition, but not so much as to reveal the main subject.

■ VIGNETTE? YOU BET

Here again, we've taken a traditional camera or darkroom effect and, instead of wielding it like a blunt battle ax, we'll control it like a svelte Samurai sword. Vignette was traditionally applied in-camera. A neutral-density filter had a circular shape cut out of the middle and was then placed over the lens. It was a little clumsy, at best, and the dark edges were often quite obvious. The effect worked, however, because it really drew your eye to the subject—and minimized distracting background areas.

Along with digital fill flash, this is one of those techniques that is hard to live without. It's simple to apply but makes an impressive improvement to many images. It adds depth and directs attention where it should be. When applied subtly, it can be used on almost every image—especially portraits—and no one will be the wiser. They'll just look better. Generally, this technique should be applied last in your enhancing workflow. Make sure you have also set your tool preferences as described in chapter 7, as they will affect how this technique works.

1. Select the top layer in your Layers palette (Opt/Alt+Shift+]).

2. Select the elliptical Marquee tool and drag a circular shape around the main subject. Release the mouse when the shape is just right. If you don't like the shape, simply start dragging a new one or go to Select>Transform Selection. Adjustment handles will appear around your selection. Pull them to reshape the selection, then hit Enter.

3. Enter Quick Mask mode by simply typing a Q. Or, if you prefer to click things, it's the right-most circle under the color swatches in the tool bar.

4. The elliptical selection area should now be a red blob that is 100% opaque. (If not, you may not have set your preferences as mentioned in chapter 7.) This blob represents your selection. It is an accurate visual way to work with selections, rather than using dotted-line approximations.

We want to soften our selection border, so we'll soften the red blob (Quick Mask) with the Gaussian Blur filter. Go to Filter>Blur>Gaussian Blur.

5. In the Gaussian Blur dialog box, set the Radius as high as possible without allowing your main subject area to show through the red blob. The goal is to achieve as much of a soft transition on the edges as possible without seeing through to the main subject. Try 200–250 pixels. Click OK.

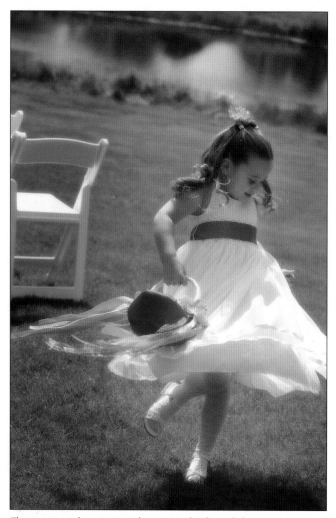

The image with a vignette has more depth, and the main subject is emphasized.

border and mat looks can also be printed that way. It is a good option when an image needs to be kept full-frame, yet printed within a standard size paper—like 8"x10"—which would normally crop the full-frame image considerably.

The first step is to create a larger canvas area around the image. We'll make an even border all around the image so there is room for a simple keyline border or film-like sloppy border. We'll start with a keyline.

1. Select the background layer. If the layer name Background appears in italics, double-click on the name, then click OK. This creates a floating layer.
2. Go to Image>Canvas Size. In the New Size section of the dialog box, select Percent in the measurement pull-down menus.
3. If the image is vertical, enter 108 in the Height box and 112 in the Width box. Swap these numbers if the image is horizontal. This will give you an even border all the way around the image area. This is the pseudo "mat" area. Make sure Relative is not checked. Click OK.

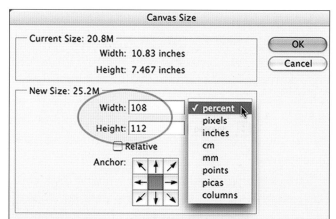

Changing the canvas size by percent allows for consistent border sizes.

6. Type Q again to leave Quick Mask mode and return to Selection mode. You'll now see the marching ants roughly representing your selection.
7. Inverse the selection (Cmd/Ctrl+Shift+I).
8. Create a new Levels adjustment layer and move the middle gray slider to the right to darken the edges. Click OK.
9. Wonderful! The result is a beautiful effect that is subtle yet very effective.

■ BORDERS AND EDGES

With all these wonderful artistic enhancements complete, it would be best to display the images properly. No photographer worth their weight in memory cards would present a fine image without a mat or frame of some sort. Why should online or screen images receive anything less than royal treatment? Photos with built-in

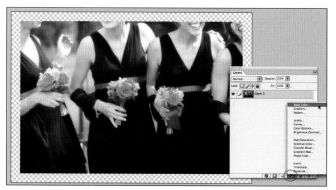

Create a new Color Fill adjustment layer.

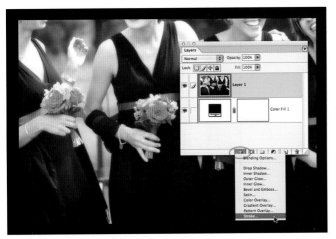

Adding a Stroke layer style to the image.

4. Your image will now have a small mat with a checkerboard pattern, which represents transparent areas. We need to fill the border with a mat color. On the Layers palette, create a new Color Fill adjustment layer.

5. Choose a color from the Color Picker for the mat. Your image is temporarily obscured, but don't worry. Click OK to close the Color Picker dialog box.

6. Type Cmd/Ctrl+Shift+[to move the Color Fill layer to the bottom of your layer stack. (Or you can just drag it down, if you feel like being a drag.)

7. Nice. Now let's add the keyline. Select the image layer and add a Stroke layer style. In the dialog box, choose Inside for the position, and use the Size slider to change the width.

8. Click on the Color box to change the color of the keyline. You can choose a color from the palette or click anywhere in your image to sample a color from it to use on the keyline. Slick.

Keep in mind that if your image has a black & white adjustment layer above this layer, it will be converting your keyline to black & white as well, so you won't see a color on the image, only shades of gray. Click OK.

The background mat and the keyline colors can easily be changed at any time by double-clicking on their respective layers and choosing a new color.

Adding a mat and keyline in this fashion gives a finished look. It also enhances the presentation—especially for images that will first be seen online or in a slide show.

The final presentation is much more polished—just like a framed image.

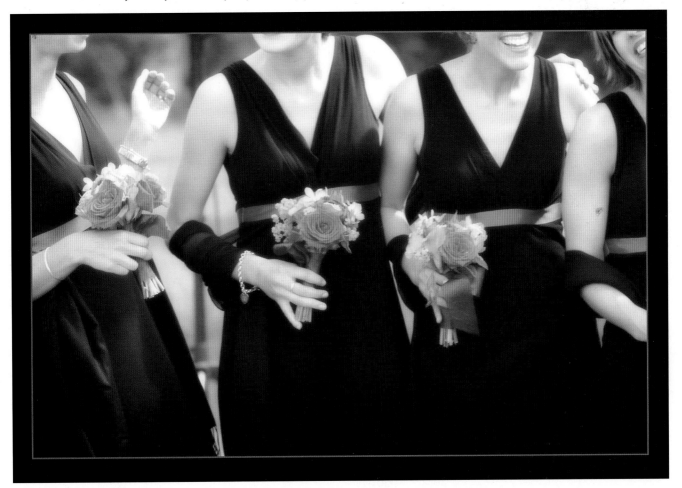

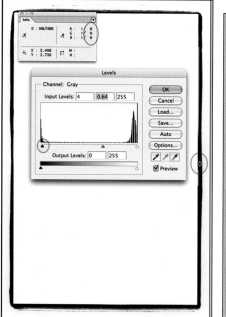
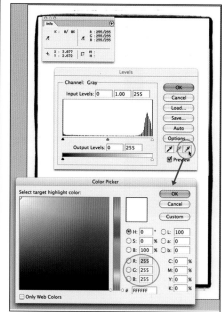
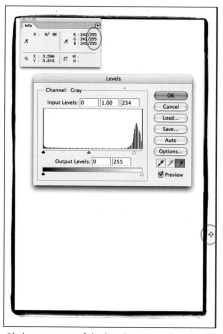

Move your cursor over the black border to see when the values are all 0, 0, 0.

Set your white eyedropper to pure white.

Click any areas of the border image that should be pure white, not dingy white or gray.

Another popular effect is to use a film-type "sloppy border" on digital images. There are stand-alone programs and plug-ins for Photoshop that are designed just for making borders. Many of them are overkill for the relatively few borders that most photographers like to use. You can make your own sloppy border template to use on any image.

The first step is to acquire a sloppy-border image. We like to use real sloppy-border edges, so we created blank frames in a darkroom, printed them, and scanned them. (If you don't have access to a darkroom, never fear: you can download a free sloppy border. See page 8.)

A. With the sloppy-border image open in Photoshop, make a selection around the inside of your border to eliminate the image area. Delete it.

B. Go to Image>Adjustments>Levels and pull the black triangle in toward the center until the inner black edge of your border is a true black. Verify this by moving your cursor over the image area and checking the values on your Info palette. The R, G, and B values should all be 0. (If your Info palette is not visible, go to Window>Info.)

C. Double-click on the white eyedropper, and in the Color Picker that comes up, enter 255, 255, 255 for the R, G, and B values. Click OK to close the dialog box.

D. Click in the image outside your black border and again inside the center area. Click on any area that should be white but may have a light-gray tone. This will push any dingy white area to pure white. Click OK.

E. Change the layer's blend mode to Multiply.

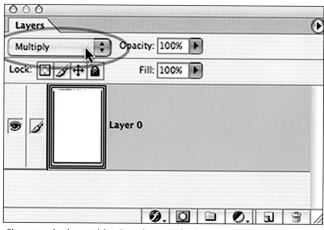

Changing the layer's blend mode to Multiply mode will make the white areas disappear when placed over another image.

F. Save this file as your sloppy-border template. Keep it in PSD format. Now that this file is saved, it can be opened at any time and applied to any image. It will only need resizing and possible rotation. Open an image that you want to apply the border to and increase the canvas size to 112% by 108% as described on page 100.

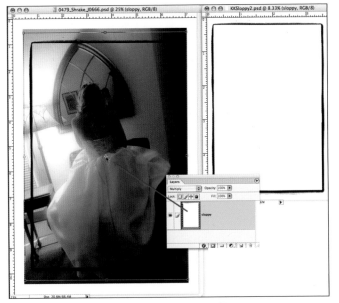

Drag the layer icon from your border-template file onto any image.

a. With both the border template and your image file open, click on the border layer on the Layers palette.

b. Hold the Shift key down and drag the layer icon from the border to your main image. Release the mouse, then release the Shift key.

c. Choose Edit>Free Transform (Cmd/Ctrl+T) and grab each corner handle to size the border to the image. (If you can't see your border transform handles, zoom out so your image is small. Pull the handles in and size the border to the image.)

d. When the image is sized just right, hit Enter to set the transform.

If you need to apply a sloppy border to an image that is oriented differently, you can rotate it before setting the transform. Put your cursor outside the border area and,

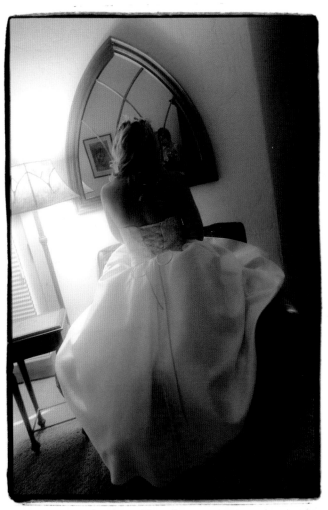

The final image with a classic film technique.

when you see the curved, double arrow, drag to rotate 90°. Holding Shift while you drag will snap the rotation to exactly 90°.

With these powerful tools, you may become a tweaking addict! Don't worry, you're not alone. We have a support hotline for those in need: 877-330-4330. (Relationship counseling not included.)

10. PHOTOSHOP ACTIONS

No man ever said on his deathbed, "I wish I had spent more time at the office."

—Senator Paul Tsongas

Now that you've mastered all the steps to creating beautiful images, what if we told you they can be automated? Don't throw anything! Your brain is richer, and it's important to know what's happening when you create in Photoshop—after all, that's how new techniques are discovered. Once you are familiar with what can be done, however, it's time to start thinking about how you can automate your repetitive steps using Photoshop actions.

Actions are recordings of processes you do, places you click, and menu items you choose. They can be saved and replayed on other images. In creating actions, Photoshop records the steps you do, much like a tape recorder. They can also be used in batches, to process folders of images in one sitting—without any further interaction from the user. Actions are tremendous time savers! They also help to ensure consistency in your images, as each one can be processed the same way.

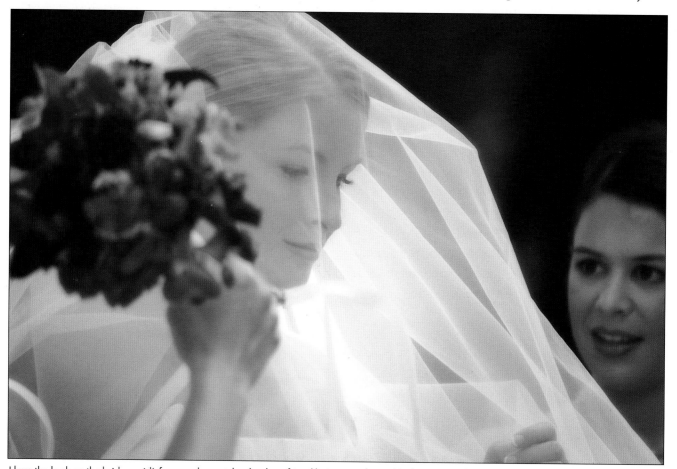

I love the look on the bridesmaid's face as she watches her best friend being transformed. Nikon D70 with 70–200mm lens at 200mm.

As we all know, computers aren't really very smart, they just do what they're told—most of the time. So, keep in mind that an action can't do things that require some interactive thinking—like adjusting a color to your liking or looking for a neutral reference point on your image. It can, however, be told to stop and wait for you to make an adjustment before it continues on its merry way. Here are just a few examples of things that can be done with actions:

- Automatically convert a folder full of high-resolution images into lower-resolution JPEG copies in black & white with a mat and keyline border and light sharpening.
- Save multiple versions of a completed image into different formats and sizes, each in different folders.
- Convert a color image to black & white using a favorite formula.
- Create a 13"x19" page at 240dpi, then open twenty-one images, size them to 3" across, sharpen them, and place them all in a three-image by seven-image grid centered on the page. Add a text title in your favorite font. Save as a PSD and JPEG file for print.
- Take really bad photos and turn them into works of art. (Okay, I'm just kidding.)

How much time can you save with actions? If you can save merely an hour per day using actions, which is completely feasible, then based on 8760 hours in a year it would only take thirty-six-and-a-half years to save a whole year! Assuming you work with Photoshop from birth to age seventy-five, you'll add over two years to your life. Now that's exciting. But seriously, the time savings with actions is undeniable. Spend time creating new images and less time repeating mindless steps.

■ THE ACTIONS PALETTE

Let's take a look at the Actions palette piece by piece. If it's not visible, go to Window>Actions.

The folder icon represents an action set, which can be used to help you organize your actions into logical groups. If you load a set of actions that you purchase (or the actions available to accompany this book; see page 8), they will appear within a folder in the list. In each

---

CAUTIONARY NOTE

There's a little "feature" in Photoshop CS and older that allows you to really mess up your actions if you're not careful—so take heed! If you click on the check box or dialog icon in the first two left-hand columns of the Actions palette, you could easily activate or deactivate every single step and/or dialog message in the Actions list. I can't think of any practical reason why someone would want to do this, other than to play a cruel practical joke by sabotaging another person's computer, so be careful. Only click on these columns if you are very comfortable working with the Actions palette. This issue has been fixed in Photoshop CS2.

---

folder are the actual actions. A folder can hold as many actions as needed, and you can save your own action sets, which can be loaded on any computer with Photoshop installed.

Clicking on the triangle next to the action name will open the action, revealing the steps that were recorded as part of the action. Clicking the triangle next to a step will reveal the settings used in that step. Juicy morsels of information are available here! Opening the actions, steps, and settings is a good way to learn more about techniques in Photoshop. If you get an action set from someone and like what an action does, open it up and see what went into making it. You can learn all sorts of new tricks this way.

At the top-right corner of the Actions palette is the Action menu options button. Clicking on it will reveal a menu of handy possibilities. For a full description, consult your Photoshop documentation. We'll cover some of the immediately useful options below.

Record Again. When you have a certain action step selected, choosing Record Again will rerecord just that one step, not the entire action. This is great for fine-tuning an action after it's been created.

Insert Menu Item. Sometimes Photoshop may not accurately record picking an item from menus using the mouse. However, any selection from the menus can be added manually as an action step using this feature.

Insert Stop. Tells the action to stop running and display a dialog box. This can simply be a note to yourself

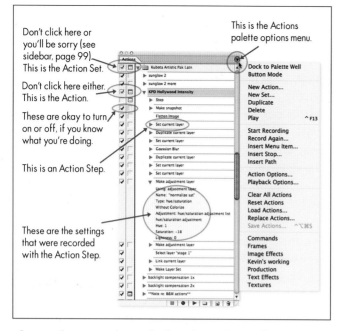

Don't click here or you'll be sorry (see sidebar, page 99). This is the Action Set.

Don't click here either. This is the Action.

These are okay to turn on or off, if you know what you're doing.

This is an Action Step.

These are the settings that were recorded with the Action Step.

This is the Actions palette options menu.

about why you exist and what the action is for, or directions to complete a step manually before continuing.

Load Actions. This is where you can install an action set that you purchased or have previously saved.

Save Actions. It's a good idea to save your action sets periodically as separate files (also known as ATN files). These saved action files are very small and can be easily stored or moved. Whenever you quit Photoshop, all the actions in the Actions palette are saved internally in Photoshop and will be there the next time you open the program. However, for portability and backup purposes, it's a good idea to save them separately on a regular basis.

■ THE BATCH DIALOG BOX

We'll cover how to make an action in just a bit, but first let's look at one more important dialog box. The Batch dialog box is accessible through File>Automate>Batch. In order to run actions on an entire folder of images, or selected images within the File Browser, certain options need to be set in this dialog box.

Play. Select the action to run from the list.

Source. Choose Folder if you have all the images you need to process inside one folder on your computer. The action will run on every image in the folder. If you want to select certain images within a folder, select them in the Browser first, then choose File Browser from this menu.

Suppress Color Profile Warnings. If your Photoshop Color Settings have been set to Preserve Color Profiles, then this will open all images with this option as your default—without asking for your confirmation. It's necessary to have this box checked if you plan to run a batch unattended.

Destination. Choose Folder if you want to make copies of the images you process and put them into a new folder. Click the Choose button to specify where the folder is. You can also select Save and Close to run the action on an image and resave it, so that it replaces itself.

Override Action "Save As" Commands. This option is a bit tricky to comprehend, but it's very important to understand. If your action includes a Save step—specifying a place, file type, and compression settings—then this option will use the recorded file type and compression settings but override the save location with the one specified above. Note that if you don't have a Save step recorded and check this box, the batch won't work as expected. If you have a Save step recorded and don't check this box, the batch won't work as expected.

Whenever you plan to use an action in a batch process, it's a good idea to record a Save step with the action, specifying your file type and compression set-

The Batch dialog box determines how an action will behave on multiple images.

Create a new action set to organize your actions.

Creating a new action.

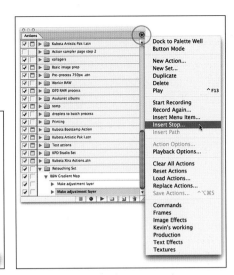

From the Action drop-down menu, choose Insert Stop to pause the action when played back and display a message.

tings. The location for the saved images can be overridden each time the action is run.

Most problems that people run into with running actions in batches have something to do with the Override Action "Save As" Commands box not being checked or unchecked appropriately.

File Naming. This can usually be left at the default, which uses the original image's name plus the appropriate file-type extension.

■ CREATING A BASIC ACTION

We'll cover a couple of simple actions to help get you started on the road to action hero or heroine status. This action will convert your image to black & white, add a little contrast, then display a message.

1. Go to Window>Actions to access the Actions palette.
2. At the bottom of the palette, click on the Create New Set icon. Name the set anything you want.
3. Next, click on the New Action icon, name the action B&W with Snap, and click Record.
4. Photoshop is now recording your every move and everything you say, so hurry up and be nice! Okay—this isn't really the case—it just waits patiently for you to do something. The speed at which you create the action has nothing to do with how quickly it replays. Take your time.
5. Switch to your Layers palette and create a black & white image using a Gradient Map adjustment layer.

6. Now, create a new Curves adjustment layer and shape the curve into an S to add contrast.
7. Add a message window to write yourself a love note. From the Actions drop-down menu (accessed by clicking the arrow at the top-right corner of the Actions palette), select Insert Stop.
8. In the Stop dialog box, write: "Adjust the curve layer for more or less contrast. Click the eyeball to turn it off completely. Think *peace* and have a groovy day." Leave the Allow Continue box unchecked.
9. Great. Click on the square Stop Recording button in the Actions palette to end the action.

Now all that's left is to reap the rewards of your efforts and play that action! Revert to the image's original color form or open another image. Click the Play triangle on the Actions palette and watch your image quickly transform. Read your note and do what it says. Can you think of a few hundred fun ways to use this?

A More Complex Action. Let's take this a step further and create an action that could be used in a batch process—for example, to transform a folder full of high-resolution images into low-resolution copies for proofing or on-screen presentations.

When using actions in batches, there are a few steps that should be included to ensure it will always run correctly, without stopping, on any type of image. Here are a few of the "safety" steps that should generally be included in actions intended for batch processes:

Flatten Image. Run this as a first step. This ensures the action will work predictably on previously layered files.

Convert to Profile. This ensures that images intended for on-screen display will look their best.

Flatten Image (Again). If your action creates layers and you want to save the result as a JPEG file, you'll need to flatten the image before saving it to avoid interruptions.

Save. This ensures that your file will be saved with the file type and compression settings you want.

Keep in mind that extra steps that have no effect on an image will simply be ignored, so it doesn't hurt to add them in as insurance.

Now let's build the action. This one will open a full-resolution file, run the Clarify effect, resize the image to 1200 maximum pixel dimension, sharpen the image, add a little color saturation, convert it to the sRGB color space, then save it as a high-quality JPEG file.

A. Open a full-sized image.

B. Create a new action, call it Make Low-Resolution Proofs, then click Record.

C. Choose Filter>Sharpen>Unsharp Mask. Use the settings: 20, 60, 4. Click OK. This is the "Clarify Effect."

D. Choose File>Automate>Fit Image. Enter 1200 in the Width and Height boxes. This will fit your image into an imaginary 1200-pixel box. It won't make it a square; horizontals will be 1200 pixels wide, and verticals will be 1200 pixels tall.

E. Choose Filter>Sharpen>Unsharp Mask. This time, use settings of 225, 0.3, 8 (for sharpening a low-resolution image).

F. Add a new Hue/Saturation adjustment layer. Increase the saturation by 10 points. Click OK.

G. Go to Layer>Flatten Image.

H. Go to Image>Mode>Convert to Profile. Select sRGB as the destination (this is best for on-screen and web images). Click OK.

I. Go to File>Save As. Put the image on your desktop for now (this is just a dummy copy of the image, which you can later throw away). Choose JPEG as the file type and select the highest-quality setting.

J. Press the square button to stop recording.

Note that we didn't need to create an adjustment layer for the Hue/Saturation since the image was going to be flattened anyway. We could have done it directly via Image>Adjustments>Hue/Saturation. However, we wanted to include a Flatten Image step, and this can't be recorded unless the image actually has a layer to flatten.

Speaking of the Flatten Image step, we need to duplicate this step so that it happens twice in our action—once immediately when the image opens (in case it's a layered file to begin with) and again near the end. It's easy to copy an existing step in your action and place it elsewhere. Here's how:

a. Open your newly created action by clicking on the triangle next to its name.

b. Click once on the Flatten Image step.

c. While holding down your Opt/Alt key, drag the step up just above the first Unsharp Mask step. This will copy your step so that it appears twice.

The action is now ready to use in a batch process. Keep in mind that if you run it on a single image without using the File>Automate>Batch dialog box, the image will be saved to your desktop, since that's where you told the action to save initially. When you use the Batch dialog box, the location can be overridden with the Override Action "Save As" Commands check box.

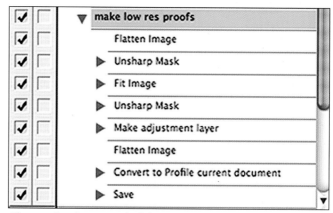

The completed action with all the steps in place.

Finally, let's save the actions so that they can be transferred to other computers if necessary—and to create and keep a backup copy. Click on the name of your action set. Go to Actions>Save Actions. Put the file in a memorable place, and you're all set. To bring this action

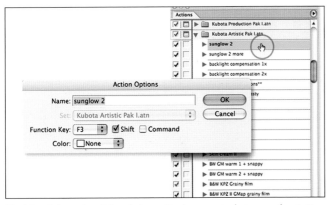

Double-click to the right of the action's name to bring up the Action Options box. You can assign a function key here.

set into another computer, choose Load Actions from the same menu. Here are some last-minute action tips.

- You can select multiple steps at a time in an action list to either copy or delete them. Press Cmd/Ctrl and click on all the action steps you want included.
- Drag selected steps up or down to rearrange them. Dragging them into another set will automatically copy them to that set.
- Before running a new or unfamiliar action, open it up and inspect the steps. Look for Flatten Image and Save steps that could mess up your image.
- Temporarily turn steps off (like the above-mentioned Flatten Image or Save) if you need to by unchecking the box next to that step in the left-most column. This is helpful to turn off Save steps when you run the action on a single image that is already open.
- If you want to play an action one step at a time instead of running it all the way through, click on the first step, then press Cmd/Ctrl and press the Play button. The program will walk through the steps one at a time. This is helpful for troubleshooting actions.
- Keep in mind that sometimes the main image layer needs to be selected first before running an action, or unexpected results may occur. (E.g., if your action is playing a step to sharpen an image but you start running it with an adjustment layer selected, nothing will happen. The Sharpen step will run on the adjustment layer instead of the actual image.)
- Double-click to the right of the action name to bring up the Action Options window. You can assign a function key here so that your favorite actions can be

run by pressing a single key. Bam! Now that's a time saver!

- Actions can be recorded to play other actions. Using this, you could make a new action that plays a series of your other favorite actions, one after the other.

By now, you should be feeling like a super action hero. With the power of actions, you can easily rule the world—or at least your little corner of it.

◼ CREATING A DROPLET

Droplets are actions that are saved as mini programs. They can be icons on your desktop (or anywhere that you can drop an image or images onto). When an image is dropped onto the icon, Photoshop will open, run the action, then save and close the file. This is great for applying your favorite actions, like a black & white conversion, from another program like iView. Here's how.

1. Create the action, if you don't already have one. Be sure to include a Flatten Image and Save step to specify the file type that will be saved.
2. Go to File>Automate>Create Droplet.
3. Apply the settings as shown below and save your droplet to a convenient location.

Now, all you need to do is drop images on the droplet, and they will be converted using the action. Keep in mind that the image you drop will actually be converted, so make sure you have a backup copy if it's an original file. Usually you'll use droplets on proof files that you'll want converted anyway.

The droplet settings

11. PRINTING AND PRESENTING

To me art in order to be truly great must, like the beauty of Nature, be universal in its appeal.
It must be simple in its presentation and direct in its expression, like the language of Nature.

—Mohandas Gandhi

Ironically, learning to print and present your images effectively will keep you completely out of "chapter 11," if you know what I mean. By printing and presenting your images more effectively you'll see increased sales and repeat business—the goal of any studio.

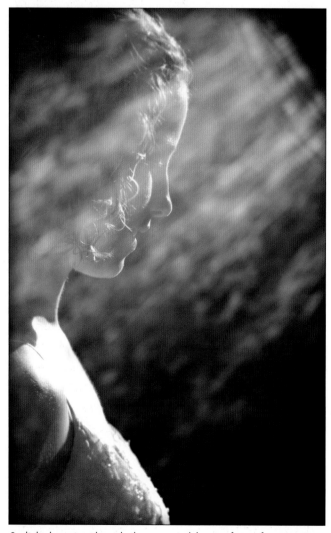

Sunlight beaming through the uncoated lens surface of a prototype Lensbaby created this ethereal image.

Shooting digitally means that you are only a few steps away from one of the best ways to present your images—up on a big screen or wall in your sales room (which may very well be your living room too, and that's okay). Digital projectors are becoming commonplace in photo studios and are an effective tool for making the best first impression possible—and making the best first impression possible is key.

Even if you use other proofing and presentation tools, like proof prints, booklets, web proofing, or CD-ROMs, these should all be supplementary to a nice in-studio presentation. Many photographers, our studio included, initially got lazy and thought that web proofing meant we would never have to sit down with and sell to a client ever again. We thought we could upload the images and the orders would just pour in from around the world while we slept or lounged by the pool with our kids. Not!

Web proofing, as we'll discuss in more detail later, is a great supplementary sales tool. But its real benefit, in our opinion, is as a vehicle for exposure and acquiring new clients.

Nothing beats face-to-face soft-selling with images larger than life and quality controlled. Emotional impact and the mood of the sales room is vital to a successful order—and equally important, the clients' enjoyment of their images and impression of you as a photographer and businessperson. Focus on the first impression and main presentation first—the rest is gravy.

Bill Sorenson, a very successful photographer and educator from Portland, Oregon, once told me, "When they cry, they buy." How true. When you've created the perfect mood in your studio and can passionately present beautiful images, the sales will happen. You don't have to be pushy or apply used-car salesman's techniques. Of course, pricing structures and packaging are all part of the equation too—which is part of Bill's area of expertise.

◼ CREATING THE PERFECT MOOD

Imagine this: you're the client and walk up to the studio door, the handle you grab is a solid, high-quality crafted shape. You come in and a pleasant scent of candles breezes over you—not too sweet, not too strong. The lights are low except for perfectly placed spots highlighting beautiful images—a baby's face, a cheerful bride, an expectant mother, a family in a loving embrace. Someone immediately and cheerfully walks over to grab your hand and welcome you in. A large, cozy leather chair looks ever so inviting, and you're offered it straight away. Now you start to sense the aroma of really good coffee brewing, and before your mouth has a chance to start watering, the offer comes, "I've got fresh coffee ready, decaf as well, can I interest you?" You spy a little plate of cookies on the end table too and imagine it wouldn't be too hard to acquire one.

How do you feel now? Maybe a little hesitant, anticipating a typical sales pitch for a stack of photos you really don't need. After all, you really just had the session done for one nice photo of your kids. You feel pretty comfortable, overall, though, and start to relax a little.

Let's continue with our fantasy: the background music is subtle and sophisticated—how did they know you love jazz? The photographer, or studio manager, shares a brief bit of casual conversation about their day or a recent event, then asks you some light and easy questions about your day, and maybe pays a sincere compliment about your new shoes or leopard-skin bikini (scratch that one). The photographer then tells you how excited they are about the images they have to share and how much they enjoyed meeting your children and family. You believe it because it is sincere and enthusiastic. This makes you feel good. You like your family too.

"Shall we look at the images? I can't wait to show you." Hmm . . . the photographer didn't say "photos" or "pictures," your subconscious notices. You relax back in your big comfy chair as the lights dim slightly. A movie screen appears from the ceiling on the wall in front of you and slowly lowers into place. A black page appears with a title in elegant white type, *"The family is one of nature's masterpieces.—George Santayana."* Beautiful images of your children begin to fade in and out, one after the other. Their faces are large, glowing, and almost touchable—big, joyous smiles and all the subtle little expressions that you cherish every day. You instantly realize this is going to be an expensive day, but some of the best money ever spent.

Does this sound good? It's certainly an idealized scenario but is not unrealistic or uncommon by any means. It doesn't take much to make people comfortable and set them at ease. Once they have relaxed, you can appeal to their emotions. And—whether you are presenting children's images, families, or their wedding day—the purchasing decisions are primarily emotional in nature. Nobody really needs more than one little photo of their kids or family, do they?

◼ PRESENTATION INGREDIENTS

So, let's take a look at what's involved in creating that first, all important, impression—from a technical standpoint.

Digital Projectors. If it fits in your budget and space, a digital projector can easily pay for itself in a short amount of time. You should see an immediate increase in sales volume and larger print size orders when projection is used properly.

For studio use where the room can be darkened somewhat, a projector with 1200 lumens (the brightness measurement) should be sufficient. XGA resolution is important (1024x768) for sharp images at full screen size. Look for a model with good, natural color that is fully adjustable. We have had good experiences with Mitsubishi and NEC (made by the same company) projectors as they offer great quality and color matching to the sRGB color space.

Slide Shows. Slide shows can be created in iView once the low-resolution images have all been tweaked and color corrected. iView has beautiful slide show functionality.

You may want to play music to accompany your slide show. If you are going to use music in a business environment, you'll probably need to get some sort of licensing rights. Common resources for this would be ASCAP, BMI, and SESAC. The Professional Photographers of America (PPA) website has some helpful information on music licensing. The loopholes and contingencies for how and where popular music can be used can be a little confusing, so it's best to read the information pages carefully.

A great solution for music that you'd like to include on DVDs or CD-ROM slide shows that you give your client is to contact local musicians who write original music. Offer to photograph their band or CD covers in exchange for rights to use some of their original songs on your slide shows. If you offer to include a credit line at the end of all your shows, giving them increased exposure, they'll probably be more than happy to oblige. If you have decent musicians in your town, this is not too difficult.

If your town is musically challenged, then try finding royalty-free music on websites like www.musicbakery.com. This is one of the better royalty-free sites (most sound like elevator music), and you only pay a moderate fee for unlimited usage in your slide shows. Quick and easy.

■ MAKING AN IVIEW SLIDE SHOW

Once the images are prepared and in an iView catalog, the slide show can be made instantly and on the fly. It's also a nice touch to add a title to your show and a few black frames, to help ease your viewer in and out of the presentation. You may also want to add a quote to help get them in the mood. All of these extra pages can easily be created in Photoshop and saved as separate JPEG files, which can be added to your catalog in the appropriate places.

To create the title pages in Photoshop, follow these steps:

1. Create a new, blank document sized to the same dimensions as your low-resolution images (e.g., 750x488 @ 72 pixels/inch). Go to Edit>Fill>Color, and fill the page with black.

2. Select the Text tool, set the text color as you like, type text for your title page, then format the text. Turn the eyeball off for now to hide the layer visibility.

3. Repeat step 2 to make a text layer for an opening quote. Turn the eyeball off for now.

4. Repeat step 2 to make a "The End" page. You may also want to place your logo or studio name on the last page. Turn the layer visibility off for now as well.

5. Now, with only the black page visible, use Save As to make a JPEG file of this black page. Save a second copy the same way. This will be your closing page.

6. Turn the eyeball on for the title-page layer, use Save As to make a JPEG file of this, and call it Title.jpg. Turn the eyeball off again.

7. Turn the eyeball on for the quote, use Save As to make a JPEG file of this as well.

8. Repeat for the final text/logo page.

A title page in Photoshop sized to the dimensions of the proof images.

When all your title and blank pages have been made, import them into iView like you would any other image. Drag them into the proper place in sequence and you're ready to make the show. Here are the basic steps for the slide show. Configure them beforehand, and all your shows will use the same defaults.

A. Open your iView catalog and click on the first image.

B. Go to Make>Slide Show Options.

C. In the dialog box, input the following—Duration: 4 seconds, Color: Black, Transition: Cross Fade, and Scaling: Scale to Fit. Obviously, you can experiment with the settings you like best.

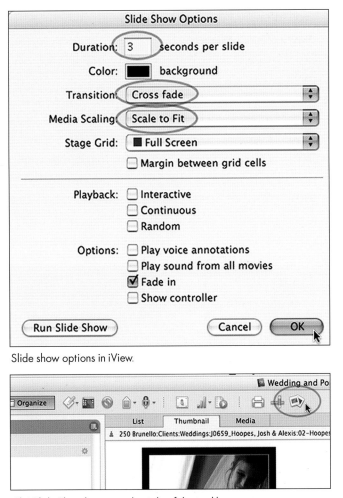

Slide show options in iView.

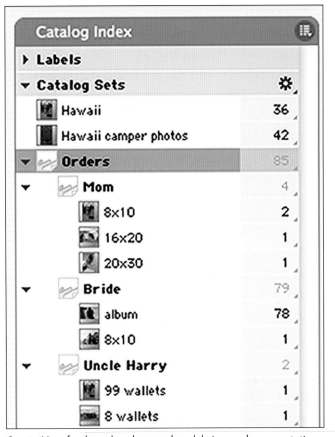

Sets in iView for the orders that are placed during a sales presentation.

The Slide Show button on the right of the tool bar.

D. Click OK to save these settings. You are now ready for the client. Save your catalog.

E. When the client is ready, open your catalog and simply click on the Slide Show button.

If you want your music to play when you start the slides, save your music file in a common format, like MP3, and add it to your catalog. Make it the first file in the list and it will start playing, then begin your slides. The music will play through to the end, then quit, so you may want to test the length before running the show. You can add additional sound files anywhere in the catalog, and they will start playing when they come up in the show.

iView can also be used as a sales tool, after the presentation. Usually it's effective to run the show all the way through, without interruption, then make another pass through, marking images as possible orders. This can be done by showing the controller when in the sec-

ond pass of the slide show. While the show is playing, just hit the Enter key. A control palette will pop up, giving options for show timing, transitions, etc. You can also see the images in a list. When a "keeper" image comes up on screen, tap the space bar. This will pause the show. You can now type 1, 2, 3, etc. on your keyboard to assign the corresponding label to the image, just like you did during the editing process. Decide on a labeling system beforehand, like 3 for keeper, 4 for maybe. Tap the space bar again to continue playing the show.

When you've gone through all the images, return to the normal catalog view, click on your labels for the "maybe" images to show only those thumbnails, then narrow down the selection further—assigning them a label of 3 if they are deemed keepers.

When the final selection of images has been narrowed down, create sets for the orders. You can make a set for Mom, Uncle Harry, the bride, etc. Then, in each set, you can create a subset for the print sizes. Simply drag an image into any set to assign it that size and to a particular recipient. Of course, you can put the same image into any number of different sets, so the organizational flexibility is endless.

Clicking on each set will show only the items in that set; this is helpful for reviewing the selections. The order can then be summarized and written up to an order form.

■ A COMPLETE DIGITAL SALES SOLUTION

For the busy studio, or one looking to become busy, give a more powerful sales and presentation tool a try. There are several on the market, with new ones emerging all the time. However, a product called ProSelect, from a company named TimeExposure (www.TimeExposure .com) in Australia, warrants a trial. The software is brilliant in its simplicity. It has a clean, elegant, uncluttered interface and is very intuitive to use. The programmers have worked closely with photographers to create a program that thoughtfully covers almost every possible scenario. We've found that ProSelect works beautifully in tandem with iView and Photoshop. After our images are edited, corrected, and prepared in iView, we can quickly load them into ProSelect for the client presentation. After the presentation, the images are passed to Photoshop for final preparation for the lab.

There are myriad ingenious features in the program, but here are a few that we particularly like:

• Images loaded into ProSelect are automatically copied and converted to low-resolution versions. All

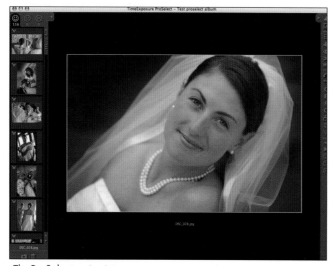

The ProSelect main view.

these files are kept together in a single "album," so they never get separated.

• Side-by-side image comparisons are very easy to make. Up to six images at a time can be compared.

• For projection, the program can easily be calibrated so that images will display at actual size on the screen if desired.

• Composite album pages and multi-image mats can easily be created and saved. Simply drag and drop images into the preset openings, allowing you to create whole album designs, image collages, and loose print orders quickly and easily with the client.

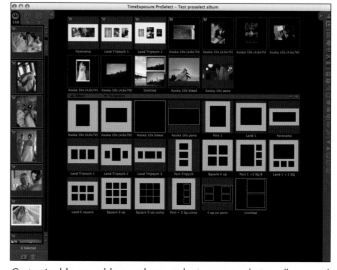

Customizable, reusable templates make it easy to design albums and presentations. Images are dragged and dropped into the openings.

Clicking on the shopping cart icon brings up the Place Order page, making it quick and easy to add it all up. You can customize price lists to your heart's content.

- Images can easily be converted to black & white, sepia, or even processed with your favorite Photoshop actions, from directly within the program!
- Slide shows with music are easy to create and are beautiful.
- Multiple, fully customizable price lists and an intuitive ordering system make the ordering process quick and painless. A summary of the order, along with thumbnails of the images, can easily be printed for the client and production person.

This program actually makes the sales and presentation process fun! The beautiful interface and simplified order system are impressive to clients as well.

■ PRINTING PROOF BOOKLETS

Booklets have become a popular alternative to loose proof prints for a number of reasons. They are less expensive to produce, allow for quick and easy browsing, clients are less likely to make reproductions of the images, and we have many stylish options for presenting them.

All of the programs mentioned will create printable proof pages, but each has its strengths. Photoshop's Contact Sheet II feature unfortunately has very little usefulness. ProSelect makes very nice proof sheets, and it does them quickly. The layout options are somewhat limited, but the basic presentation is clean and functional. Images look very crisp and the color is accurate.

iView has the best proof sheet functionality of any program. The header and footer are customizable—you can add the client or event name at the top and the studio contact and copyright information at the bottom. You can even add footers to either side of the printouts for additional information.

Here are some tips for printing your proof sheets from iView:

- Choose your settings as indicated for high-quality, quick-printing proofs. The Grid setting determines how many images display on the page.
- It is helpful to set your margins for extra room on the left side. A .75" inside left margin will do for

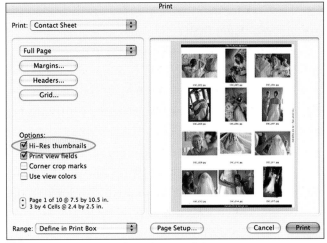

The print settings in iView for making proof sheets.

You can customize the headers and footers in just about whatever way necessary.

binding the finished booklet. This setup works for single-sided printing.
- To center your text in the headers, insert the special Indent symbol first.

If your iView catalog contained the low-resolution proof images, then printing proof booklets should be fairly quick and painless. Inkjet printers work great for proofing as well as final prints. The Canon series of printers are very fast and make excellent choices for proofing. Color laser printers can also be very effective for proofing. The cost per page is much lower than inkjets, although the quality of the output is lower as well. For proofing purposes, however, many photographers consider them more than acceptable.

When presenting the final booklet, you can add a nice cover image. Be sure to include order forms and cropping information in the back of the booklet. You can then have it bound at a copy center with a coil binding (it looks better than spiral binding).

The debate will always go on over whether or not it is good practice to give your clients proofs to take home. Many contend that this allows them to copy the images, put off purchasing, or lose the excitement (pressure) of making decisions in the studio. Some find the proof booklet concept a reasonable compromise, as they aren't large enough to copy or use for display prints, but they give the client something tangible to look at and make further buying decisions from. Each photographer has their own philosophy on this, and there is no right answer.

If you prefer to have your proof pages printed at a lab, rather than on an inkjet or laser printer, you have a few options. Many labs now offer proofing services for digital images—either in the form of traditional proof prints or proof pages. You can simply upload all your images and they will make the proof pages on photographic paper. They charge an extra fee for this service, above the cost of the page it's printed on, but it's a solution if you have the time to deal with the upload process and want the prints made on photographic paper.

Another option is to create a PDF file of your proof printout from iView and then convert that file into 8.5"x11" JPEG pages in Photoshop. These can then be uploaded to the lab for standard photographic prints. You can easily turn any printable document into a PDF file. Here's how:

1. On a Mac, simply choose Save as PDF instead of Print in the print dialog box. On the PC, you'll need to install a utility to be able to print to PDF, but many options, including free software, are available online. Here's a free program that works well: Primo PDF (www.PrimoPDF.com).

2. Once you have created the PDF file on either platform, open it with Photoshop. You will be asked to rasterize the file, so choose an appropriate resolution for your printer. Also be sure to choose the RGB color space.

3. Once in Photoshop, you may need to assign a different color profile to the image to make it look right. Try sRGB or your monitor profile.

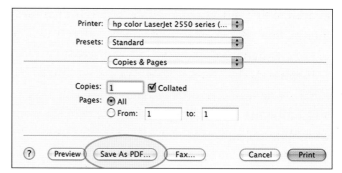

The print dialog box on Mac OS X has a Save As PDF option.

Rasterize settings when opening the PDF with Photoshop.

4. Save the newly converted images as standard JPEG files for your lab.

■ ONLINE PROOFING AND SELLING

As mentioned earlier, setting up web proofing and selling is definitely worth the time and effort. However, don't expect dramatic sales increases right away. With the right marketing and promotion techniques, many photographers have reported excellent additional sales through the web. You can't just "put it up there"—you need to put it up *and* promote it.

Benefits do come from increased exposure to potential new clients. When your work is good and all your client's friends and relatives see the images, chances are they'll be calling you when they have a need for a photographer. Consider it an on-going marketing expense and the cost is easily justified. To ensure that as many people as possible view the images online, plan to help your clients spread the word about the website. Some ideas include:

A Pre-Event Website. This can be a simple yet elegantly designed web page that is customized for your new client. They can announce their event to all the guests, have an RSVP page, and post helpful information about the event. Of course, there will also be a link to see the final images and the photographer's contact information. Make sure the client lists this web address in their invitations or on "save the date" cards.

Website Access Cards. These are given out at the event. Make sure that everyone there knows the images will be online for viewing or ordering. Simple cards with the web address and login information can be passed out or placed in a conspicuous place.

Give extra access cards to the client after the event. These can be put into thank-you cards by the client. An option is to create photo thank-you cards for the client for an additional charge, or include it in the package price. The card will have your web address and the event login as well.

Another benefit to web posting is its value to your client. They really appreciate the convenience of sharing the images with friends and family online. In fact, many clients expect it these days. It is a positive selling point for your studio.

Web proofing can be used for almost any type of photography. Commercial clients are always connected via high-speed networks and are quite used to viewing images online. Clients that come from out of town (for reunions, for example) often book family portrait sessions. They come from all over the country and usually have to leave within a day or two. If you can't make a sales presentation to them while they are all local, web proofing eases their concerns and also gives your studio a booking advantage. Business portraits can be shot, then prepared and posted online almost by the time the person returns to their office. It allows for quick service but also allows the studio to edit and prepare the files properly. There are basically three levels of proofing:

1. Posting directly to an area of your existing website using web page building software in Photoshop or iView. Benefits include: relative ease of posting, and no cost to implement. Limitations include: no online sales capabilities or image security, other than watermarking; limited viewing features.
2. Using an existing service through a lab (like ProShots). Benefits include: ease of use and a direct link to your lab for order fulfillment, basic image security. Limitations: the client has to go to a sepa-

rate site that doesn't look like yours, and the site's design could be confusing or cluttered; orders must be processed by the hosting lab, and commissions and fees for event hosting can be high.
3. Custom shopping cart system for your site (like EyeSelect; see Resources for more info). Benefits: the system is integrated with your site's look and feel, and the client never leaves your site; the system is feature-rich and can be elegantly designed; there are low monthly fees and no commissions taken on sales; orders can be processed in studio or sent to any lab; image security; and the approach is more cost effective and flexible in the long run. Considerations include: initial setup fee, more complex to set up, may require hiring a web designer for customization of the look, if you're not comfortable with a web design program.

GIVE EXTRA ACCESS CARDS TO THE CLIENT AFTER THE EVENT.

The three types of solutions will be covered briefly in the following sections, with some tips for making the most of each option.

Creating Websites with iView or Photoshop. Both programs allow for instant creation of websites, and both have some very useful built-in templates to get you started. You'll probably want to customize these, however, and it can be done fairly easily with Adobe GoLive or Macromedia's Dreamweaver or Contribute—however, any HTML-editing program should work. Here are some tips for creating your own proofing site:

1. Size your larger view images to 450 to 550 pixels for a good compromise of download speed and detail viewing.
2. Watermark large images with your studio website address.
3. Establish an "online until" time frame so people are encouraged to make a decision by a deadline.
4. Add an e-mail link directly on each page so viewers can contact you easily. The text is easy to add in any

HTML editor: "mailto:me@mywebsite.com." This will simply show up as: me@mywebsite.com and when they click on it, their e-mail program opens with a blank message addressed and ready to go.

All that's needed to use this basic type of web proofing page is, of course, your own website and FTP access to the site directory on the server. It works well to have a sub-folder labeled Clients in the root directory. Each client will then have their own folder, which contains the components you created above. When you give the web address to your client, it will look something like this: www.KubotaPhotoDesign.com/clients/smith.

Working with a Photo-Posting Service. Using an online hosting service can often be the easiest way to get started proofing and selling your images online. While it's not ideal (in that the client has to go to another vendor's website), most services are fairly well designed. Some of these types of services will do order fulfillment for the photographer as well by taking the orders direct-

ly from the clients, then sending the finished prints to them. This can be very helpful for high-volume studios with less need for quality control; however, other studios find it very disconcerting to have images sent to clients without the photographer's final inspection and approval. You need to use a lab that you trust 100%

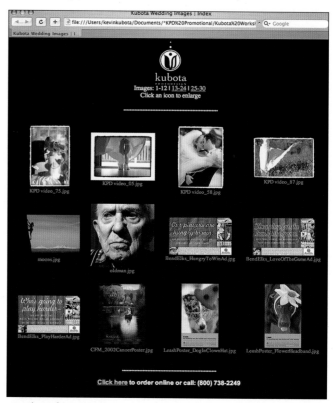

A website from iView customized with a studio logo.

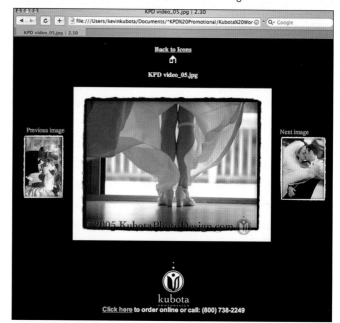

The full image view also allows viewers to browse forward and back in the list of images.

WATERMARKS

It's important to use watermarks on your images when you create simple websites like these because the images can easily be copied or printed. When a custom shopping cart system is used, they generally have other built-in protection methods, so watermarking is less critical, but still a good idea. iView has a nice feature allowing it to automatically place a watermark image, not just text, over the photos. This can be used for your logo or website info.

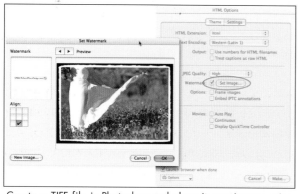

Create a TIFF file in Photoshop and place it over images using iView's watermark feature. To make the logo partially transparent, make sure to check Save Transparency in the TIFF options dialog box when you save it.

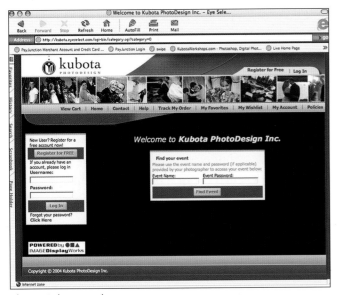
The EyeSelect store login page.

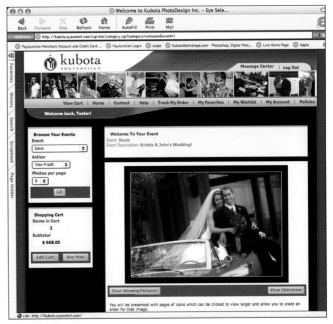
The EyeSelect main event page.

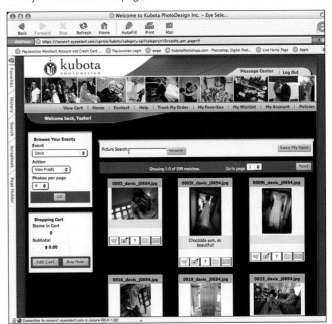
Thumbnail browsing in EyeSelect also has many purchasing options available.

before relying on their fulfillment services. This workflow also precludes the studio from making custom prints, or tweaks, of the images when ordered, as the lab will generally create "straight" prints only.

Every service has unique specifications for how they prefer images to be submitted and how they handle sales commissions, so they won't be covered in detail here. Make sure to read the fine print.

Building Your Own Proofing and Selling System. You won't actually have to build the system yourself—there are packages that are premade, with easy-to-edit templates that can be customized to match the look and feel of your existing website. The shopping cart part of the system can be hosted on your server or the service's, but the transition from your main site to the proofing/cart system is seamless. The client won't notice that they've left the main photography site.

To integrate this type of system into your website requires some setup. This can easily be done by the service that sells the system or by your web designer. It is usually not very expensive or complicated. Once the setup is complete, the studio has complete control over the events that are uploaded; they are transferred directly from the studio at any time. The studio sets pricing, shipping, up-sell items, gift certificates, can download full sales reports, etc.—everything is under their control.

Another benefit of this type of system is that the cart is dedicated to your uses and clients only, speeding up access to the images and reducing network traffic jams. You are not sharing the same shopping cart with hundreds or thousands of other photographers' clients.

One system of this type that we like (partly because we helped to design the basic feature set many years ago) is from a company called Make-A-Store. The product is EyeSelect, and it is truly one of the most feature-rich shopping-cart systems available, designed specifically for the needs of photo buyers and studios. Whenever we look for products for our own studio, we have found that the most important qualities are:

- ease of use
- innovative ideas
- professional design appeal
- cost effectiveness
- excellent and dependable customer support.

Make-A-Store excels in these areas and produced an excellent product in EyeSelect. More information on Eye Select can be found at: www.KubotaWorkshops .com.

■ CD-ROM AND DVD SLIDE SHOWS

Slide shows are quickly becoming a popular way to present images from an event. Many of our clients tell us that this is their favorite way to enjoy the images we've created for them. They pop that DVD in and watch it over and over again.

Traditionalists may take issue with the idea of selling slide shows, as some feel that it detracts from print sales after the event. This may be true, but how can we argue with the fact that clients love the slide shows? It may take some adjustment to traditional thinking, shifting the product line a little, and of course pricing the slide show products so that they are profitable as well. The times they are a changin', and digital photographers need to go with the flow.

SLIDE SHOWS ARE BECOMING A POPULAR WAY TO PRESENT IMAGES.

Here again, because of the popularity of digital slide shows, there are numerous programs on the market for creating slide shows. Your choice will depend on the computer platform you use and the amount of control over the look and feel of the show that you want to take. With CD-ROM slide shows, the format of the actual show file is important to consider as well. On the PC, there are several options for making slide shows into self running EXE files—but Macs can't use those. Unless you are sure that all your clients use PCs, then it may be

better to look at other options. Shows in QuickTime and Flash format are better for bridging the computer-platform gap. They are universal and also can be imported into other programs for use in various projects—a DVD, for example. In this case, QuickTime is the most reliable and universal.

Essentially, there are two ways to present the slide show: as a movie file on a CD-ROM that can only be played on computers or as a DVD that can be played on most televisions as well as computers. Making the DVD will require special DVD-authoring software, which is generally not very expensive. Mac computers with a built-in DVD burner have iDVD included free, and this happens to be one of the best-quality authoring pieces available. PC users have several options, ranging from cheap to fairly expensive. See the Resources for a list.

If you decide to use QuickTime as the file format, the file can be used for both a CD-ROM slide show and imported into most DVD-authoring programs directly. This same file can also be kept on your computer for a stand-alone presentation or portfolio. We keep several different demo slide shows on our computers for client meetings.

Making the QuickTime Slide Show. iView has the ability to make QuickTime slide shows directly from your catalog. Mac users also have the ability to make nice slide shows from iPhoto, another free and included piece of software. Slide shows come in two basic types—rendered (which is typical for converting to a video format or DVD) and un-rendered. Most programs that create slide shows, including iView, create the rendered flavor. Rendered means that it behaves like video, displaying many frames per second in order for transitions to appear smooth. Generally, 30 frames per second (fps) is considered TV quality. The inherent problem here is that for every second the image stays on screen, it actually requires thirty copies of your image (hence the term: 30fps)! Can you see how a long show can really grow in file size?

There are many variables to this process, and for slide show purposes usually 15fps will look good enough through the transitions. Fortunately, iView hides all the complicated stuff from the user and simply offers a few easy choices: Normal, Better, Best.

Non-rendered movies, in contrast, do not need a specific frame rate. The software simply tells the computer to "hold" an image on screen for three seconds then use a transition to the next image and hold it for the specified time. In this way, only one image file is needed for a three-second display versus forty-five images for the rendered version (at 15fps). Resulting movies are considerably smaller and take less time to create. iPhoto creates un-rendered movies, although the image quality (because of the compression it automatically selects) is not quite as good as the Better quality from iView. The file size savings and shorter rendering time may be worth the quality tradeoff, however. PC users will need to use iView or find another program that creates slide shows in QuickTime format.

Images that will be displayed on a standard TV screen work best when set up beforehand. Most TV displays have a 640x480 resolution, and because of the picture tube design, an area around the edges gets cropped off. Because of this, about 50 pixels around the edges will be hidden when played on a tube-type TV. The area that is seen is called the "TV-safe zone." LCD TVs, Plasma, and other new digital types do not have this problem. Most people still have tube-type TVs, however, so it's best to design for the least common denominator.

To size your images for the TV-safe zone, it's best to follow these guidelines:

1. Reduce your images to fit 425x425 pixels using Photoshop's Fit Image function.
2. Add a black background to fill up the extra space to 640x480.
3. Save the resulting file as a new JPEG for TV.

You can use a Photoshop action droplet to automatically do these steps.

On the Mac or PC, iView can create beautiful QuickTime slide shows. Here are the steps involved.

A. Load your TV-safe images into an iView catalog.
B. Arrange them in the display order you want.
C. Add your titles, logo, blank, and end pages as desired.
D. Go to Make>Slide Show Options to set your slide show preferences.

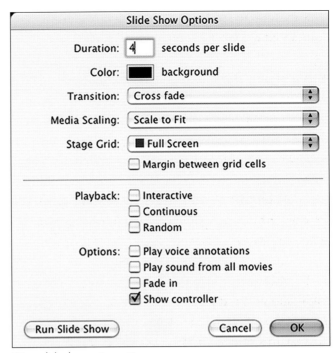

iView slide show setup options.

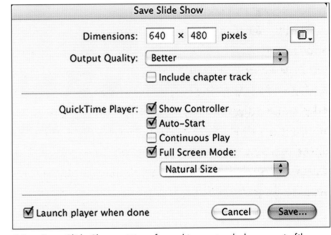

iView Save Slide Show settings for making a stand-alone movie file.

E. The same settings you use for an on-screen show straight from iView will also apply to exported QuickTime slide shows.
F. Choose Make>Save Slide Show as Movie and enter these settings:
    a. Dimensions: 640x480
    b. Output Quality: Better
    c. QuickTime Player: Check on Show Controller, Auto-Start, and Full Screen Mode>Natural Size.
G. Using these settings, a typical slide show created at 640x480 resolution (normal TV size) on a 733MHz Mac for a movie of 513 images takes 25

minutes to render. The resulting movie file is about 415MB.

The resulting show is ready to import into a DVD-authoring program, play directly on screen, or be copied to a CD-ROM. Mac users can also use iPhoto, as mentioned earlier, to make more compact slide shows a little quicker. Both rendered and un-rendered versions will work the same when imported into a DVD-authoring program, and the difference will be miniscule. Here are the steps for creating the un-rendered slide show in iPhoto:

a. Import the images into iPhoto.
b. Arrange them by title (View>Sort Photos>by

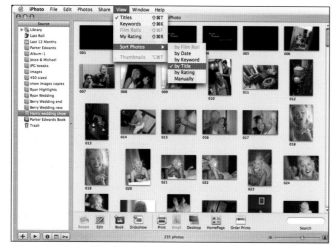

Arranging photos by title in iPhoto.

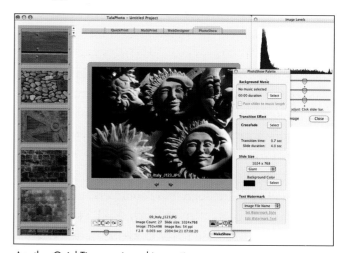

iPhoto export to QuickTime settings.

Title) so they are in proper order.
c. Select all images.
d. Go to File>Export.
e. Go to the QuickTime tab.
f. Apply these settings in the dialog box— Width: 640, Height: 480, Display image for: 3 seconds.
g. Click Export.

The show will also be a QuickTime format, ready to play or import to your DVD-authoring program.

Another QuickTime Movie-Making Option. Finding a simple program to make a basic QuickTime slide show doesn't seem like it should be that hard, but finding a program with all the right ingredients is actually quite challenging. After searching through dozens of programs to find a simple solution, we found TalaPhoto by TalaSoft (www.TalaSoft.com). This program is compatible with both Mac and Windows platforms and creates beautiful QuickTime movies in an un-rendered format. It also creates simple web pages and can print contact sheets or single prints with on-the-fly sizing. It even has a surprisingly good image levels adjuster for last-minute adjustments.

The program is very easy to use, well thought out, and of course has some very clever features—like the ability to automatically display the image file name (or any other information) during the show. And, as we hoped, the company has great tech support. Two thumbs way up! Oh, did I mention it's only $29, which includes lifetime upgrades?

Another QuickTime movie-making option.

Adding Music to Your Slide Show. A slide show is not as emotional without music, so you'll probably want to include a soundtrack with your presentation. (See Resources for links to music and licensing info.)

The easiest way to include music is to add your music files to the sequence (in iView) or import one into iPhoto. This way it will be part of the QuickTime slide show you export. Simple enough. But wait, you're probably a tweaker and a closet music-video producer at heart—so of course you'll want to mix audio and time it to key events just like a master DJ.

Unfortunately, to inexpensively mix audio sources and apply them to a high-quality QuickTime movie on either Mac or PC requires more than one piece of software. Complete authoring packages, like Roxio's Easy Media Creator (PC), will easily let you combine photos and mix music, but they are generally $80 and up. They output to DVD quite easily, but saving the files as QuickTime movies for on-screen display is not always supported. So, to get the best of both worlds, on both platforms and inexpensively, requires a little creative use of a couple different programs, but it's not that hard! Let's first see how it's done on a Mac.

To edit your QuickTime movies, on both Mac and PC, will require an upgrade to QuickTime Pro ($29; see Resources). The basic QuickTime player is free and available for any computer, but you don't have the ability to edit, or combine a slide show with audio—which we want to do. Download the Pro upgrade and you're well on your way.

1. We'll use iMovie *just* for the audio mixing. Don't add images to iMovie—the resulting shows don't look crisp. This demo was done using iMovie 5.0.

2. Create a new project and open the timeline view. Drag songs to the timeline and start to roughly position them.

3. Open the images-only slide show QuickTime file that you created earlier and position it so you can see it behind the iMovie window. You'll be switching back and forth between these windows.

4. Notice the time markers for each. We'll use these to synchronize our soundtrack to events in the slide show.

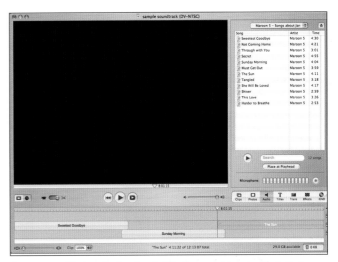

Songs are added to the timeline in iMovie to synchronize their timing.

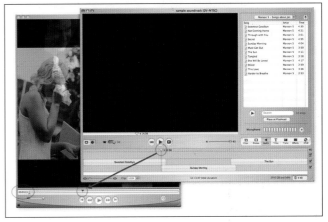

The timeline markers can be matched to coordinate music with images.

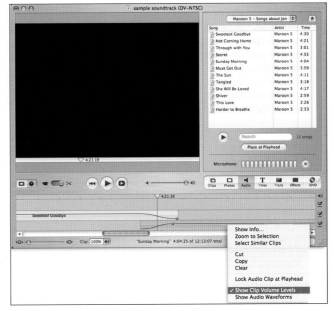

Song volume can be faded or cross-faded with the next song.

5. Right-click/press Ctrl and click on the music in the timeline, and make sure Show Clip Volume Levels is

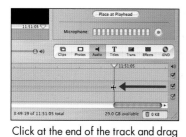

Click at the end of the track and drag to where you want it to end early.

Open the hidden package contents to access the soundtrack.

Open the hidden soundtrack in the iMovie project.

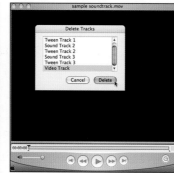

Using QuickTime Pro, you can do simple edits to movies.

Remove the blank video track to leave an audio-only movie.

The soundtrack only in a QuickTime MOV file.

selected. You can then adjust the volume line to make them cross-fade by clicking on the volume line in the track and moving the adjustment balls down and apart to create the fades.

6. A simple workflow is to switch to your movie in QuickTime, move the play head to a key point, then return to iMovie and move the play head to the same position. You will then be able to see and hear the song that will play at that point. Adjust your soundtrack as necessary.

7. If you need to end your soundtrack before a song is over, fade the song out. Next, right-click/press Ctrl and click on a track and make sure Show Clip Volume Levels is *not* selected.

8. Click on the end of the song and drag the bar inward to shorten the track duration.

9. When you're finish adding tracks and editing, you're ready to combine the audio soundtrack with the slide show you created.

10. Go to File>Save.

We're going to use a cool trick now to extract the audio so it can be combined with the slides using QuickTime Pro.

   A. Locate your iMovie project, with the soundtrack you just made, in the Finder.

   B. Right-click/press Ctrl and click on the project file, then choose Show Package Contents.

   C. Inside the package contents window you'll see a folder called Shared Movies, and in that iDVD, and in that will be your soundtrack with an .mov extension.

   D. Double-click the MOV file to open your soundtrack with QuickTime.

Now you'll have a soundtrack with a black window. This black area is your nonexistent video track (we didn't create any video in iMovie, remember?). This is where QuickTime Pro steps in. When you upgrade to Pro, the player application will look basically the same; the difference is that some of the menu options that were previously grayed out will now be available, meaning that you can edit QuickTime MOV files.

We're going to delete the blank video track so that we are only left with audio. Then we'll combine this audio with the slide show you created earlier.

   a. Go to Edit>Delete Tracks.

   b. Scroll to the bottom of the track list and select Video Track. Click Delete.

   c. Now you're left with an audio-only QuickTime MOV file.

   d. Go to Edit>Select All.

e. Go to Edit>Copy.

f. Switch to your slide show window.

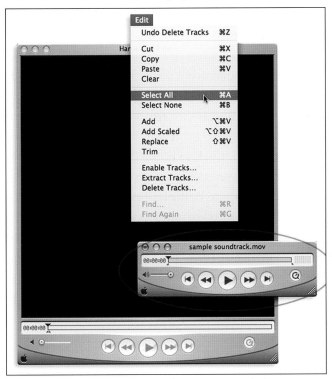

When the soundtrack has been copied, switch to the image slideshow and add the music. Be sure to put the playhead at the start.

Adding the sound to the slides movie file.

g. Move the play head to the beginning, if it's not already there.

h. Choose Edit>Add.

i. Ta da! Click Play to test your new show. The music should now be in perfect sync with the slide show. All that's left is to save your final piece. Choose Save As from your File menu.

Now you have a stand-alone QuickTime movie that can be imported into a DVD-authoring program or played directly from your presentation computer.

The preceding process may seem a little involved, but once you've done it once or twice, it really is quite easy and can be completed very quickly. The hardest part is deciding what music to use. If you have a collection of royalty-free music that you use for every presentation, the process can be completed in a few minutes.

On the PC, the steps are nearly identical, except PC users have a free program from Microsoft called Windows Movie Maker (www.Microsoft.com). First, the slide show is created in iView and saved as a QuickTime movie (.mov file extension), then the soundtrack is built in Windows Movie Maker, which functions similarly to iMovie. The resulting soundtrack is saved as a WMA audio file, then converted to MP3 or AIF (see Resources for audio-conversion programs). The resulting audio file is opened in QuickTime Player and the slides and music are combined just like on the Mac.

Putting it All Together. You're almost a full-fledged movie producer now. The QuickTime movie you saved will play beautifully on its own or can be imported into most DVD-authoring programs for conversion to TV/DVD format.

The specific instructions for making the DVD will depend on the software you use, but most are essentially the same. Just drag your QuickTime movie into it, create titles and a start button, and click Burn. Here are a few extra tips for creating DVDs:

• Use high-quality DVD media to avoid burn errors. Ritek brand is generally very reliable, although others work well too. You may need to experiment a little to find a brand that works best in your system.

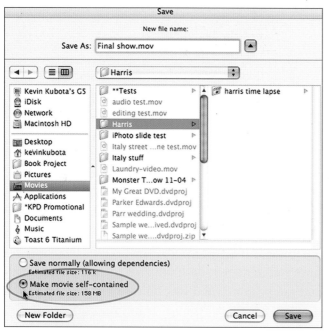

When saving the new file, select "make movie self contained." This puts all the pictures and audio into one portable file.

- Keep in mind that not all consumer DVD players will play home-authored DVDs. Most newer units will be compatible, but older machines can occasionally refuse to play them. If you continually have clients who cannot play your DVDs, consider trying another authoring program. Each implements the DVD standards slightly differently.
- Printable-surface DVDs look professional when adorned with an image and your logo. Try the silver surface discs, they look really slick! Low-cost inkjets designed for direct disc printing are readily available.

The DVD is a great add-on sale item, especially right after the the clients have seen their images in a slide show in your studio! The impression is lasting, and people are generally very multimedia savvy these days—they enjoy seeing their images in this new presentation. Suggest they buy multiple copies as gifts for family and friends. The reproduction cost is less than $1 once you've created the master DVD. Charge appropriately for your images, however. Remember: we're still selling images, not the material they're presented on.

■ ALBUMS AND OTHER PRESENTATIONS

Alas! The album is not dead by any means. With all this multimedia tantalizing our clients' senses, you might think the album would disappear forever. Not true. People still love to have something to hold in their hands, to be able to flip pages, and to touch and feel. The look of the album and the presentation style is changing, however, and for the better. No longer are we locked into creating traditional post-bound books with standard mat openings and gold-tipped pages. The sky's the limit now, and our product lines have taken a major leap forward in quality.

While new products are being introduced at every major trade show, here are some items and ideas that are particularly interesting:

- handmade, bound albums filled with fine-art inkjet-paper prints
- wood and metal covers, fun and funky colors in silks and leathers
- magazine-style layouts within any type of album
- book-bound albums that look like store-bought art books
- collections of image mats, instead of albums, that can be displayed in rotation
- images in bevel-cut mats within albums

Digital photography really opened the door for what is commonly referred to as magazine-style layouts. This refers to pages that are designed in Photoshop, often with multiple images, but printed out as one print. This is cost effective for the photographer, since only one print is made, and the design options are unlimited. Layouts can be as graphic and modern as desired, or kept simple and timeless. While the graphically exciting books may be fun today, they have the potential to look dated in a few years. While designs with more of a classic feel may not be as "modern bride," they will more likely stand the test of time. You certainly don't want people looking at your current albums ten years from now and saying, "Oh, those are soooo new millennium." Neither design style is "bad," but just keep the issue in mind.

■ ALBUM GALLERY

Here are some cool new coffee-table books from a company called Asukabook USA. We love these books for

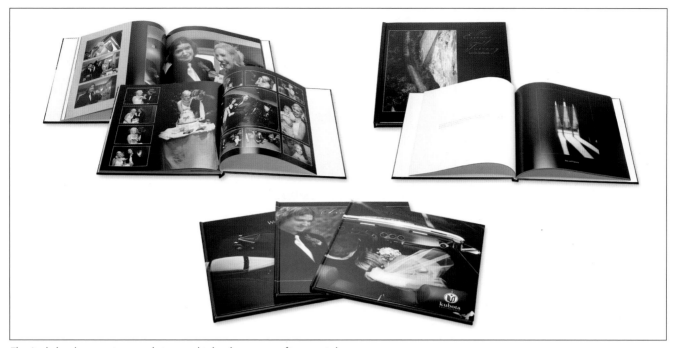

The Asukabooks come in several sizes and in hard-cover or soft-cover styles.

the coffee-table book styling and exceptional pricing on single-book production. They work great for portfolios, companion wedding albums, family portrait books, senior photo sessions—you name it. Our clients love these books because they look like store-bought art books. See the full line of products at www.Asuka book.com.

■ MAGAZINE-STYLE ALBUMS AND COLLAGES

Now that you're a Photoshop expert, you can not only create beautiful images, but you can also use the program to create beautiful page layouts. While having Photoshop skills won't necessarily make you a graphic designer, you can create basic layouts for magazine-style albums and image collages, both of which are very popular and cost effective to produce.

While a course in album design could fill an entire book in itself (hey, that's a good idea), we can still offer some helpful tips for creating your own layouts. Begin with the proper page specifications from your album company. Generally you only need to know the print size, the resolution, the trimmed sized, and the gutter amount—if any. Print size will be a standard print dimension, like 10"x10". Trimmed size may be $1/8$" smaller all around or similar. You may also need to allow an extra $3/8$"–$1/2$" or so in the center to accommo-

date the gutter, so important image details aren't swallowed up in the center of the book.

Set up a blank page in Photoshop, selecting the proper resolution and color profile for the lab you will be sending the pages to. Make your rulers visible and drag guides in from the edges for your trim lines. It is often a good idea to add additional guides about $1/2$" in from the trim as well. This is your true "safe" zone; important image information should not go beyond this point. Select View>Snap To>Guides, then drag out a vertical and horizontal center line. They should "snap" at the center of the page.

Select View>Snap To>Guides so that images can be quickly aligned on a page layout.

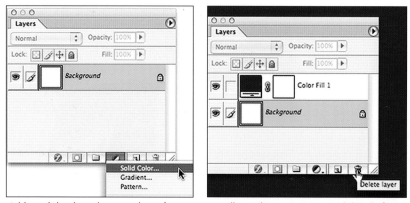
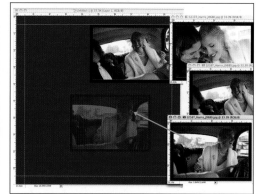

Add a solid-color adjustment layer (Create New Fill or Adjustment Layer>Solid Color) and delete the blank Background layer.

Images can be dragged onto a page layout and arranged as needed.

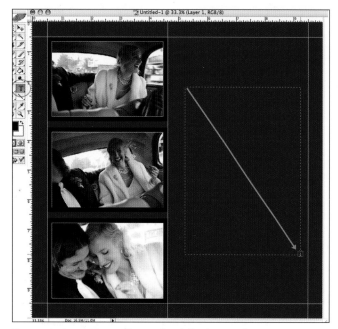

Drag out a box with your Text tool to define an area for type.

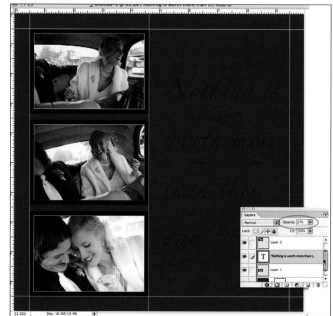

Fading the type layer is a nice, subtle effect.

1. Add a solid-color adjustment layer to your image. Choose the color for the page background. You can delete the blank background layer.
2. Open an image and drag its layer icon to your new page.
3. If the image needs to be resized, use Edit>Free Transform. Grab a corner handle to resize. Be sure to also hold the Shift key while sizing to maintain proportions.
4. Position the image as desired using the Move tool .
5. Add additional images and transform as needed.
6. Images snap to your guides to help with alignment. Tip: to temporarily stop an image from snapping to guides or the page border, hold down the Ctrl key while dragging (Mac only).

Once you have your images positioned and sized, you may want to add some text to the pages as well.

A. Click and drag with the Text tool to size a text box.
B. Enter your text.
C. Double-click on the text icon in Layers palette to select all the text on that layer.
D. Trick: click once in the Font or Size box in the options bar. Then, use the up or down arrow keys on your keyboard to change the font style or size.
E. Position text with the Move tool.

Move Tool Cool Trick. With multiple images on a page, you can become confused when trying to select the appropriate layer to move images into different positions. Here's a trick: select your Move tool (V), then click the check box labeled Auto Select Layer in the options bar. Now, when you simply click on any image, its layer is automatically selected so you can drag it where you please.

Right-click/press Ctrl and click on an image to see a menu of all the layers beneath the top image to select a different one if needed.

You can also press Shift and click on multiple images to link them all together in the Layers palette. This allows you to move them together as a unit. Press Shift and click again on each image to unlink them.

When you have completed your page design, save two files: a PSD master file with the layers intact and a copy in JPEG format to send to your lab. The same techniques can be used to create image collages for framing. By the way, these collages are excellent promotional items to give any vendors you work with. Display images of their products or services, along with your logo, and give them a free print. It's a win–win deal.

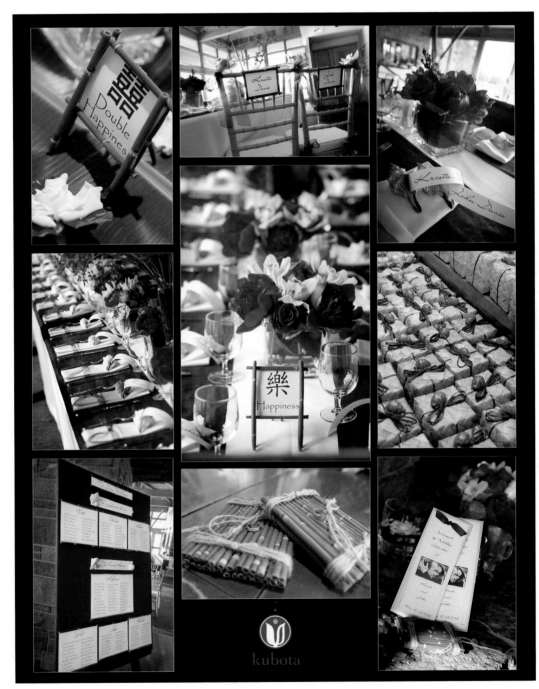

Creating a photo collage for a vendor is great marketing for you and is much appreciated by them.

12. THE BIG PICTURE

The meaning of life is finding your gift; the purpose of life is giving it away.

—Joy J. Golliver

With all the tools and techniques available to us, it's easy to become swept away in the day-to-day process of just keeping up. Technology can make your head spin—it's a constant learning process, and you know what? It always will be. Photography will never be the same. It's entered the dig-ital, computer world that inherently changes at an expo-nential rate. It will never go back. And that's okay—change is good.

When do we find time to think about the future? Do you set aside time every day or week to do some market-ing and planning? Do we make time, even in the busiest

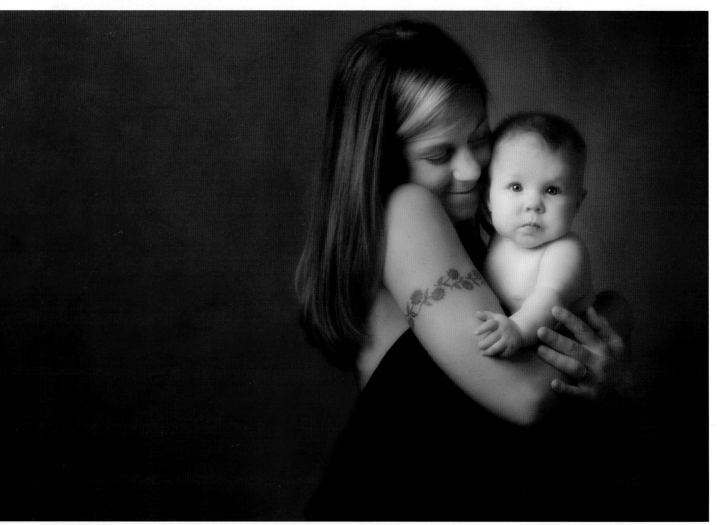

The most beautiful thing in the world.

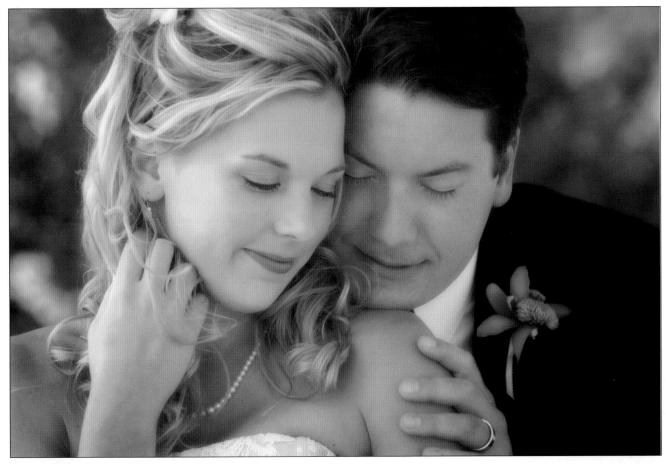

Photographers often tend to underestimate themselves and the power they have to change the world.

of seasons, to give a little back to our communities and friends in need? Many photographers find the time to plan for marketing and promotional events, but what about pure charity work?

This is always a struggle—if we're *so* busy we can barely keep up with the work that's paying the bills, how can we begin to think about doing work that pays absolutely nothing (maybe "why?" is the better question). Well, we all have a responsibility to make the world a better place—to try and leave it a little nicer than we found it when we came in. "Giving back" needs to be a normal and regular part of our business practice.

Photographers often tend to underestimate themselves and the power they have to change the world. Photojournalists may be more aware of their influence as their images affect millions of people every day. They can move people to tears, move them to act—out of compassion, frustration, or even anger. They bring joy, laughter, awareness, and reverence to everyday people. Yet, every photographer has this gift. It only takes a

belief in oneself and a desire to make a difference. That's all.

Portrait photographers witness these feelings often too—people cry when they see the beautiful images of their children, or they relive the wonderful moments from their wedding day. People cry when they look at a sensitive image of a loved one, now passed. You help to evoke that emotion; this is a good thing, and it is your gift. Strengthening the bonds of family and reinforcing the value of treating people well while they are still on this earth—that is a powerful gift. Don't underestimate the importance of your services.

■ WHAT CAN YOU DO?

I know many photographers who make charitable work a part of their normal business model. But let's convince all photographers to do this. Do you think we can? Wouldn't it be great if photographers the world over were recognized as the most generous and compassionate of all business types?

Spread the word. There's a movie called *Pay it Forward,* a moving film about a young boy who decided to try an experiment for a school project. He wanted to see what would happen if everyone stopped and did just one nice thing—even for a total stranger—without any thought of benefit or recognition. They just went out of their way to help someone in need and only asked in return that the receiving person "pay it forward," doing the same for someone else. The results were amazing, and "miracles" started to spread all over the world.

So what can you do? Start in your own hometown. Everyone (hopefully) has their own favorite charity or cause. Call them right now (okay—wait until you finish the book), and ask if they need photos for any of their promotional events or projects. Offer to take some really nice portraits of their staff or volunteers to put up on the wall. A great, professional photo makes people feel good and important, and that is key to keeping volunteers motivated.

Whenever a charity has a community awareness project, offer to be there to take documentary photos. They can use them in their newsletters and websites to boost their business image and thereby increase public interest, respect, and involvement.

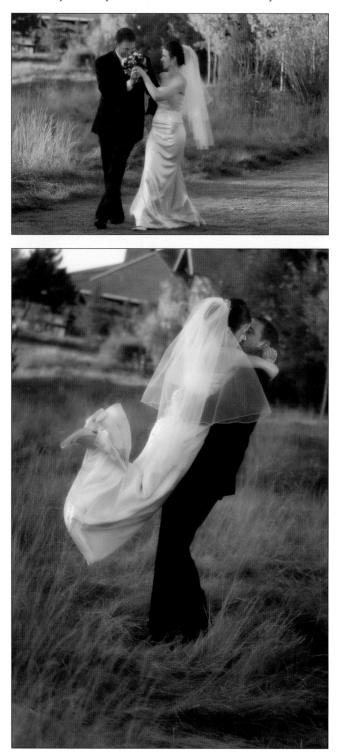

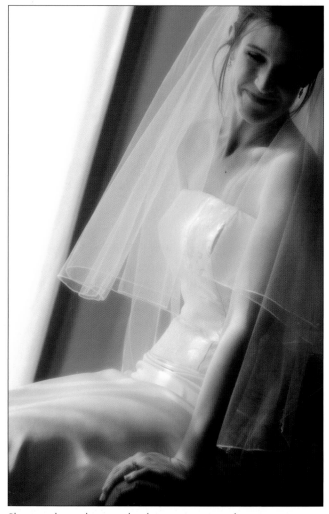

Photography can bring joy, laughter, awareness, and reverence to everyday people.

Donate gift certificates for photography services to any legitimate fund-raising auctions in your community. This one is somewhat self-serving, as it will bring you new clients, but it is a win–win proposition.

Give the gift of a family portrait to families that cannot afford it. Everyone should have a family portrait—even if the family only consists of a runaway teenage mother and her three-month-old baby. Portraits make people proud of who they are. They give them a joyful reminder when they feel down or when life is especially challenging. They give them an image to cherish should the unthinkable happen and they lose someone in the portrait.

Every year in our hometown we coordinate and host an event called "Family Photos in the Park." We contact a list of charitable organizations in our community—like Habitat for Humanity, the Family Resource Center, Sparrow Clubs, Grandmother's House, HeadStart, church shelters, etc., and ask them to sign up families that they feel are in a challenging situation. These families can come down to the park, on a date and time we specify, and receive a free family portrait and print package. There are no strings attached, and we even give them the digital files so they can take them to Costco for cheap reprints.

We enlist the help of other local photographers to photograph families and receive donations from local caterers and stores for supplies. We make a big party of it and spend a Sunday in the park taking pictures together—it's great fun. The families are extremely thankful, the photographers bond as a group, and they go home feeling warm and fuzzy, knowing they've used their gifts to better the world.

This project is something that I am very proud of. Since its inception, many other photographers have taken the suggestion and started similar programs in their hometowns, all across the country. I hope someday that every community in the country will embrace a "Family Photos in the Park" day—and have their local photographers to thank for it. If you'd like more details on this program, as well as helpful information on how to get it started in your area, please e-mail us.

There is one other charitable project that deserves attention, if only because it goes straight to the core of

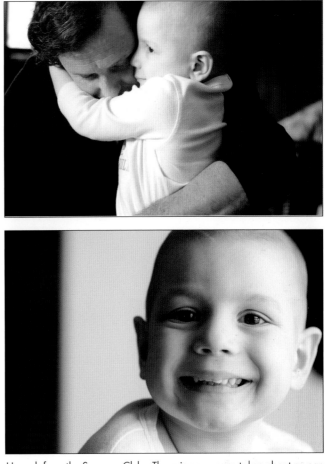

Hannah from the Sparrow Clubs. These images were taken about a year ago. At the time of this writing, her family said she had just a few days—maybe a week or two—left. Her amazing spirit, and the deep love of her family, is felt throughout the community.

what is needed to build a better future for our world. It encourages children to feel compassion for others—and to gain a sense of pride in return. This program is called the Sparrow Clubs (www.SparrowClubs.org).

Sparrow Clubs USA promotes school-based service projects of kids helping kids in medical need. A child with a serious medical crisis is chosen as the "sparrow," then children in a local school form a club to support this sparrow through community service projects, fundraisers, and all-around moral support. It is truly amazing how effectual these kids can be. They raise surprising amounts of money and give the sick children the support and camaraderie that is so vital to their mental well-being.

Sick children and their families are supported in critical ways, and school kids learn the value of caring and community involvement. Isn't this the way to ensure a better future for all of us?

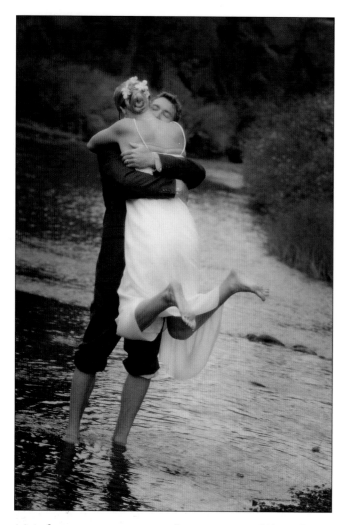

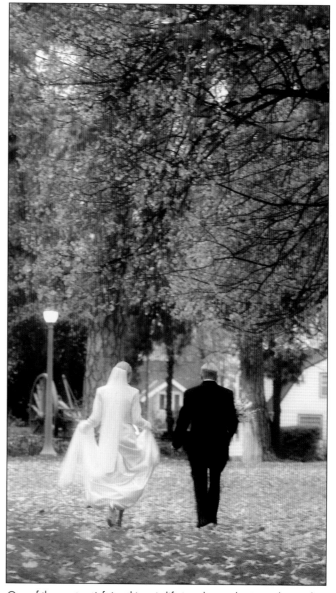

One of the most satisfying things in life is to have a business doing what you love

A few years ago, one of our past wedding clients called us and, with some hesitation in her voice, told us she was the new coordinator for the Sparrow Clubs. She wanted to know if we'd be at all interested in taking some portraits of the sick children to use at an upcoming fund-raiser event. We were honored to be asked and gladly took the project. I was hesitant, however, because I knew that what I had to photograph would be painful for me. I'm a big crybaby anyway, and this would only make me worse.

What I discovered, contrary to my expectations, was an amazing beauty and strength in the children and families I photographed. They all opened their homes and their hearts to us—and those who could smile, smiled brightly. The parents were full of hope and positive thoughts, and the children showed courage and acceptance. It put my whole world in perspective, and I felt almost ashamed of myself for all the weight I sometimes put on my trivial problems.

It has been a life-changing experience, for both my wife and I, to be involved with the Sparrow Clubs. They are graciously thankful for the ongoing photography work we do for them, and we are grateful to be humbled and enlightened by these precious little sparrows. As the club motto says, "we have found our wings."

Photography can change the world. Just as every little person can change the world with a simple action or suggestion. Each thing we do to make the world a better place becomes contagious—it spreads and grows. Set the example by doing whatever you can do, and soon you'll see others doing the same. It's time for us all to pay it forward.

■ THE KEYS TO SUCCESS

We've identified some keys to success and have used them to successfully grow our business every year. It helps us to feel a deep-rooted sense of happiness and satisfaction for our place in this world. Everyone, of course, has their own set of goals and values—a mission statement for life, if you will. The mission statement could be written down, or simply a part of your being—that doesn't matter much—but it helps to recognize it, and ensure that it is actively a part of life and business.

- Integrity in everything you do.
- Commitment to giving back to your community. This involves charitable work locally and sharing your knowledge with peers in business.
- Trust in your intuition and creative voice.
- Balance—in work and personal life. In business there should a be balance of creativity, inspiration, technology, technique, and presentation.

One of the most satisfying things in life is to have a business doing what you love; and, by its very nature, your business also contributes to making people happy and bettering your little corner of the universe.

Bettering your skills as a photographer should not be the goal, but rather, bettering them for the sake of what you can ultimately create and give from those skills.

I hope that this book has been valuable to you and your business. I enjoy teaching and sharing my experience as much as I enjoy creating images. If you've learned something great, pay it forward. Help someone else out—if for no other reason than to see them prosper. If you have any experiences or feedback to share, I'd love to hear about it. Please e-mail me at kevin@Kubota Workshops.com.

And remember, you can't create in a vacuum—unless you want to suck.

Nothing is worth more than this day.

—Goethe

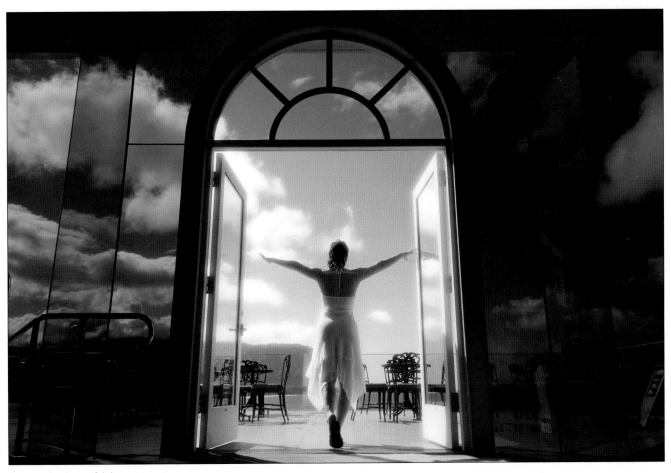

Just another beautiful day in Hawaii.

RESOURCES

Albums and Presentation Products
Albums Australia—www.Albumsaustralia.com.au
Asukabook—www.AsukaBook.com
JonesBook—www.Jonesbook.com
Leather Craftsmen—www.Leathercraftsmen.com
Stone Editions—available through
   www.RiceStudioSupply.com

LCD Monitors
www.Formac.com—Very high-quality and affordable
   LCD monitors. We use these in our studio. They represent some of the best deals in the industry.
www.LaCie.com—Known for their high-quality graphics products.
www.Mac.com—Apple monitors are arguably some of
   the most beautifully designed on the planet. We also
   use these in our studio.

Music for Slide Shows
www.ASCAP.com—The American Society of
   Composers, Author, and Publishers.
www.BMI.com—Broadcast Music Inc.
www.LJ3Entertainment.com—Custom music production for photographers.
www.MusicBakery.com—royalty-free music for reasonable, fixed prices.
www.PPA.com—FAQs and licensing information, general photographers' resource.
www.SESAC.com—Performing rights organization.

Software
iDVD—DVD-authoring software for Macs. Free with
   computer.
PC Audio conversion programs—www.wma-mp3.com.
   View a partial list of some useful applications here.

ProSelect—www.timeexposure.com. Sales and
   Presentation software.
QuickTime Pro—www.Apple.com. Edit QuickTime
   movies and audio.
Roxio Easy Media Creator—www.Roxio.com. DVD-
   authoring software for PCs.
TalaPhoto—www.TalaSoft.com. Used for making un-
   rendered QuickTime movies.
Ulead DVD MovieFactory—www.Ulead.com. DVD-
   authoring software for PCs.
Free actions for readers of this book—see download
   instructions on page 8.
Action sets and digital training programs—
   www.KubotaWorkshops.com

Online Forums for Photographers
www.digitalweddingforum.com
www.DPReview.com—New product announcements,
   reviews, general forums. One of the best informa-
   tional sites on new cameras.
www.Nikonians.com—Nikon camera forum.
www.photography-on-the.net—Canon digital photography forum.

Miscellaneous
Digital Photographers Bootcamp—
   www.KubotaWorkshops.com.
EyeSelect—more info at www.KubotaWorkshops.com.
   Custom shopping cart and proofing system for
   photographers.
Lensbaby—www.Lensbabies.com. Inexpensive tilt-
   swing selective-focus lens for Canon and Nikon
   cameras.

TROUBLESHOOTING

PROBLEM	POSSIBLE SOLUTION
Camera times not correct or synchronized after job is shot	You can adjust the actual capture date that is embedded in the image file. Mac users can download the free Applescript for iView. See page 8. PC users can use the handy program ExifUtils from www.hugsan.com.
Memory cards won't read in computer	Unplug and re-plug the card reader. Also try reading the cards on a different computer or using a different method—like camera direct to computer through a USB cable.
Camera locks up while shooting	Bad memory card. Make a note of which card was in use each time the camera locks. Try to narrow it to the suspect card. Pull the card and do not use it again until images are downloaded. Also, a low or old battery can cause erratic behavior. Check with camera manufacturer to see if newer firmware is available for your camera.
Soft black spots on images	Dust on the CCD. Send to repair service for cleaning or do it yourself using products specifically made for cleaning the CCD. Products available at www.Photosol.com and www.Visibledust .com.
RAW files won't open in Photoshop	Make sure you have the latest update to the ACR (Adobe Camera Raw) plugin. Visit www.Adobe.com for updates.
Image colors don't look right	Ensure proper white balance at capture time using a custom white balance. Use a gray card or ExpoDisc. Use a high-quality monitor designed for photographic work. Check that your monitor is properly calibrated and profiled using a hardware device on a regular basis (three to four weeks).
Prints never match the monitor	Use a high-quality monitor designed for photographic work. Check that your monitor is properly calibrated and profiled using a hardware device on a regular basis (three to four weeks). Formac (www.Formac.com) makes great LCD monitors (Mac and PC compatible). Use printer profiles properly with inkjet printers (see chapter 6).
I accidentally deleted images from the card!	Doh! Do not use the card! Adding new images could make the others permanently unrecoverable. Use image-recovery software to restore the images. Try PhotoRescue from www.Datarescue.com.
Focus is consistently off (usually farther back than the area that's supposed to be in focus)	Back focus is a common problem. It can usually be fixed by a competent repair service. Many users have reported success in fixing it themselves. We do not recommend this procedure, but details can be found under Tips & Tricks at www.kubotaworkshops.com.
My kids know more about Photoshop than I do!	This is totally unacceptable! Get yourself some training as soon as possible. Visit www.kubotaworkshops.com.
When I hang upside-down from my ankles, I lose consciousness	Don't hang upside-down from your ankles.

INDEX

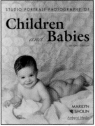

WEDDING PHOTOGRAPHY
CREATIVE TECHNIQUES FOR LIGHTING, POSING, AND MARKETING, 3rd Ed.

Rick Ferro

Creative techniques for lighting and posing wedding portraits that will set your work apart from the competition. Covers every phase of wedding photography. $29.95 list, 8½x11, 128p, 125 color photos, index, order no. 1649.

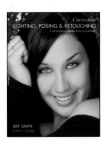

STUDIO PORTRAIT PHOTOGRAPHY OF CHILDREN AND BABIES, 2nd Ed.

Marilyn Sholin

Work with the youngest portrait clients to create cherished images. Includes techniques for working with kids at every developmental stage, from infant to preschooler. $29.95 list, 8½x11, 128p, 90 color photos, order no. 1657.

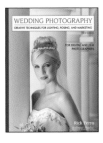

CORRECTIVE LIGHTING, POSING & RETOUCHING FOR DIGITAL PORTRAIT PHOTOGRAPHERS, 2nd Ed.

Jeff Smith

Learn to make every client look his or her best by using lighting and posing to conceal real or imagined flaws—from baldness, to acne, to figure flaws. $34.95 list, 8½x11, 120p, 150 color photos, order no. 1711.

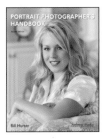

PORTRAIT PHOTOGRAPHER'S HANDBOOK, 2nd Ed.

Bill Hurter

Bill Hurter has compiled a step-by-step guide to portraiture that easily leads the reader through all phases of portrait photography. This book will be an asset to experienced photographers and beginners alike. $29.95 list, 8½x11, 128p, 175 color photos, order no. 1708.

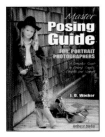

MASTER POSING GUIDE FOR PORTRAIT PHOTOGRAPHERS

J. D. Wacker

Learn the techniques you need to pose single portrait subjects, couples, and groups for studio or location portraits. Includes techniques for photographing weddings, teams, children, special events, and much more. $29.95 list, 8½x11, 128p, 80 photos, order no. 1722.

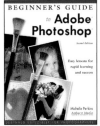

BEGINNER'S GUIDE TO ADOBE® PHOTOSHOP®, 2nd Ed.

Michelle Perkins

Learn to effectively make your images look their best, create original artwork, or add unique effects to any image. Topics are presented in short, easy-to-digest sections that will boost confidence and ensure outstanding images. $29.95 list, 8½x11, 128p, 300 color images, order no. 1732.

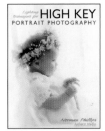

PROFESSIONAL TECHNIQUES FOR
DIGITAL WEDDING PHOTOGRAPHY, 2nd Ed.

Jeff Hawkins and Kathleen Hawkins

From selecting equipment, to marketing, to building a digital workflow, this book teaches how to make digital work for you. $29.95 list, 8½x11, 128p, 85 color images, order no. 1735.

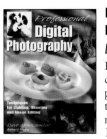

LIGHTING TECHNIQUES FOR
HIGH KEY PORTRAIT PHOTOGRAPHY

Norman Phillips

Learn to meet the challenges of high key portrait photography and produce images your clients will adore. $29.95 list, 8½x11, 128p, 100 color photos, order no. 1736.

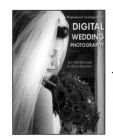

PROFESSIONAL DIGITAL PHOTOGRAPHY

Dave Montizambert

From monitor calibration, to color balancing, to creating advanced artistic effects, this book provides those skilled in basic digital imaging with the techniques they need to take their photography to the next level. $29.95 list, 8½x11, 128p, 120 color photos, order no. 1739.

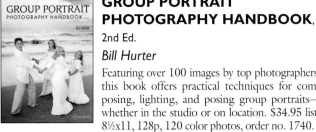

GROUP PORTRAIT PHOTOGRAPHY HANDBOOK, 2nd Ed.

Bill Hurter

Featuring over 100 images by top photographers, this book offers practical techniques for composing, lighting, and posing group portraits—whether in the studio or on location. $34.95 list, 8½x11, 128p, 120 color photos, order no. 1740.

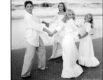

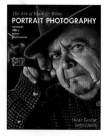

THE ART OF BLACK & WHITE PORTRAIT PHOTOGRAPHY

Oscar Lozoya

Learn how master photographer Oscar Lozoya uses unique sets and engaging poses to create black & white portraits that are infused with drama. Includes lighting strategies, special shooting techniques, and more. $29.95 list, 8½x11, 128p, 100 duotone photos, order no. 1746.

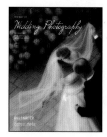

THE BEST OF WEDDING PHOTOGRAPHY, 2nd Ed.

Bill Hurter

Learn how the top wedding photographers in the industry transform special moments into lasting romantic treasures with the posing, lighting, album design, and customer service pointers found in this book. $34.95 list, 8½x11, 128p, 150 color photos, order no. 1747.

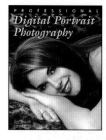

PROFESSIONAL DIGITAL PORTRAIT PHOTOGRAPHY

Jeff Smith

Because the learning curve is so steep, making the transition to digital can be frustrating. Author Jeff Smith shows readers how to shoot, edit, and retouch their images—while avoiding common pitfalls. $29.95 list, 8½x11, 128p, 100 color photos, order no. 1750.

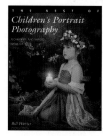

THE BEST OF CHILDREN'S PORTRAIT PHOTOGRAPHY

Bill Hurter

Rangefinder editor Bill Hurter draws upon the experience and work of top professional photographers, uncovering the creative and technical skills they use to create their magical portraits of these young subejcts. $29.95 list, 8½x11, 128p, 150 color photos, order no. 1752.

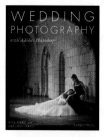

WEDDING PHOTOGRAPHY WITH ADOBE® PHOTOSHOP®

Rick Ferro and Deborah Lynn Ferro

Get the skills you need to make your images look their best, add artistic effects, and boost your wedding photography sales with savvy marketing ideas. $29.95 list, 8½x11, 128p, 100 color images, index, order no. 1753.

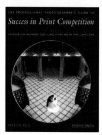

PROFESSIONAL PHOTOGRAPHER'S GUIDE TO
SUCCESS IN PRINT COMPETITION

Patrick Rice

Learn from PPA and WPPI judges how you can improve your print presentations and increase your scores. $29.95 list, 8½x11, 128p, 100 color photos, index, order no. 1754.

PHOTOGRAPHER'S GUIDE TO
WEDDING ALBUM DESIGN AND SALES

Bob Coates

Enhance your income and creativity with these techniques from top wedding photographers. $29.95 list, 8½x11, 128p, 150 color photos, index, order no. 1757.

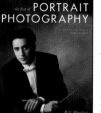

THE BEST OF PORTRAIT PHOTOGRAPHY

Bill Hurter

View outstanding images from top professionals and learn how they create their masterful images. Includes techniques for classic and contemporary portraits. $29.95 list, 8½x11, 128p, 200 color photos, index, order no. 1760.

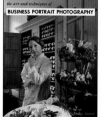

THE ART AND TECHNIQUES OF
BUSINESS PORTRAIT PHOTOGRAPHY

Andre Amyot

Learn the business and creative skills photographers need to compete successfully in this challenging field. $29.95 list, 8½x11, 128p, 100 color photos, index, order no. 1762.

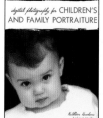

DIGITAL PHOTOGRAPHY FOR CHILDREN'S AND FAMILY PORTRAITURE

Kathleen Hawkins

Discover how digital photography can boost your sales, enhance your creativity, and improve your studio's workflow. $29.95 list, 8½x11, 128p, 130 color images, index, order no. 1770.

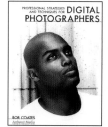

PROFESSIONAL STRATEGIES AND TECHNIQUES FOR DIGITAL PHOTOGRAPHERS

Bob Coates

Learn how professionals—from portrait artists to commercial specialists—enhance their images with digital techniques. $29.95 list, 8½x11, 128p, 130 color photos, index, order no. 1772.

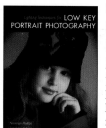

LIGHTING TECHNIQUES FOR
LOW KEY PORTRAIT PHOTOGRAPHY

Norman Phillips

Learn to create the dark tones and dramatic lighting that typify this classic portrait style. $29.95 list, 8½x11, 128p, 100 color photos, index, order no. 1773.

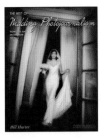

THE BEST OF WEDDING PHOTOJOURNALISM

Bill Hurter

Learn how top professionals capture these fleeting moments of laughter, tears, and romance. Features images from over twenty renowned wedding photographers. $29.95 list, 8½x11, 128p, 150 color photos, index, order no. 1774.

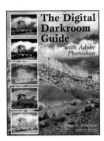

THE DIGITAL DARKROOM GUIDE WITH ADOBE® PHOTOSHOP®

Maurice Hamilton

Bring the skills and control of the photographic darkroom to your desktop with this complete manual. $29.95 list, 8½x11, 128p, 140 color images, index, order no. 1775.

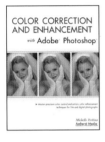

COLOR CORRECTION AND ENHANCEMENT WITH ADOBE® PHOTOSHOP®

Michelle Perkins

Master precision color correction and artistic color enhancement techniques for scanned and digital photos. $29.95 list, 8½x11, 128p, 300 color images, index, order no. 1776.

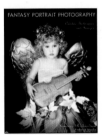

FANTASY PORTRAIT PHOTOGRAPHY

Kimarie Richardson

Learn how to create stunning portraits with fantasy themes—from fairies and angels, to 1940s glamour shots. Includes portrait ideas for infants through adults. $29.95 list, 8½x11, 128p, 60 color photos index, order no. 1777.

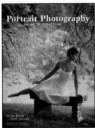

PORTRAIT PHOTOGRAPHY

THE ART OF SEEING LIGHT

Don Blair with Peter Skinner

Learn to harness the best light both in studio and on location, and get the secrets behind the magical portraiture captured by this award-winning, seasoned pro. $29.95 list, 8½x11, 128p, 100 color photos, index, order no. 1783.

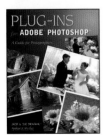

PLUG-INS FOR ADOBE® PHOTOSHOP®

A GUIDE FOR PHOTOGRAPHERS

Jack and Sue Drafahl

Supercharge your creativity and mastery over your photography with Photoshop and the tools outlined in this book. $29.95 list, 8½x11, 128p, 175 color photos, index, order no. 1781.

POWER MARKETING FOR WEDDING AND PORTRAIT PHOTOGRAPHERS

Mitche Graf

Set your business apart and create clients for life with this comprehensive guide to achieving your professional goals. $29.95 list, 8½x11, 128p, 100 color images, index, order no. 1788.

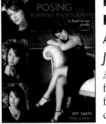

POSING FOR PORTRAIT PHOTOGRAPHY

A HEAD-TO-TOE GUIDE

Jeff Smith

Author Jeff Smith teaches surefire techniques for fine-tuning every aspect of the pose for the most flattering results. $29.95 list, 8½x11, 128p, 150 color photos, index, order no. 1786.

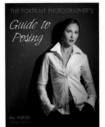

THE PORTRAIT PHOTOGRAPHER'S
GUIDE TO POSING

Bill Hurter

Posing can make or break an image. Now you can get the posing tips and techniques that have propelled the finest portrait photographers in the industry to the top. $29.95 list, 8½x11, 128p, 200 color photos, index, order no. 1779.

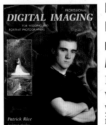

MASTER LIGHTING GUIDE

FOR PORTRAIT PHOTOGRAPHERS

Christopher Grey

Efficiently light executive and model portraits, high and low key images, and more. Master traditional lighting styles and use creative modi-fications that will maximize your results. $29.95 list, 8½x11, 128p, 300 color photos, index, order no. 1778.

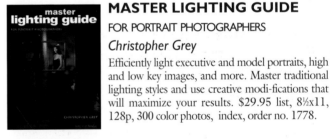

PROFESSIONAL DIGITAL IMAGING FOR WEDDING AND

PORTRAIT PHOTOGRAPHERS

Patrick Rice

Build your business and enhance your creativity with practical strategies for making digital work for you. $29.95 list, 8½x11, 128p, 200 color photos, index, order no. 1780.

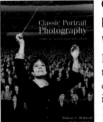

CLASSIC PORTRAIT PHOTOGRAPHY

William S. McIntosh

Learn how to create portraits that truly stand the test of time. Master photographer Bill McIntosh discusses some of his best images, giving you an inside look at his timeless style. $29.95 list, 8½x11, 128p, 100 color photos, index, order no. 1784.

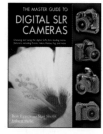

THE MASTER GUIDE TO DIGITAL SLR CAMERAS
Stan Sholik and Ron Eggers

What makes a digital SLR the right one for you? What features are available? What should you look out for? These questions and more are answered in this helpful guide. $29.95 list, 8½x11, 128p, 180 color photos, index, order no. 1791.

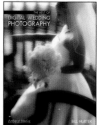

DIGITAL INFRARED PHOTOGRAPHY
Patrick Rice

The dramatic look of infrared photography has long made it popular—but with digital it's actually *easy* too! Add digital IR to your repertoire with this comprehensive book. $29.95 list, 8½x11, 128p, 100 b&w and color photos, index, order no. 1792.

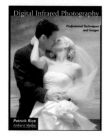

THE BEST OF DIGITAL WEDDING PHOTOGRAPHY
Bill Hurter

Explore the groundbreaking images and techniques that are shaping the future of wedding photography. Includes dazzling photos from over 35 top photographers. $29.95 list, 8½x11, 128p, 175 color photos, index, order no. 1793.

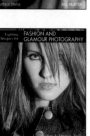

LIGHTING TECHNIQUES FOR FASHION AND GLAMOUR PHOTOGRAPHY
Stephen A. Dantzig, PsyD.

In fashion and glamour photography, light is the key to producing images with impact. With these techniques, you'll be primed for success! $29.95 list, 8½x11, 128p, over 200 color images, index, order no. 1795.

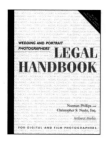

WEDDING AND PORTRAIT PHOTOGRAPHERS' LEGAL HANDBOOK
N. Phillips and C. Nudo, Esq.

Don't leave yourself exposed! Sample forms and practical discussions help you protect yourself and your business. $29.95 list, 8½x11, 128p, 25 sample forms, index, order no. 1796.

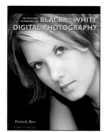

PROFESSIONAL TECHNIQUES FOR BLACK & WHITE DIGITAL PHOTOGRAPHY
Patrick Rice

Digital makes it easier than ever to create black & white images. With these techniques, you'll learn to achieve dazzling results! $29.95 list, 8½x11, 128p, 100 color photos, index, order no. 1798.

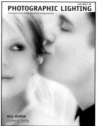

THE BEST OF PHOTOGRAPHIC LIGHTING
Bill Hurter

Top professionals reveal the secrets behind their successful strategies for studio, location, and outdoor lighting. Packed with tips for portraits, still lifes, and more. $34.95 list, 8½x11, 128p, 150 color photos, index, order no. 1808.

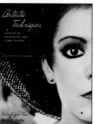

MARKETING AND SELLING TECHNIQUES
FOR DIGITAL PORTRAIT PHOTOGRAPHERS
Kathleen Hawkins

Great portraits aren't enough to ensure the success of your business! Learn how to attract clients and boost your sales. $34.95 list, 8½x11, 128p, 150 color photos, index, order no. 1804.

ARTISTIC TECHNIQUES WITH ADOBE® PHOTOSHOP® AND COREL® PAINTER®
Deborah Lynn Ferro

Flex your creative skills and learn how to transform photographs into fine-art masterpieces. Step-by-step techniques make it easy! $34.95 list, 8½x11, 128p, 200 color images, index, order no. 1806.